Richard Steele

The Tender Husband

A Comedy

Richard Steele

The Tender Husband
A Comedy

ISBN/EAN: 9783744661591

Printed in Europe, USA, Canada, Australia, Japan

Cover: Foto ©Thomas Meinert / pixelio.de

More available books at **www.hansebooks.com**

SIR,

YOU will be surprized, in the midst of a daily and familiar conversation, with an address which bears so distant an air as a public dedication : But to put you out of the pain which I know this will give you, I assure you I do not design in it, what would be very needless, a panegyrick on yourself, or what, perhaps, is very necessary, a defence of the play. In the one I should discover too much the concern of an author, in the other too little the freedom of a friend.

My purpose, in this application, is only to show the esteem I have for you, and that I look upon my intimacy with you, as one of the most valuable enjoyments of my life. At the same time I hope I make the town no ill compliment for their kind acceptance of this comedy, in acknowledging that it has so far raised my opinion of it, as to make me think it no improper memorial of an inviolable friendship.

I should not offer it to you as such, had I not been very careful to avoid every thing that might look ill-

natured, immoral, or prejudicial to what the better part of mankind hold sacred and honourable.

Poetry, under such restraints, is an obliging service to human society; especially when it is used, like your admirable vein, to recommend more useful qualities in yourself, or immortalize characters truly heroic in others. I am, here, in danger of breaking my promise to you, therefore shall take the only opportunity that can offer itself of resisting my own inclinations, by complying with yours.

I am, Sir,

Your most faithful humble servant,

RICHARD STEELE.

SIR RICHARD STEELE.

Was of the number of brilliant yèt eccentric geniusses, who have conferred by their birth the fame of producing wit, in a more than equal degree, upon the kingdom of Ireland. In the county of Wexford his family possessed a considerable property.

Sir RICHARD, however, was of the British Charter-House, and thence he went to Merton-College, Oxford. What proficiency he made has been sufficiently obvious. As a classical prose writer of his time, he yields only to ADDISON. If he be considered as a dramatist, he cannot rank high; for he is not an original: he drew from French models, and the dialogue of his pieces was more distinguished by sentiment than by wit or humour. His characters are none of them new, nor are they marked with much strength of conception or peculiarity of diction—*Ex uno disce omnes.*—BEVIL indeed is the dramatic GRANDISON, humane, tender, delicate and honourable.

STEELE's thoughts seem to have, in despite of his life and manners, tended always to virtue; and if indulgence may be extended to any man who acts against internal evidence, STEELE may deserve the commiseration of him, who can sigh over the records of indiscretion, and resolve to become better himself.

He was connected with the fluctuating parties in the reign of Queen ANNE; and, as the one or the other triumphed, he was in place to day, and in poverty to-morrow. He was now theatrically a manager of Drury-Lane House, but he managed there as he managed in his own house, which long together he did not keep *over his head.* He was concerned in a variety of periodical publications—The Tatler, Spectator, Guardian, Spinster, Reader, Theatre, &c. &c.

GEORGE I. conferred upon him the honour of knighthood, April 28, 1715, and WALPOLE ordered him Five Hundred Pounds for especial services. He ended a life discriminated with nearly endless incursions of misery and returns of affluence, at his seat of Langunnor, near Caermarthen, September 21, 1729, and was interred in the church of Caermarthen.

His plays are in number six, two of which are yet unpublished:

Funeral; or, *Grief A-la-mode*, 1702.
The Tender Husband; or, *The Accomplished Fools*, 1704.
The Lying Lover; or, *The Ladies' Friendship*, 1706.
The Conscious Lovers, 1721.
The Gentlemen, N. D.
The School of Action, N. D.

TENDER HUSBAND.

THE character of this Comedy may be extracted from the general character of STEELE'S plays, as mentioned in the life. It, in the present times, has not much theatrical attraction, though it certainly may be read with great pleasure. The incidents are many of them borrowed, and the Husband who solicits his own dishonour, tastes of *Ford* in the Merry Wives of Windsor. The language is very pure and neat.

PROLOGUE.

WRITTEN BY MR. ADDISON.

IN the first rise and infancy of farce,
When fools were many, and when plays were scarce,
The raw, unpractised authors could with ease,
A young and unexperienced audience please:
No single character had e'er been shown,
But the whole herd of fops was all their own;
Rich in originals, they set to view,
In every piece, a coxcomb that was new.

But now our British Theatre can boast
Drolls of all kinds, a vast unthinking host!
Fruitful of folly and of vice, it shows
Cuckolds, and cits, and bawds, and pimps, and beaux;
Rough country knights are found of every shire,
Of every fashion, gentle fops appear;
And punks of different characters we meet,
As frequent on the stage as in the pit:
Our modern wits are forc'd to pick and cull,
And here and there, by chance glean up a fool:
Long ere they find the necessary spark,
They search the town, and beat about the park:

To all his most frequented haunts resort,
Oft dog him to the ring, and oft to court ;
As love of pleasure, or of place invites :
And sometimes catch him taking snuff at White's.

Howe'er, to do you right, the present age
Breeds very hopeful monsters for the stage,
That scorn the paths their dull forefathers trod,
And won't be blockheads in the common road.
Do but survey this crowded house to night :
——Here's still encouragement for those that write.

Our author to divert his friends to day,
Stocks with variety of fools his play ;
And that there may be something gay, and new,
Two ladies errant has exposed to view :
The first a damsel, travell'd in romance ;
The t'other more refin'd ; she comes from France :
Rescue, like courteous knights, the nymph from danger,
And kindly treat, like well-bred men, the stranger.

A SONG.

Designed for the FOURTH ACT, but not set.

SEE Britons, see with awful eyes,
Britannia from her seas arise!
" Ten thousand billows round me roar
* While winds and waves engage,*
That break in froth upon my shore
* And impotently rage.*
Such were the terrors, which of late
Surrounded my afflicted state ;
* United fury thus was bent*
On my devoted seats,
* 'Till all the mighty force was spent*
In feeble swells, and empty threats.

But now with rising glory crown'd,
My joys run high, they know no bounds ;
* Tides of unruly pleasure flow*
Through every swelling vein,
* New raptures in my bosom glow,*
And warm me up to youth again.
* Passing pomps my streets adorn ;*
* Captive spoils in triumph born,*

Standards of Gauls, in fight subdued
Colours in hostile blood embrued,
  Ensigns of tyrannic might,
  Foes to equity and right,
In courts of British justice wave on high,
Sacred to law and liberty.
My crowded theatres repeat,
In songs of triumph, the defeat.
  Did ever joyful mother see
  So bright, so brave a progeny!
  Daughters with so much beauty crown'd,
  Or sons for valour so renown'd!

But oh, I gaze, and seek in vain
To find amidst this warlike train
My absent sons, that us'd to grace
With decent pride this joyous place:
Unhappy youths! How do my sorrows rise,
Swell my breast and melt my eyes,
  While I your mighty loss deplore,
Wild and raging with distress
I mourn, I mourn my own success,
  And boast my victories no more.
Unhappy youths! far from their native sky,
On Danube's banks interr'd they lie.
Germania, give me back my slain,
Give me my slaughter'd sons again.
Was it for this they ranged so far,
To free thee from oppressive war!"
    Germania, &c.

Tears of sorrow while I shed,
O'er the manes of my dead,
Lasting altars let me raise
To my living heroes praise;
Heaven give them a longer stay,
As glorious actions to display,
Or perish on as great a day.

Dramatis Personae.

DRURY-LANE.

Men.

Sir HARRY GUBBIN, - - - - -	Mr. Baddeley.
HUMPHRY GUBBIN, - - -	Mr. Dodd,
Mr. TIPKIN, - - - - - - - -	Mr. Parsons.
CLERIMONT, Sen. - - - -	Mr. Packer.
Captain CLERIMONT, - - - - -	Mr. Brereton.
Mr. POUNCE, - - - - - -	Mr. Aickin.

Women.

Mrs. CLERIMONT, - - - - - -	Mrs. Ward.
AUNT, - - - - - - -	Mrs. Hopkins.
NIECE, - - - - - - - - -	Miss Farren.
FAINLOVE, - - - - -	Mrs. Wells.
JENNY Maid to Mrs. Clerimont, - -	Miss Tidswell.

COVENT-GARDEN.

Men.

Sir HARRY GUBBIN, - -	Mr. Quick.
HUMPHRY GUBBIN, - - - - -	Mr. Edwin.
Mr. TIPKIN, - - - -	Mr. Wewitzer.
CLERIMONT, Sen. - - - - -	Mr. Farren.
Captain CLERIMONT, - -	Mr. Lewis.
Mr. POUNCE, - - - - - -	Mr. Fearon.

Women.

Mrs. CLERIMONT, - - - - -	Mrs. Mattocks.
AUNT, - - - - -	Mrs. Webb.
NIECE, - - - - - - - - -	Mrs. Abington.
FAINLOVE. - - - -	Mrs. Bernard.
JENNY, Maid to Mrs. Clerimont, - -	Miss Brangin.

TENDER HUSBAND.

ACT I. SCENE I.

The Park. **Enter** CLERIMONT, *Sen. and* FAINLOVE.

Clerimont, Sen.

WELL, Mr. Fainlove, how do you go on in your amour with my wife?

Fain. I am very civil and very distant; if she smiles or speaks, I bow and gaze at her—Then throw down my eyes, as if opprest by fear of offence, then steal a look again till she again sees me—This is my general method.

Cler. Sen. And 'tis right—For such a fine lady has no guard to her virtue, but her pride; therefore you must constantly apply yourself to that: But dear Lucy, as you have been a very faithful, but a very costly wench to me, so my spouse also has been constant to my bed, but careless of my fortune.

B ij

Fain. Ah! my dear, how could you leave your poor Lucy, and run into France to see sights, and show your gallantry with a wife? Was not that unnatural?

Cler. Sen. She brought me a noble fortune, and I thought she had a right to share it: therefore carried her to see the world, forsooth, and make the tour of France and Italy, where she learned to lose her money gracefully, to admire every vanity in our sex, and contemn every virtue in her own; which, with ten thousand other perfections, are the ordinary improvements of a travell'd lady. Now I can neither mortify her vanity that I may live at ease with her, or quite discard her, till I have catch'd her a little enlarging her innocent freedoms, as she calls 'em: for this end I am content to be a French husband, tho' now and then with the secret pangs of an Italian one; and therefore, sir, or madam, you are thus equipt to attend and accost her ladyship: it concerns you to be diligent: if we wholly part—I need say no more: if we do not—I'll see thee well provided for.

Fain. I'll do all I can, I warrant you, but you are not to expect I'll go much among the men.

Cler Sen. No, no, you must not go near men, you are only (when my wife goes to a play) to sit in a side-box with pretty fellows—I don't design you to personate a real man, you are only to be a pretty gentleman——Not to be of any use or consequence in the world, as to yourself, but merely as a property to others ; "such as you see now and then have a "life in the intail of a great estate, that seem to have "come into the world only to be tags in the, pedigree "of a wealthy house."—You must have seen many of that species.

Fain. I apprehend you, such as stand in assemblies, with an indolent softness and contempt of all around 'em ; who make a figure in public, and are scorn'd in private ; I have seen such a one with a pocket glass to see his own face, and an affeĉted perspeĉtive to know others.   [*Imitates each.*

Cler. Sen. Aye, aye, that's my man—Thou dear rogue.

Fain. Let me alone—I'll lay my life I'll horn you, that is, I'll make it appear I might if I could.

Cler. Sen. Aye, that will please me quite as well. '

Fain. To shew you the progress I have made, I last night won of her five hundred pounds, which I have brought you safe.   [*Giving him bills.*

Cler. Sen. Oh the damn'd vice ! That women can imagine all household care, regard to posterity, and fear of poverty, must be sacrificed to a game at cards —Suppose she had not had it to pay, and you had been capable of finding your account another way—

Fain. That's but a suppose——

Cler. Sen. I say, she must have complied with every thing you ask'd——

Fain. But she knows you never limit her expences —I'll gain him from her for ever if I can.   [*Aside.*

Cler. Sen. With this you have repaid me two thou- '

B iij

sand pounds, and if you did not refund thus honestly, I, could not have supplied her——We must have parted.

Fain. Then you shall part—if t'other way fails. [*Aside.*] However, I can't blame your fondness of her, she has so many entertaining qualities with her vanity—Then she has such a pretty unthinking air, while she saunters round a room, and prattles sentences—

Cler. Sen. That was her turn from her infancy; she always had a great genius for knowing every thing but what it was necessary she should—" The " wits of the age, the great beauties, and short-lived " people of vogue, were always her discourse and " imitation"—Thus the case stood when she went to France; but her fine follies improved so daily, that, tho' I was then proud of her being call'd Mr. Clerimont's wife, I am now as much out of countenance to hear myself call'd Mrs. Clerimont's husband, so much is the superiority of her side.

Fain. I am sure if ever I gave myself a little liberty, I never found you so indulgent.

Cler. Sen. I should have the whole sex on my back, should I pretend to retrench a lady so well visited as mine is—Therefore I must bring it about that it shall appear her own act, if she reforms; or else I shall be pronounced jealous, and have my eyes pull'd out for being open—But I hear my brother Jack coming, who, I hope, has brought yours with him——Hist, not a word.

Enter Captain CLERIMONT *and* POUNCE.

Capt. I have found him out at last, brother, and brought you the obsequious Mr. Pounce; I saw him at a distance in a crowd, whispering in their turns with all about him—He is a gentleman so received, so courted, and so trusted——

Pounce. I am very glad if you saw any thing like that, if the approbation of others can recommend me (where I much more desired it) to this company—

Capt. Oh the civil person—But, dear Pounce, you know I am your profest admirer; " I always cele-
" brated you for your excellent skill and address,
" for that happy knowledge of the world, which
" makes you seem born for living with the persons
" you are with, wherever you come"——Now my brother and I want your help in a business that requires a little more dexterity than we ourselves are masters of.

Pounce. You know, sir, my character is helping the distrest, which I do freely, and without reserve; while others are for distinguishing rigidly on the justice of the occasion, and so lose the grace of the benefit——Now 'tis my profession to assist a free-hearted young fellow against an unnatural long-lived father—to disencumber men of pleasure of the vexation of unwieldy estates, to support a feeble title to an inheritance, to——

Cler. Sen. I have been well acquainted with your merits ever since I saw you, with so much compassion, prompt a stammering witness in Westminster-hall——that wanted instruction——I love a man that can venture his ears with so much bravery for his friend.

Pounce. Dear sir, spare my modesty, and let me know to what all this panegyric tends.

Cler. Sen. Why, sir, what I would say is in behalf of my brother the Captain here, whose misfortune it is that I was born before him.

Pounce. I am confident he had rather you should have been so, than any other man in England.

Capt. You do me justice, Mr. Pounce——But though 'tis to that gentleman, I am still a younger brother, and you know we that are so, are generally condemn'd to shops, colleges, or inns of court.

Pounce. But you, sir, have escaped 'em; you have been trading in the noble mart of glory——

Capt. That's true—But the general makes such haste to finish the war, that we red coats may be soon out of fashion—and then I am a fellow of the most easy, indolent disposition in the world; I hate all manner of business.

Pounce. A composed temper, indeed!

Capt. In such case, I should have no way of livelihood, but calling over this gentleman's dogs in the country, drinking his stale beer to the neighbourhood, or marrying a fortune.

Cler. Sen. To be short, Pounce——I am putting Jack upon marriage; and you are so public an envoy, or rather plenipotentiary, from the very different nations of Cheapside, Covent-Garden, and St. James's; you have, too, the mien and language of each place so naturally, that you are the properest instrument I know in the world, to help an honest young fellow to favour in one of 'em, by credit in the other.

Pounce. By what I understand of your many prefaces, gentlemen, the purpose of all this is—That it would not, in the least, discompose this gentleman's easy, indolent disposition, to fall into twenty thousand pounds, tho' it came upon him never so suddenly.

Capt. You are a very discerning man——How could you see so far through me, as to know I love a fine woman, pretty equipage, good company, and a clean habitation?

Pounce. Well, though I am so much a conjuror— What then?

Cler. Sen. You know a certain person, into whose hands you now and then recommend a young heir, to be relieved from the vexation of tenants, taxes, and so forth——

Pounce. What! my worthy friend, and city patron, Hezekiah Tipkin, banker, in Lombard-street; would the noble captain lay any sums in his hands?

Capt. No—But the noble captain would have treasure out of his hands—You know his niece.

Pounce. To my knowledge, ten thousand pounds in money.

Capt. Such a stature! such a blooming countenance! so easy a shape!

Pounce. In jewels of her grandmother's five thousand——

Capt. Her wit so lively, her mien so alluring!

Pounce. In land a thousand a year.

Capt. Her lips have that certain prominence, that swelling softness, that they invite to a pressure ; her eyes that languish, that they give pain, though they look only inclined to rest——Her whole person that one charm——

Pounce. " Raptures! raptures!

" *Capt.* How can it, so insensibly to itself, lead us " through cares it knows not, through such a wilder- " ness of hopes, fears, joys, sorrows, desires, de- " spairs, ecstacies, and torments, with so sweet, yet " so anxious vicissitude !*

" *Pounce.*" Why I thought you had never seen her——

Capt. No more I ha'n't.

Pounce. Who told you, then, of her inviting lips, her soft sleepy eyes ?——

Capt. You yourself——

Pounce. Sure you rave ; I never spoke of her before to you.

Capt. Why, you won't face me down—Did you not just now say, she had ten thousand pounds in money, five in jewels, and a thousand a year ?

Pounce. I confess my own stupidity, and her charms—Why, if you were to meet, you would certainly please her ; you have the cant of loving ; but, pray, may we be free—That young gentleman—

Capt. A very honest, modest gentleman of my acquaintance : one that has much more in him than he appears to have ; you shall know him better, sir ; this is Mr. Pounce. Mr. Pounce, this is Mr. Fainlove ; I must desire you to let him be known to you, and your friends.

Pounce. I shall be proud—Well, then, since we may be free, you must understand, the young lady, by being kept from the world, has made a world of her own.—She has spent all her solitude in reading romances ; her head is full of shepherds, knights, flowery meads, groves, and streams ; so that if you talk like a man of this world to her, you do nothing.

Capt. Oh let me alone—I have been a great traveller in fairy land myself ; I know Oroondates, Cassandra ; Astrea and Clelia are my intimate acquaintance.

" Go, my heart's envoys, tender sighs make haste,
" And with your breath swell the soft Zephyr's
        blast :
" Then near that fair one, if you chance to fly,
" Tell her, in whispers, 'tis for her I die."

Pounce. That would do, that would do——her very language.

Cler. Sen. Why then, dear Pounce, I know thou art the only man living that can serve him.

Pounce. Gentlemen, you must pardon me, I am soliciting the marriage settlement between her and a country booby, her cousin, Humphry Gubbin, Sir

Harry's heir, who is come to town to take possession of her.

Cler. Sen. Well, all that I can say to the matter is, that a thousand pounds on the day of Jack's marriage to her, is more than you'll get by the dispatch of those deeds.

Pounce. Why a thousand pounds is a pretty thing, especially when 'tis to take a lady fair out of the hands of an obstinate ill-bred clown, to give her to a gentle swain, a dying enamour'd knight.

Cler. Sen. Ay, dear Pounce—consider but that—the justice of the thing.

Pounce. Besides, he is just come from the glorious Blenheim! Look ye, Captain, I hope you have learn'd an implicit obedience to your leaders.

Capt. 'Tis all I know.

Pounce. Then, if I am to command—make no one step without me—And since we may be free—I am also to acquaint you, there will be more merit in bringing this matter to bear than you imagine—Yet right measures make all things possible.

Capt. We'll follow yours exactly.

Pounce. But the great matter against us is want of time, for the nymph's uncle, and 'Squire's father, this morning met, and made an end of the matter—But the difficulty of a thing, captain, shall be no reason against attempting it.

Capt. I have so great an opinion of your conduct that I warrant you we conquer all.

1

Pounce, I am so intimately employ'd by old Tipkin, and so necessary to him, that I may, perhaps, puzzle things yet.

Cler. Sen. I have seen thee cajole the knave very dextrously.

Pounce. Why, really, sir, generally speaking, 'tis but knowing what a man thinks of himself, and giving him that, to make him what else you please——Now Tipkin is an absolute Lombard-street wit, a fellow that drolls on the strength of fifty thousand pounds: he is called on 'Change, Sly-boots, and by the force of a very good credit, and very bad conscience, he is a leading person : but we must be quick, or he'll sneer old Sir Harry out of his senses, and strike up the sale of his niece immediately.

Capt. But my rival, what's he——

Pounce. There's some hopes there, for I hear the booby is as averse, as his father is inclined to it—One is as obstinate, as the other cruel.

Cler. Sen. He is, they say, a pert blockhead, and and very lively out of his father's sight.

Pounce. He that gave me his character, call'd him a docile dunce, a fellow rather absurd, than a direct fool—When his father's absent, he'll pursue any thing he's put upon—But we must not lose time—Pray be you two brothers at home to wait for any notice from me—While that pretty gentleman and I, whose face I have known, take a walk and look about for 'em—So, so—Young lady——[*Aside to* Fainlove.]

[*Exeunt.*

C

Enter Sir HARRY GUBBIN *and* TIPKIN.

Sir Har. Look ye, brother Tipkin, as I told you before, my business in town is to dispose of an hundred head of cattle, and my son.

Tip. Brother Gubbin, as I signified to you in my last, bearing date September 13th, my niece has a thousand pounds per annum, and because I have found you a plain-dealing man, (particularly in the easy pad you put into my hands last summer,) I was willing you should have the refusal of my niece, provided that I have a discharge from all retrospects while her guardian, and one thousand pounds for my care.

Sir Har. Aye, but brother, you rate her too high, the war has fetch'd down the price of women : the whole nation is over-run with petticoats ; our daughters lie upon our hands, brother Tipkin ; girls are drugs, sir, mere drugs.

Tip. Look ye, sir Harry—Let girls be what they will—a thousand pounds a year, is a thousand pounds a year ; and a thousand pounds a year is neither girl nor boy.

Sir Har. Look ye, Mr. Tipkin, the main article with me is, that foundation of wives rebellion, and husbands cuckoldom, that cursed pin-money—Five hundred pounds per annum pin-money.

Tip. The word pin-money, sir Harry, is a term.—

Sir Har. It is a term, brother, we never had in our family, nor ever will—make her jointure in widowhood accordingly large, but four hundred pounds a year is enough to give no account of.

Tip. Well, sir Harry, since you can't swallow these pins, I will abate to four hundred pounds.

Sir Har. And to molify the article—as well as specify the uses, we'll put in the names of several female utensils, as needles, knitting-needles, tape, thread, scissars, bodkins, fans, play-books, with other toys of that nature. And now, since we have as good as concluded the marriage, it will not be improper that the young people see each other.

Tip. I don't think it prudent 'till the very instant of marriage, lest they should not like one another.

Sir Har. They shall meet——As for the young girl she cannot dislike Numps; and for Numps, I never suffer'd him to have any thing he liked in his life. He'll be here immediately; he has been train'd up from his childhood under such a plant as this in my hand——I have taken pains in his education.

Tip. Sir Harry, I approve your method; for since you have left off hunting, you might otherwise want exercise, and this is a subtile expedient to preserve your own health, and your son's good manners.

Sir Har. It has been the custom of the Gubbins to preserve severity and discipline in their families— I myself was caned the day before my wedding.

Tip. Aye, sir Harry, had you not been well cud-gelled in youth, you had never been the man you are.

Sir Har. You say right, now I feel the benefit of it——There's a crab-tree, near our house, which flourishes for the good of my posterity, and has brusht our jackets, from father to son, for several generations——

Tip. I am glad to hear you have all things necessary for the family within yourselves——

Sir Har. Oh! yonder, I see Numps is coming—— I have drest him in the very suit I had on at my own wedding; 'tis a most becoming apparel.

Enter HUMPHRY GUBBIN.

Tip. Truly, the youth makes a good marriageable figure.

Sir Har. Come forward, Numps, this is your uncle Tipkin, your mother's brother, Numps, that is so kind as to bestow his niece upon you. (Don't be so glum, sirrah.) Don't bow to a man, with a face as if you'd knock him down, don't, sirrah.

Tip. I am glad to see you cousin Humphry—He is not talkative, I observe already.

Sir Har. He is very shrewd, sir, when he pleases. Do you see this crab-stick, you dog: [*Apart.*] Well, Numps, don't be out of humour. Will you talk? [*Apart.*] Come, we're your friends, Numps, come, lad.

Hump. You are a pure fellow for a father. This is always your trick, to make a great fool of one before company.   [*Apart to his father.*]

Sir Har. Don't disgrace me, sirrah: you grim graceless rogue. [*Apart.*]—Brother, he has been bred up to respect and silence before his parents——Yet did you but hear what a noise he makes sometimes in the kitchen, or the kennel, he's the loudest of 'em all.

Tip. Well, sir Harry, since you assure me he can speak, I'll take your word for it.

Hump. I can speak when I see occasion, and I can hold my tongue when I see occasion.

Sir Har. Well said, Numps—sirrah, I see you can do well if you will. [*Apart.*]

Tip. Pray walk up to me, cousin Humphry.

Sir Har. Aye, walk to and fro between us, with your hat under your arm. Clear up your countenance. [*Apart.*]

Tip. I see, sir Harry, you han't set him a capering under a French dancing-master: he does not mince it: he has not learn'd to walk by a courant, or a boree——His paces are natural——sir Harry.

Hump. I don't know but 'tis, so we walk in the West of England.

Sir Har. Aye, right, Numps, and so we do——Ha, ha, ha! Pray, brother, observe his make, none of your lath-back'd wishy washy breed——come hither, Numps. Can't you stand still?

[Apart, measuring his shoulders.

Tip. I presume this is not the first time, sir Harry, you have measured his shoulders with your cane.

Sir Har. Look ye, brother, two feet and an half in the shoulders.

Tip. Two feet and an half! we must make some settlement on the younger children.

Sir Har. Not like him, quotha'!

Tip. He may see his cousin when he pleases.

Hump. But hark ye, uncle, I have a scruple I had better mention before marriage than after.

Tip. What's that? what's that?

Hump. My cousin, you know, is a-kin to me, and I don't think it lawful for a young man to marry his own relations.

Sir Har. Hark ye, hark ye, Numps, we have got a way to solve all that : sirrah! consider this cudgel! Your cousin! Suppose I'd have you marry your grandmother; what then? [*Apart.*]

Tip. Well has your father satisfied you in the point, Mr. Humphry?

Hump. Aye, aye, sir, very well: I have not the least scruple remaining; no, no—not in the least, sir.

Tip. Then hark ye, brother; we'll go take a whet, and settle the whole affair.

Sir Har. Come, we'll leave Numps here——he knows the way. Not marry your own relations, sirrah! [*Apart.*]   [*Exeunt Sir* Harry *and* Tipkin.

Hump. Very fine, very fine ; how prettily this park is stockt with soldiers, and deer, and ducks, and ladies ——Ha! where are the old fellows gone; where can they be, tro'——I'll ask these people——

Enter POUNCE *and* FAINLOVE.

Hump. Ha, you pretty young gentleman, did you see my father?

Fain. Your father, sir?

Hump. A weezel-faced cross old gentleman, with spindle shanks?

* *Fain.* No, sir.

Hump. A crab-tree stick in his hand?

Pounce. We ha'n't met any body with these marks, but sure I have seen you before——Are not you Mr. Humphry Gubbin, son and heir to sir Henry Gubbin?

Hump. I am his son and heir——But how long I shall be so, I can't tell, for he talks every day of disinheriting me.

Pounce. Dear sir, let me embrace you——Nay, don't be offended if I take the liberty to kiss you; Mr. Fainlove, pray [Fainlove *kisses.*] kiss the gentleman—Nay, dear sir, don't stare and be surprized, for I have had a desire to be better known to you ever since I saw you one day clinch your fist at your father, when his back was turn'd upon you—For I must own I very much admire a young gentleman of spirit.

Hump. Why, sir, would it not vex a man to the heart, to have an old fool snubbing a body every minute afore company——

Pounce. Oh fye, he uses you like a boy.

Hump. Like a boy! He lays me on, now and then, as if I were one of his hounds—You can't think what a rage he was in this morning because I boggled a little at marrying my own cousin.

Pounce. A man can't be too scrupulous, Mr. Humphry; a man can't be too scrupulous.

Hump. Sir, I could as soon love my own flesh and blood, we should squabble like brother and sister; do.you think we should not, Mr.——? Pray, gentlemen, may I crave the favour of your names?

Pounce. Sir, I am the very person that have been employed to draw up the articles of marriage between you and your cousin.

Hump. Aye, say you so? Then you can inform me in some things concerning myself?——Pray, sir, what estate am I heir to?

Pounce. To fifteen hundred pounds a year, an intailed estate——

Hump. I am glad to hear it, with all my heart; and can you satisfy me in another question—Pray how old am I at present?

Pounce. Three and twenty last March.

Hump. Why, as sure as you are there they have kept me back. I have been told by some of the neighbourhood, that I was born the very year the pigeon-house was built, and every body knows the pigeon-house is three and twenty—Why, I find there has been tricks play'd me; I have obey'd him all along, as if I had been obliged to it.

Pounce. Not at all, sir; your father can't cut you out of one acre of fifteen hundred pounds a year.

Hump. What a fool have I been to give him his head so long!

Pounce. A man of your beauty and fortune may find out ladies enough that are not a-kin to you.

Hump. Look ye, Mr. What-d'ye-call—As to my

beauty, I don't know but they may take a liking to that—But, sir, mayn't I crave your name?

Pounce. My name, sir, is Pounce, at your service.

Hump. Pounce, with a P——!

Pounce. Yes, sir, and Samuel with an S——.

Hump. Why, then, Mr. Samuel Pounce, do you know any gentlewoman that you think I could like? For to tell you truly, I took an antipathy to my cousin ever since my father proposed her to me—And since every body knows I came up to be married, I don't care to go down and look baulkt.

Pounce. I have a thought just come into my head ——Do you see this young gentleman? he has a sister, a prodigious fortune—'faith you two shall be acquainted—

Fain. I can't pretend to expect so accomplish'd a gentleman as Mr. Humphry for my sister! but, being your friend, I'll be at his service in the affair.

Hump. If I had your sister, she and I should live like too turtles.

Pounce. Mr. Humphry, you shan't be fool'd any longer. I'll carry you into company; Mr. Fainlove, you shall introduce him to Mrs. Clerimont's toilet.

Fain. She'll be highly taken with him, for she loves a gentleman whose manner is particular.

Pounce. What, sir, a person of your pretensions, a clear estate, no portions to pay! 'Tis barbarous, your treatment—Mr. Humphry, I'm afraid you want money—There's for you—What, a man of your accomplishments!   [*Giving a purse.*

Hump. And yet you see, sir, how they use me—
Dear sir, you are the best friend I ever met with in
all my life—Now I am flush of money bring me to
your sister, and I warrant you for my behaviour—A
man's quite another thing with money in his pocket—
you know.

Pounce. How little the oaf wonders why I should
give him money! You shall never want, Mr. Humphry, while I have it—Mr. Humphry; but, dear
friend, I must take my leave of you, I have some
extraordinary business on my hands; I can't stay;
but you must not say a word—

Fain. But you must be in the way half an hour
hence, and I'll introduce you at Mrs. Clerimont's.

Pounce. Make 'em believe you are willing to have
your cousin Bridget, 'till opportunity serves: Farewell, dear friend.   [*Exeunt* Pounce *and* Fainlove.

Hump. Farewell, good Mr. Samuel Pounce—But
let's see my cash——'tis very true, the old saying, a
man meets with more friendship from strangers, than
his own relations——Let's see my cash, 1, 2, 3, 4,
there on that side—1, 2, 3, 4, on that side; 'tis a
foolish thing to put all one's money in one pocket, 'tis
like a man's whole estate in one county—These five
in my fob—I'll keep these in my hand, lest I should
have present occasion—But this town's full of pick
pockets—I'll go home again.   [*Exit whistling.*

ACT II.   SCENE I.

Continues.   Enter POUNCE, *and Captain* CLERIMONT *with his arm in a scarf.*

Pounce.

YOU are now well enough instructed both in the aunt and niece to form your behaviour.

Capt. But to talk with her apart is the great matter.

Pounce. The antiquated virgin has a mighty affectation for youth, and is a great lover of men and money—One of these, at least, I am sure I can gratify her in, " by turning her pence in the annuities, " or the stocks of one of the companies ;" some way or other I'll find to entertain her, and engage you with the young lady.

Capt. Since that is her ladyship's turn, so busy and fine a gentleman as Mr. Pounce must needs be in her good graces.

Pounce. So shall you too—But you must not be seen with me at first meeting; I'll dog 'em, while you watch at a distance.   [*Exeunt.*

Enter AUNT *and* NIECE.

Niece. Was it not my gallant that whistled so charmingly in the parlour, before he went out this morning ? He's a most accomplish'd cavalier.

Aunt. Come, niece, come—You don't do well to make sport with your relations, especially with a young gentleman that has so much kindness for you.

Niece. Kindness for me! What a phrase is there to express the darts and flames, the sighs and languishings of an expecting lover!

Aunt. Pray, niece, forbear this idle trash, and talk like other people. Your cousin Humphry will be true and hearty in what he says, and that's a great deal better than the talk and compliment of romances.

Niece. Good madam, don't wound my ears with such expressions : do you think I can ever love a man that's true and hearty! What a peasant-like amour do these coarse words import? True and hearty! Pray, aunt, endeavour a little at the embellishment of your stile.

Aunt. Alack-a-day, cousin Biddy, these idle romances have quite turn'd your head.

Niece. How often must I desire you, madam, to lay aside that familiar name, cousin Biddy? I never hear it without blushing—Did you ever meet with an heroine, in those idle romances as you call 'em, that was term'd Biddy?

Aunt. Ah! Cousin, cousin—These are mere vapours, indeed—Nothing but vapours—

Niece. No, the heroine has always something soft and engaging in her name—Something that gives us a notion of the sweetness of her beauty and behaviour. A name that glides through half a dozen tender syllables, as Elismunda, Clidamira, Deidamia, that runs upon vowels of the tongue, not hissing through one's teeth, or breaking them with consonants.——'Tis strange rudeness those familiar names they give us, when there is Aurelia, Saccharissa, Gloriana, for people of condition; and Celia, Chloris, Corinna, Mopsa, for their maids and those of lower rank.

Aunt. Look ye, Biddy, this is not to be supported —I know not where you learn'd this nicety; but I can tell you, forsooth, as much as you despise it, your mother was a Bridget afore you, and an excellent housewife.

Niece. Good madam, don't upbraid me with my mother Bridget, and an excellent housewife.

Aunt. Yes, I say, she was, and spent her time in better learning than ever you did—not in reading of fights and battles of dwarfs and giants; but in writing out receipts for broths, possets, caudles, and surfeit-waters, as became a good country gentlewoman.

Niece. My mother, and a Bridget!

Aunt. Yes, niece, I say again your mother, my sister, was a Bridget! the daughter of her mother Margery, of her mother Cicely, of her mother Alice.

Niece. Have you no mercy? O the barbarous genealogy!

Aunt. Of her mother Winifred, of her mother Joan.

Niece. Since you will run on, then I must needs tell you I am not satisfied in the point of my nativity. Many an infant has been placed in a cottage with obscure parents, 'till by chance some ancient servant of the family has known it by its marks.

Aunt. Aye, you had best be search't——That's like your calling the winds the fanning gales, before I don't know how much company; and the tree that was blown by it, had, forsooth, a spirit imprison'd in the trunk of it.

Niece. Ignorance!

Aunt. Then a cloud this morning had a flying dragon in it.

Niece. What eyes had you that you could see nothing? For my part, I look upon it to be a prodigy, and expect something extraordinary will happen to me before night——But you have a gross relish of things. What noble descriptions in romances had been lost, if the writers had been persons of your *gout?*

Aunt. I wish the authors had been hang'd, and their books burnt, before you had seen 'em.

Niece. Simplicity!

Aunt. A parcel of improbable lies,

Niece. Indeed, madam, your raillery is coarse——

Aunt. Fit only to corrupt young girls, and fill their heads with a thousand foolish dreams of I don't know what.

Niece. Nay, now, madam, you grow extravagant.

Aunt. What I say is not to vex, but advise you for your good.

Niece. What, to burn Philocles, Artaxerxes, Oroondates, and the rest of the heroic lovers, and take my country booby, cousin Humphry, for an husband!

Aunt. Oh dear, Oh dear, Biddy! Pray, good dear,

learn to act and speak like the rest of the world; come, come, you shall marry your cousin, and live comfortably.

Niece. Live comfortably! What kind of life is that? A great heiress live comfortably! Pray, aunt, learn to raise your ideas——What is, I wonder, to live comfortably?

Aunt. To live comfortably, is to live with prudence and frugality, as we do in Lombard-street.

Niece. As we do——That's a fine life indeed, with one servant of each sex——Let's see how many things our coachman is good for——He rubs down his horses, lays the cloth, whets the knives, and sometimes makes beds.

Aunt. A good servant should turn his hand to every thing in a family.

Niece. Nay, there's not a creature in our family, that has not two or three different duties; as John is butler, footman, and coachman; so Mary is cook, laundress, and chamber-maid.

Aunt. Well, and do you laugh at that?

Niece. No—not I—nor at the coach-horses, tho' one has an easy trot for my uncle's riding, and t'other an easy pace for your side-saddle.

Aunt. And so you jeer at the good management of your relations, do you?

Niece. No, I'm well satisfied that all the house are creatures of business; but, indeed, was in hopes that my poor lap-dog might have lived with me upon my fortune without an employment; but my uncle threatens every day to make him a turnspit, that he too, in his sphere, may help us to live comfortably——

Aunt. Hark ye, cousin Biddy.

Niece. I vow I'm out of countenance, when our butler, with his careful face, drives us all stowed in a chariot drawn by one horse ambling, and t'other trotting with his provisions behind for the family, from Saturday night till Monday morning, bound for Hackney——Then we make a comfortable figure indeed.

Aunt. So we do, and so will you always, if you marry your cousin Humphry.

Niece. Name not the creature.

Aunt. Creature! what your own cousin a creature!

Niece. Oh, let's be going, I see yonder another creature that does my uncle's law business, and has, I believe, made ready the deeds, those barbarous deeds.

Aunt. What, Mr. Pounce a creature too! Nay, now I'm sure you're ignorant—You shall stay, and you'll learn more wit from him in an hour, than in a thousand of your foolish books in an age—Your servant, Mr. Pounce.

Enter POUNCE.

Pounce. Ladies, I hope I don't interrupt any private discourse.

Aunt. Not in the least, sir.

Pounce. I should be loth to be esteemed one of those who think they have a privilege of mixing in all companies, without any business, but to bring forth a loud laugh, or vain jest.

Niece. He talks with the mien and gravity of a Pa-
ladin.   [*Aside.*

Pounce. Madam, I bought the other day at three
and an half, and sold at seven.

Aunt. Then pray, sir, sell for me in time. Niece,
mind him : he has an infinite deal of wit—

Pounce. This that I speak of was for you——I never neglect such opportunities to serve my friends.

Aunt. Indeed, Mr. Pounce, you are, I protest, without flattery, the wittiest man in the world.

Pounce. I assure you, madam, I said last night,
before an hundred head of citizens, that Mrs. Barsheba Tipkin was the most ingenious young lady in
the liberties,

Aunt. Well, Mr. Pounce, you are so facetious—
But you are always among the great ones——'Tis no
wonder you have it.

Niece. Idle! idle!

Pounce. But, madam, you know Alderman Grey-
Goose, he's a notable joking man——Well, says he,
here's Mrs. Barsheba's health——She's my mistress.

Aunt. That man makes me split my sides with
laughing, he's such a wag——(Mr. Pounce pretends
Grey-Goose said all this, but I know 'tis his own wit,
for he's in love with me.)   [*Aside.*

Pounce. But, madam, there's a certain affair I
should communicate to you.   [*Apart.*

Aunt. Aye, 'tis certainly so—He wants to break
his mind to me.   [*Captain Clerimont passing.*

Pounce. Oh, Captain Clerimont, Captain Clerimont,
D iij

——Ladies, pray let me introduce this young gentleman, he's my friend, a youth of great virtue and
goodness, for all he is in a red coat.

Aunt. If he's your friend, we need not doubt his
virtue.

Capt. Ladies, you are taking the cool breath of the
morning.

Niece. A pretty phrase.   [*Aside.*

Aunt. That's the pleasantest time this warm weather.

Capt. Oh, 'tis the season of the pearly dews, and
gentle zephyrs.

Niece. Aye! pray mind that again, Aunt. [*Aside.*

Pounce. Shan't we repose ourselves on yonder seat,
I love improving company, and to communicate.

Aunt. 'Tis certainly so——He's in love with me,
and wants opportunity to tell me so—I don't care if
we do——He's a most ingenious man.   [*Aside.*

[*Exeunt* Aunt *and* Pounce.

Capt. We enjoy here, madam, all the pretty land-
scapes of the country, without the pains of going
thither.

Niece. Art and nature are in a rivalry, or rather a
confederacy, to adorn this beauteous park with all
the agreeable variety of water, shade, walks, and air.
—What can be more charming than these flowery
lawns?

Capt. Or these gloomy shades?——

Niece. Or these embroider'd vallies?——

Capt. Or that transparent stream?——

Niece. Or these bowing branches on the banks of it, that seem to admire their own beauty in the crystal mirror?

Capt. I am surprized, madam, at the delicacy of your phrase——Can such expressions come from Lombard-street?

Niece. Alas! sir, what can be expected from an innocent virgin, that has been immured almost one and twenty years from the conversation of mankind, under the care of an Urganda of an aunt?

Capt. Bless me, madam, how have you been abused! many a lady before your age has had an hundred lances broken in her service, and as many dragons cut to pieces in honour of her.

Niece. Oh, the charming man!   [*Aside.*

Capt. Do you believe Pamela was one and twenty before she knew Musidorus?

Niece. I could hear him ever.——   [*Aside.*

Capt. A lady of your wit and beauty might have given occasion for a whole romance in folio before that age.

Niece. Oh, the powers! Who can he be? Oh, youth unknown! But let me, in the first place, know whom I talk to, for, sir, I am wholly unacquainted both with your person and your history—You seem, indeed, by your deportment, and the distinguishing mark of your bravery which you bear, to have been in a conflict—May I not know what cruel beauty obliged you to such adventures, till she pitied you?

Capt. Oh, the pretty coxcomb ! [*Aside.*] Oh, Blenheim ! Oh, Cordelia, Cordelia!

Niece. You mention the place of battle—I would
fain hear an exact description of it—Our public papers are so defective, they don't so much as tell us
how the sun rose on that glorious day——Were there
not a great many flights of vultures before the battle
began ?

Capt. Oh, madam, they have eaten up half my acquaintance.

Niece. Certainly never birds of prey were so feast-
ed—By report, they might have lived half a year on
the very legs and arms our troops left behind 'em.

Capt. Had we not fought near a wood, we should
ne'er have got legs enough to have come home upon.
The Joiner of the Foot Guards has made his fortune
by it.

Niece. I shall never forgive your general—He has
put all my ancient heroes out of countenance ; he has
pulled down Cyrus and Alexander, as much as Louis
le Grand—But your own part in that action ?

Capt. Only that slight hurt, for the astrologer said
at my nativity—Nor fire, nor sword, nor pike, nor
musquet shall destroy this child, let him but avoid
fair eyes—But, madam, mayn't I crave the name of
her that has captivated my heart ?

Niece. I can't guess whom you mean by that description ; but if you ask my name—I must confess
you put me upon revealing what I always keep as the

greatest secret I have—for, would you believe it—
they have call'd me—I don't know how to own it,
but have call'd me—Bridget. -

Capt. Bridget?

Niece. Bridget.

Capt. Bridget?

Niece. Spare my confusion, I beseech you, sir, and
if you have occasion to mention me, let it be by Parthenissa, for that's the name I have assumed ever
since I came to years of discretion.

Capt. The insupportable tyranny of parents, to fix
names on helpless infants which they must blush at
all their lives after! I don't think there's a sirname
in the world to match it.

Niece. No! what do you think of Tipkin?

Capt. Tipkin! Why, I think if I was a young lady
that had it, I'd part with it immediately.

Niece. Pray how would you get rid of it?

Capt. I'd change it for another—I could recommend to you three very pretty syllables——What do
you think of Clerimont?

Niece. Clerimont! Clerimont! Very well——But
what right have I to it?

Capt. If you will give me leave, I'll put you in
possession of it. By a very few words I can make it
over to you, and your children after you.

Niece. Oh, fye! Whither are you running! You
know a lover should sigh in private, and languish
whole years before he reveals his passion; he should
retire into some solitary grove, and make the woods

and wild beasts his confidants—You should have told
it to the echo half a year before you had discovered it
even to my hand-maid.   And yet besides—to talk to
me of children—Did you ever hear of an heroine with
a big belly?

Capt. What can a lover do, madam; now the race
of giants is extinct? Had I lived in those days, there
had not been a mortal six feet high, but should have
own'd Parthenissa for the paragon of beauty, or measured his length on the ground——Parthenissa should
have been heard by the brooks and deserts at midnight—the echo's burden, and the river's murmur.

Niece. That had been a golden age, indeed! But
see, my aunt has left her grave companion, and is
coming towards us—I command you to leave me.

Capt. Thus Oroondates, when Statira dismist him
her presence, threw himself at her feet, and implored
permission but to live.   [*Offering to kneel.*

Niece. And thus Statira raised him from the earth,
permitting him to live and love.   [*Exit Capt.* Cler.

Enter AUNT.

Aunt. Is not Mr. Pounce's conversation very improving, niece?

Niece. Is not Mr. Clerimont a very pretty name,
aunt?

Aunt. He has so much prudence.

Niece. He has so much gallantry.

Aunt. So sententious in his expressions.

Niece. So polish'd in his language.

Aunt. All he says, is, methinks, so like a sermon.

Niece. All he speaks savours of romance.

Aunt. Romance, niece? Mr. Pounce! what savours of romance?

Niece. No, I mean his friend, the accomplish'd Mr. Clerimont.

Aunt. Fye, for one of your years to commend a young fellow!

Niece. One of my years is mightily govern'd by example! You did not dislike Mr. Pounce.

Aunt. What, censorious too? I find there is no trusting you out of the house—A moment's fresh air does but make you still the more in love with strangers, and despise your own relations.

Niece. I am certainly by the power of an enchantment placed among you, but I hope I this morning employ'd one to seek adventures, and break the charm.

Aunt. Vapours, Biddy, indeed! Nothing but vapours——Cousin Humphry shall break the charm.

Niece. Name him not——Call me still Biddy, rather than name that brute. [*Exeunt* Aunt *and* Niece.

Enter Captain CLERIMONT *and* POUNCE.

Capt. A perfect Quixote in petticoats! I tell thee, Pounce, she governs herself wholly by romance—— It has got into her very blood——She starts by rule, and blushes by example——Could I have produced one instance of a lady's complying at first sight, I should have gained her promise on the spot—How am I bound to curse the cold constitutions of the Philoclea's and Statira's! I am undone for want of precedents.

Pounce. I am sure I labour'd hard to favour your conference; and plied the old woman all the while with something that tickled either her vanity or her covetousness; " I consider'd all the stocks, old and " new company, her own complexion and youth, " partners for sword-blades, chamber of London, " banks for charity, and mine adventurers, till she " told me I had the repute of the most facetious man " that ever came to Garraway's—For you must know, " public knaves and stock jobbers pass for wits at " her end of the town, as common cheats and game- " sters do at yours."

Capt. I pity the drudgery you have gone through; but what's next to be done towards getting my pretty heroine?

Pounce. What should next be done, in ordinary method of things—You have seen her, the next regular approach is, that you cannot subsist a moment, without sending forth musical complaints of your misfortune, by way of a serenade.

Capt. I can nick you there, sir, " I have a scrib- " bling army friend, that has wrote a triumphant, " rare, noisy song, in honour of the late victory, that " will hit the nymph's fantasque to a hair;" I'll get every thing ready as soon as possible.

Pounce. While you are playing upon the fort, I'll

be within, and observe what execution you do, and give you intelligence accordingly.

Capt. You must have an eye upon Mr. Humphry, while I feed the vanity of Parthenissa—For I am so experienced in these matters, that I know none but coxcombs think to win a woman by any desert of their own—No, it must be done rather by complying with some prevailing humour of your mistress, than exerting any good quality in yourself.

> *'Tis not the lover's merit wins the field,*
> *But to themselves alone the beauteous yield.*   [Exeunt.

ACT III. SCENE I.

A Chamber.   Enter Mrs. CLERIMONT, FAINLOVE, *(carrying her lap dog), and* JENNY.

Jenny.

MADAM, the footman that's recommended to you is below, if your ladyship will please to take him.

Mrs. Cler. Oh, fye; don't believe I'll think on't— It is impossible he should be good for any thing—— The English are so saucy with their liberty—I'll have all my lower servants French—There cannet be a good footman born out of an absolute monarchy,——

Jen. I am beholden to your ladyship, for believing so well of the maid-servants in England.

Mrs. Cler. Indeed, Jenny, I could wish thou wert

E

really French: for thou art plain English in spite of
example—Your arms do but hang on, and you move
perfectly upon joints.   Not with a swim of the whole
person—But I am talking to you, and have not adjusted myself to-day: what pretty company a glass
is, to have another self! [*Kisses the dog.*] The con-
verse is soliloquy!   To have company that never
contradicts or displeases us!   The pretty visible echo
of our actions. [*Kisses the dog.*]   How easy, too, it is
to be disincumber'd with stays, where a woman has
any thing like shape, if no shape, a good air—But I
look best when I'm talking.

[*Kisses the lap-dog in* Fainlove's *arms.*

Jen. You always look well.

Mrs. Cler. For I'm always talking, you mean so,
that disquiets thy sullen English temper, but I don't
really look so well when I am silent——If I do but
offer to speak—Then I may say that—Oh, bless me,
Jenny, I am so pale, I am afraid of myself——I have
not laid on half red enough——What a dough-baked
thing I was before I improved myself, and travelled
for beauty——However, my face is very prettily
design'd to-day.

Fain. Indeed, madam, you begin to have so fine an
hand, that you are younger every day than other.

Mrs. Cler. The ladies abroad used to call me Mademoiselle Titian, I was so famous for my colouring;
but pr'ythee, wench, bring me my black eye-brows
out of the next room.

Jen. Madam, I have 'em in my hand.

Fain. It would be happy for all that are to see you to-day, if you could change your eyes too.

Mrs. Cler. Gallant enough—No, hang it, I'll wear these-I have on; this mode of visage takes mightily; I had three ladies last week came over to my complexion—I think to be a fair woman this fortnight, 'till I find I'm aped too much—I believe there are an hundred copies of me already.

Jen. Dear madam, won't your ladyship please to let me be of the next countenance you leave off?

Mrs. Cler. You may, Jenny—but I assure you—it is a very pretty piece of ill-nature, for a woman that has any genius for beauty, to observe the servile imitation of her manner, her motion, her glances, and her smiles.

Fain. Aye, indeed, madam, nothing can be so ridiculous as to imitate the inimitable.

Mrs. Cler. Indeed, as you say, Fainlove, the French mien is no more to be learn'd, than the language, without going thither——Then again to see some poor ladies who have clownish, penurious English husbands, turn and torture their old clothes into so many forms, and dye 'em into so many colours, to follow me—What say'st, Jenny? What say'st? Not a word?

Jen. Why, madam, all that I can say——

Mrs. Cler. Nay, I believe, Jenny, thou hast nothing to say any more than the rest of thy country women—The spleneticks speak just as the weather lets 'em—They are mere talking barometers—Abroad the people of quality go on so eternally, and still go

E ij

on, and are gay and entertain—In England discourse
made up of nothing but question and answer—I was
t'other day at a visit, where there was a profound silence, for, I believe, the third part of a minute.

Jen. And your ladyship there?

Mrs. Cler. They infected me with their dullness.
Who can keep up their good humour at an English
visit?—They sit as at a funeral, silent in the midst of
many candles—One, perhaps, alarms the room—'Tis
very cold weather—then all the mutes play their fans
—'till some other question happens, and then the
fans go off again.———

" *Enter Boy.*

" *Boy.* Madam, your spinnet master is come.

" *Mrs. Cler.* Bring him in, he's very pretty com-
" pany.

" *Fain.* His spinnet is, he never speaks himself.

" *Mrs. Cler.* Speak, simpleton! What then, he
" keeps out silence, does not he [*Enter.*]—Oh, sir,
" you must forgive me, I have been very idle—Well,
" you pardon me, *(Master bows.)*——(Did you think
" I was perfect in the song—) *(bows)* but pray let me
" hear it once more. Let us see it.   [*Reads.*

" S O N G.

" *With studied airs, and practiced smiles,*
" *Flavia my ravish'd heart beguiles:*
" *The charms we make, are ours alone,*
" *Nature's works are not our own.*

" *Her skilful hand gives eu'ry grace,*
" *And shows her fancy in her face;*
" *She feeds with art an amorous rage,*
" *Nor fears the force of coming age.*

" You sing it very well : But, I confess, I wish you'd
" give more into the French manner.——Observe me
" hum it *à la Françoise.*

    " *With studied airs,* &c.

" The whole person, every limb, every nerve sings
" ——the English way is only being for that time a
" mere musical instrument, just sending forth a
" sound without knowing they do so——Now I'll
" give you a little of it, like an English woman——
" You are to suppose I've denied you twenty times,
" look'd silly, and all that—Then with hands and
" face insensible——I have a mighty cold.

    " *With studied airs,* &c."

Enter Servant.

Serv. Madam, Captain Clerimont, and a very
strange gentleman, are come to wait on you.

Mrs. Cler. Let him and the very strange gentleman
come in.

Fain. Oh ! madam, that's the country gentleman I
was telling you of.

Enter HUMPHRY *and Captain* CLERIMONT.

Fain. Madam, may I do myself the honour to re
E iij

commend Mr. Gubbin, son and heir to Sir Harry
Gubbin, to your ladyship's notice?

Mrs. Cler. Mr. Gubbin, I am extremely pleased
with your suit, 'tis antique, and originally from
France.

Hump. It is always lock'd up, madam, when I'm in
the country. My father prizes it mightily.

Mrs. Cler. 'Twould make a very pretty dancing
suit in a mask. Oh! Captain Clerimont, I have a
quarrel with you.

Enter Servant.

Serv. Madam, your ladyship's husband desires to
know whether you see company to-day, or not?

Mrs. Cler. Who, you clown?

Serv. Mr. Clerimont, madam.

Mrs. Cler. He may come in.

Enter CLERIMONT, *Senior.*

Mrs. Cler. Your very humble servant.

Cler. Sen. I was going to take the air this morning
in my coach, and did myself the honour, before I
went, to receive your commands, finding you saw
company.

Mrs. Cler. At any time, when you know I do, you
may let me see you. Pray how did you sleep last
night?——If I had not asked him that question, they
might have thought we lay together. [*Aside.*] [*Here*
Fainlove *looking through a perspective, bows to* Clerimont, *Senior.*] But, captain, I have a quarrel with

you—I have utterly forgot those three coupees, you promised to come again and shew me.   Your humble servant, sir.——But, oh! [*As she is going to be led by the captain.*] Have you sign'd that mortgage to pay off my Lady Faddle's winnings at Ombre?

Cler. Sen. Yes, madam.

Mrs. Cler. Then all's well, my honour's safe. [*Exit.*

Clerimont, *Sen.*] Come, captain, lead me this step—for I am apt to make a false one—you shall shew me.

Capt. I'll shew you, madam, 'tis no matter for a fiddle; I'll give you 'em the French way, in a teaching tune.   Pray, more quick——*O Mademoiselle que faitez vous—A moi*—There again—Now slide, as it were, with and without measure——There you outdid the gipsey!——and you have all the smiles of the dance to a tittle.

" *Mrs. Cler.* Why truly, I think, that the greatest
" part—I have seen an English woman dance a jig
" with the severity of a vestal virgin"——

Hump. If this be French dancing and singing, I fancy I could do it—Haw, Haw!   [*Capers aside.*

Mrs. Cler. I protest, Mr. Gubbin, you have almost the step, without any of our country bashfulness. Give me your hand—Haw, haw!   So, so a little quicker—that's right, Haw! " Captain, your brother
" deliver'd this spark to me, to be diverted here till
" he calls for him."   [*Exit Capt. Clerimont.*

Hump. This cutting so high makes one's money jingle confoundedly.   I'm resolved I'll never carry above one pocket full hereafter.

Mrs. Cler. You do it very readily—You amaze me.

Hump. Are the gentlemen of France generally so well bred as we are in England?—Are they, madam, ha! But, young gentleman, when shall I see this sister? Haw, haw, haw! Is not the higher one jumps the better?

Fain. She'll be mightily taken with you, I'm sure. One would not think 'twas in you—you're so gay—and dance so very high——

Hump. What should ail me? Did you think I was wind-gall'd? I can sing, too, if I please—but I won't 'till I see your sister. This is a mighty pretty house.

Mrs. Cler. Well, do you know that I like this gentleman extremely; I should be glad to inform him ——But were you never in France, Mr Gubbin?

Hump. No;—but I'm always thus pleasant, if my father's not by——I protest, I'd advise your sister to have me—I'm for marrying her at once—why should I stand shilly shally, like a country Bumpkin?

Fain. Mr. Gubbin, I dare say she'll be as forward as you; we'll go in and see her. [*Apart.*

Mrs. Cler. Then he has not yet seen the lady he is in love with. I protest very new and gallant—Mr. Gubbin, she must needs believe you a frank person ——Fainlove, I must see this sister too, I'm resolved she shall like him.

There needs not time true passion to discover;
The most believing is the most a lover. [*Exeunt.*

SCENE II.

The Park.. Enter NIECE, *sola.*

Niece. Oh Clerimont! Clerimont! To be struck at first sight! I'm asham'd of my weakness; I find in myself all the symptoms of a raging amour; I love solitude; I grow pale; I sigh frequently; I call upon the name of Clerimont when I don't think of it—— his person is ever in my eyes, and his voice in my ears ————methinks I long to lose myself in some pensive grove, or to hang over the head of some warbling fountain, with a lute in my hand, softening the murmurs of the water.

Enter AUNT.

Aunt. Biddy, Biddy; where's Biddy Tipkin?
Niece. Whom do you inquire for?
Aunt. Come, come, he's just a coming at the park door.
Niece. Who is coming?
Aunt. Your cousin Humphry—who should be coming? Your lover, your husband that is to be—— Pray, my dear, look well, and be civil for your credit and mine too.
Niece. If he answers my idea, I shall rally the rustic to death.
Aunt. Hist——here he is.

Enter HUMPHRY.

Hump. Aunt, your humble servant———Is that—ha! Aunt?

Aunt. Yes, cousin Humphry, that's your cousin Bridget. Well, I'll leave you together.

[*Exit* Aunt. *They sit.*

Hump. Aunt does as she'd be done by, cousin Bridget, does not she, cousin? ha! What, are you a Londoner, and not speak to a gentleman? Look ye, cousin, the old folks resolving to marry us, I thought it would be proper to see how I liked you, as not caring to buy a pig in a poke——for I love to look before I leap.

Niece. Sir, your person and address bring to my mind the whole history of Valentine and Orson: what! would they marry me to a wild man? Pray answer me a question or two.

Hump. Aye, aye, as many as you please, cousin Bridget.

Niece. What wood were you taken in? How long have you been caught?

Hump. Caught!

Niece. Where were your haunts?

Hump. My haunts!

Niece. Are not clothes very uneasy to you? Is this strange dress the first you ever wore?

Hump. How!

Niece. Are you not a great admirer of roots, and

raw flesh ?—Let me look upon your nails——Don't
you love blackberries, haws, and pig-nuts, mightily ?

Hump. How !

Niece. Can'st thou deny that thou wert suckled by
a wolf? You han't been so barbarous, I hope, since
you came amongst men, as to hunt your nurse—
Have you ?

Hump. Hunt my nurse ? Aye, 'tis so, she's distracted as sure as a gun——Hark ye, cousin, pray
will you let me ask you a question or two ?

Niece. If thou hast yet learnt the use of language,
speak, monster.

Hump. How long have you been thus ?

Niece. Thus ! what would'st thou say ?

Hump. What's the cause of it ? Tell me truly now
—Did you never love any body before me ?

Niece. Go, go, thou'rt a savage.   [*Rises.*

Hump. They never let you go abroad, I suppose.

Niece. Thou'rt a monster, I tell thee.

Hump. Indeed, cousin, tho' 'tis folly to tell thee so
—I am afraid thou art a mad woman.

Niece. I'll have thee into some forest.

Hump. I'll take thee into a dark room.

Niece. I hate thee.

Hump. I wish you did—There's no hate lost, I assure you, cousin Bridget.

Niece. Cousin Bridget, quoth'a—I'd as soon claim
kindred with a mountain bear——I detest thee.

Hump. You never do any harm in these fits, I hope
—But do you hate me in earnest ?

Niece. Dost thou ask it, ungentle forester.

Hump. Yes, for I've a reason, look ye. It happens very well if you hate me, and in your senses, for to tell you truly—I don't much care for you; and there is another fine woman, as I am inform'd, that is in some hopes of having me.

Niece. This merits my attention. '   [*Aside.*

Hump. Look ye d'ye see—as I said, I don't care for you——I would not have you set your heart on me—but if you like any body else let me know it—and I'll find out a way for us to get rid of one another, and deceive the old folks that would couple us.

Niece. This wears the face of an amour—There is something in that thought which makes thy presence less unsupportable.

Hump. Nay, nay, now you're growing fond; if you come with these maids tricks, to say you hate at first and afterwards like me,—you'll spoil the whole design.

Niece. Don't fear it——When I think of consorting with thee, may the wild boar defile the cleanly ermin, may the tiger be wedded to the kid!

Hump. When I of thee, may the pole-cat catterwaul with the civet.

Niece. When I harbour the least thought of thee, may the silver Thames forget its course!

Hump. When I like thee, may I be soused over head and ears in a horse-pond?——But do you hate me?

Enter AUNT.

Niece. For ever; and you me?

Hump. Most heartily.

Aunt. Ha! I like this———They are come to promises—and protestations.   •   [*Aside.*

Hump. I am very glad I have found a way to please you.

Niece. You promise to be constant.

Hump. 'Till death. •

Niece. Thou best of savages!

Hump. Thou best of savages! poor Biddy.

Ant. Oh the pretty couple joking on one another. Well, how do you like your cousin Humphry now?

Niece. Much better than I thought I should—He's quite another thing than what I took him for———We have both the same passions for one another.

Hump. We wanted only an occasion to open our hearts—Aunt.

Aunt. Oh, how this will rejoice my brother, and Sir Harry! we'll go to 'em.

Hump. No, I must fetch a walk with a new acquaintance, Mr. Samuel Pounce.

Aunt. An excellent acquaintance for your husband! come, Niece, come.

Niece. Farewell, rustic.

Hump. B'ye, Biddy.

Aunt. Rustic! Biddy! Ha! ha! pretty creatures.
[*Exeunt.*

F

ACT IV. SCENE I.

Continues. **Enter Captain** CLERIMONT *and* POUNCE.

Captain.

Does she expect me, then, at this very instant?

Pounce. I tell you, she ordered me to bring the painter at this very hour precisely, to draw her niece ——" for to make her picture peculiarly charming, " she has now that down-cast pretty shame, that " warm cheek, glowing with the fear and hope of " to-day's fate, with the inviting, coy affectation of " a bride, all in her face at once." Now I know you are a pretender that way.

Capt. Enough, I warrant, to personate the character on such an inspiring occasion.

Pounce. " You must have the song I spoke of per- " form'd at this window—at the end of which I'll " give you a signal——Every thing is ready for you, " your pencil, your canvas stretch'd—your——" Be sure you play your part in humour: to be a painter for a lady, you're to have the excessive flattery of a lover, the ready invention of a poet, and the easy gesture of a player.

Capt. Come, come, no more instructions; my imagination out-runs all you can say : begone, begone!

[*Exit* Pounce.

A SONG.

" *Why, lovely charmer, tell me why,*
" *So very kind, and yet so shy?*

" *Why does the cold forbidding air*
" *Give damps of sorrow and despair?*
" *Or why that smile my soul subdue,*
" *And kindle up my flames anew?*

" *In vain you strive with all your art,*
" *By turns to freeze and fire my heart:*
" *When I behold a face so fair,*
" *So sweet a look, so soft an air,*
" *My ravish'd soul is charm'd all o'er,*
" *I cannot love thee less nor more.*

" *After the Song,* POUNCE *appears beckoning the Captain.*

" *Pounce.* Captain, Captain." [*Exit* Captain.

SCENE II.

NIECE's *Lodgings.* *Enter* AUNT *and* NIECE.

Aunt. Indeed, Niece, I am as much overjoy'd to see your wedding day, as if it were my own.

Niece. But why must it be huddled up so?

Aunt. Oh, my dear, a private wedding is much better; your mother had such a bustle at her's, with feasting and fooling: besides, they did not go to bed till two in the morning.

Niece. Since you understand things so well, I wonder you never married yourself.

Aunt. My dear, I was very cruel thirty years ago, and no body ask'd me since.

F ij

Niece. Alas-a-day!

Aunt. Yet, I assure you, there were a great many matches proposed to me—There was Sir Gilbert Jolly; but he, forsooth, could not please; he drank ale, and smoak'd tobacco, and was no fine gentleman, forsooth——but, then again, there was young Mr. Peregrine Shapely, who had travell'd, and spoke French, and smiled at all I said; he was a fine gentleman—but then he was consumptive: and yet again, to see how one may be mistaken: Sir Jolly died in half a year, and my lady Shapely has by that thin slip eight children, that should have been mine; but here's the bridegroom. So, cousin Humphry!

Enter HUMPHRY.

Hump. Your servant, ladies—So, my dear—

Niece. So, my savage——

Aunt. O fye, no more of that to your husband, Biddy.

Hump. No matter, I like it as well as duck or love: I know my cousin loves me as well as I do her.

Aunt. I'll leave you together; I must go and get ready an entertainment for you when you come home.   [*Exit.*

Hump. Well, cousin, are you constant?——Do you hate me still?

Niece. As much as ever.

Hump. What an happiness it is, when people's inclinations jump! I wish I knew what to do with you: can you get no body, d'ye think, to marry you?

Niece. Oh, Clerimont, Clerimont! where art thou?

Aside.

Enter AUNT, *and Captain* CLERIMONT *disguised.*

Aunt. This, sir, is the lady whom you are to draw ——You see, sir, as good flesh and blood as a man would desire to put in colours—I must have her maiden pictures.

Hump. Then the painter must make haste—Ha, cousin!

Niece. Hold thy tongue, good savage.

Capt. Madam, I'm generally forced to new-mould every feature, and mend nature's handy-work; but here she has made so finish'd an original, that I despair of my copy's coming up to it.

Aunt. Do you hear that, Niece?

Niece. I don't desire you to make graces where you find none.

Capt. To see the difference of the fair sex——I protest to you, madam, my fancy is utterly exhausted with inventing faces for those that sit to me. The first entertainment I generally meet with, are complaints for want of sleep; they never look'd so pale in their lives, as when they sit for their pictures—— Then, so many touches and re-touches, when the face is finish'd——That wrinkle ought not to have been, those eyes are too languid, the colour's too weak, that side-look hides the mole on the left cheek. In short, the whole likeness is struck out: but in

F iij

you, madam, the highest I can come up to will be
but rigid justice.

Hump. A comical dog, this!

Aunt. Truly the gentleman seems to understand
his business.

Niece. Sir, if your pencil flatters like your tongue,
you are going to draw a picture that won't be at all
like me. Sure, I have heard that voice somewhere.

[*Aside.*

Capt. Madam, be pleased to place yourself near
me, nearer still, madam, here falls the best light——
You must know, madam, there are three kinds of
a rs which the ladies most delight in——There is
your haughty—your mild—and your pensive air——
The haughty may be exprest with the head a little
more erect than ordinary, and the countenance with
a certain disdain in it, so as she may appear almost,
but not quite, inexorable: this kind of air is generally
heightened with a little knitting of the brows—I gave
my Lady Scornwell her choice of a dozen frowns, before she could find one to her liking.

Niece. But what's the mild air?

Capt. The mild air is compos'd of a languish, and
a smile——But if I might advise, I'd rather be a
pensive beauty; the pensive usually feels her pulse,
leans on one arm, or sits ruminating with a book in
her hand——which conversation she is supposed to
choose, rather than the endless importunities of lovers.

Hump. A comical dog.

Aunt. Upon my word he understands his business

well; 'I'll tell you, Niece, how your mother was drawn——She had an orange in her hand, and a nosegay in her bosom, but a look so pure and fresh-colour'd, you'd have taken her for one of the seasons.

Capt. You seem, indeed, madam, most inclined to the pensive——The pensive delights also in the fall of waters, pastoral figures, or any rural view suitable to a fair lady, who, with a delicate spleen, has re-tired from the world, as sick of its flattery and ad-miration.

Niece. No——since there is room for fancy in a picture, I would be drawn like the Amazon Tha-lestris, with a spear in my hand, and an helmet on a table before me——At a distance behind, let there be a dwarf, holding by the bridle a milk-white pal-frey——

Capt. Madam, the thought is full of spirit; and, if you please, there shall be a Cupid stealing away your helmet, to shew that love should have a part in all gallant actions.

Niece. That circumstance may be very picturesque.

Capt. Here, madam, shall be your own picture, here the palfrey, and here the dwarf—The dwarf must be very little, or we shan't have room for him.

Niece. A dwarf cannot be too little.

Capt. I'll make him a blackamoor, to distinguish him from the other too powerful dwarf——[*Sighs.*] the Cupid—I'll place that beauteous boy near you, 'twill look very natural—He'll certainly take you for his mother Venus.

Niece. I leave these particulars to your own fancy.

Capt. Please, madam, to uncover your neck a little; a little lower still—a little, little lower.

Niece. I'll be drawn thus, if you please, sir.

Capt. Ladies, have you heard the news of a late marriage between a young lady of a great fortune and a younger brother of a good family?

Aunt. Pray, sir, how is it?

Capt. This young gentleman, ladies, is a particular acquaintance of mine, and much about my age and stature; (look me full in the face, madam;) he accidentally met the young lady, who had in her all the perfections of her sex; (hold up your head, madam, that's right;) she let him know that his person and discourse were not altogether disagreeable to her— the difficulty was, how to gain a second interview, (your eyes full upon mine, madam;) for never was there such a sigher in all the vallies of Arcadia, as that unfortunate youth, during the absence of her he loved——

Aunt. A-lack-a-day—poor young gentleman!

Niece. It must be he——what a charming amour is this!   [*Aside.*

Capt. At length, ladies, he bethought himself of an expedient; he drest himself just as I am now, and came to draw her picture; (your eyes full upon mine, pray, madam.)

Hump. A subtle dog, I warrant him.

Capt. And by that means found an opportunity of carrying her off, and marrying her.

Aunt. Indeed, your friend was a very vicious young man.

Niece. Yet perhaps the young lady was not displeased at what he had done.

Capt. But, madam, what were the transports of the lover, when she made him that confession.

Niece. I dare say she thought herself very happy, when she got out of her guardian's hands.

Aunt. 'Tis very true, Niece—There are abundance of those head-strong young baggages about town.

Capt. The gentleman has often told me, he was strangely struck at first sight ; but when she sat to him for her picture, and assumed all those graces that are proper for the occasion, his torment was so exquisite, his occasions so violent, that he could not have lived a day, had he not found means to make the charmer of his heart his own.

Hump. 'Tis certainly the foolishest thing in the world to stand shilly-shally about a woman, when one has a mind to marry her.

Capt. The young painter turn'd poet on the subject; I believe I have the words by heart.

Niece. A sonnet ! pray repeat it.

Capt. When gentle Parthenissa walks,
    And sweetly smiles, and gaily talks,
    A thousand shafts around her fly,
    A thousand swains unheeded die :

    If then she labours to be seen,
    With all her killing air and mein;

From so much beauty, so much art,
What mortal can secure his heart ?

Hump. I fancy if 'twas sung, 'twould make a very pretty catch.

Capt. My servant has a voice, you shall hear it.

[*Here it is sung.*

Aunt. Why, this is pretty. I think a painter should never be without a good singer—It brightens the features strangely—I profess I'm mightily pleased; I'll but just step in, and give some orders, and be with you presently. [*Exit.*

Niece. Was not this adventurous painter called Clerimont ?

Capt. It was Clerimont, the servant of Parthenissa; but let me beseech that beauteous maid to resolve, and make the incident I feign'd to her a real one—— consider, madam, you are environ'd by cruel and treacherous guards, which would force you to a disagreeable marriage; your case is exactly the same with the princess of the Leontines in Clelia.

Niece. How can we commit such a solecism against all rules! what, in the first leaf of our history to have the marriage ? You know it cannot be.

Capt. The pleasantest part of the history will be after marriage.

Niece. No! I never yet read of a knight that entered tilt or tournament after wedlock——'Tis not to be expected——When the husband begins, the hero ends; all that noble impulse to glory, all the gene-

rous passion for adventures is consumed in the nuptial
torch; I don't know how it is, but Mars and Hymen
never hit it.

Hump. [*Listening.*] Consumed in the nuptial torch!
Mars and Hymen! What can all this mean?—I am
very glad I can hardly read—They could never get
these foolish fancies into my head—I had always a
strong brain. [*Aside.*] Hark ye, cousin, is not this
painter a comical dog?

Niece. I think he's very agreeable company—

'*Hump.* Why then I tell you what—marry him A
painter's a very genteel calling—He's an ingenious
fellow, and certainly poor, I fancy he'd be glad on't;
I'll keep my aunt out of the room a minute or two,
that's all the time you have to consider. [*Exit.*

Capt. Fortune points out to us this only occasion
of our happiness : love's of celestial origin, and needs
no long acquaintance to be manifest. Lovers, like
angels, speak by intuition——Their souls are in their
eyes.

Niece. Then I fear he sees mine. [*Aside.*] But I
can't think of abridging our amours, and cutting off
all farther decorations of disguise, serenade, and adventure.

Capt. Nor would I willingly lose the merit of long
services, midnight sighs, and plaintive solitudes—
were there not a necessity.

Niece. Then to be seized by stealth!

Capt. Why, madam, you are a great fortune, and
should not be married the common way. Indeed,

madam, you ought to be stolen; nay, in strictness, I don't know but you ought to be ravish'd.

Niece. But then our history will be short.

Capt. I grant it; but you don't consider there's a device in other's leading you instead of this person that's to have you; and, madam, tho' our amours can't furnish out a romance, they'll make a very pretty novel——Why smiles my fair?

Niece. I am almost of opinion, that had Oroondates been as pressing as Clerimont, Cassandra had been but a pocket-book: but it looks so ordinary, to go out at a door to be married—Indeed, I ought to be taken out of a window, and run away with.

Enter HUMPHRY *and* POUNCE.

Hump. Well, cousin, the coach is at the door. If you please I'll lead you.

Niece. I put myself into your hands, good savage; but you promise to leave me.

Hump. I tell you plainly, you must not think of having me.

Pounce. [*To Capt.*] You'll have opportunity enough to carry her off? the old fellow will be busy with me —I'll gain all the time I can, but be bold and pros- per.

Niece. Clerimont, you follow us.

Capt. Upon the wings of love.

ACT V. SCENE I.

A Chamber. *Enter* CLERIMONT, *Sen. and* FAINLOVE.

Clerimont, Sen.

THEN she gave you this letter, and bid you read it as a paper of verses?

Fain. This is the place, the hour, the lucky mi-. nute—Now am I rubbing up my memory, to recollect all you said to me when you first ruin'd me, that I may attack her right.

Cler. Sen. Your eloquence would be needless—'tis so unmodish to need persuasion: modesty makes a lady embarrast—But my spouse is above that, as for example, [*Reading the letter.*] Fainlove, *you don't seem to want wit—therefore I need say no more, than that distance to a woman of the world is becoming in no man, but a husband. An hour hence, come up the back stairs to my closet.* Adieu, *Mon Mignon.*

I am glad you are punctual. I'll conceal myself to observe your interview—Oh, torture! but this wench must not see it. [*Aside.*

Fain. Be sure you come time enough to save my reputation.

Cler. Sen. Remember your orders, distance becomes no man but an husband.

Fain. I am glad you are in so good humour on the occasion; but you know me to be but a bully in love, that can bluster only 'till the minute of engagement—

G

But I'll top my part, and form my conduct by my own sentiments—If she grows coy, I'll grow more saucy—'Twas so I was won myself—

Cler. Sen. Well, my dear rival—your assignation draws nigh—you are to put on your transport, your impatient throbbing heart won't let you wait her arrival—let the dull family-thing and husband, who reckons his moments by his cares, be content to wait, but you are gallant, and measure time by extasies.

Fain. I hear her coming—to your post—good husband know your duty, and don't be in the way when your wife has a mind to be in private—to your post, into the coal hole.

Enter Mrs. CLERIMONT.

Welcome my dear, my tender charmer——Oh! to my longing arms—feel the heart pat, that falls and rises as you smile or frown——Oh, the extatic moment!

I think that was something like what has been said to me.   [*Aside.*

Mrs. Cler. Very well—Fainlove—I protest I value myself for my discerning—I knew you had fire through all the respect you shewed me—But how came you to make no direct advances, young gentleman?—why was I forced to admonish your gallantry.

Fain. Why, madam, I knew you a woman of breeding, and above the senseless niceties of an English wife—The French way is, you are to go so far, whether they are agreeable or not: If you are so happy

s to please, nobody that is not of a constrain'd behaviour, is at a loss to let you know it—Besides, if
the humble servant makes the first approaches, he
has the impudence of making a request, but not the
honour of obeying a command.

Mrs. Cler. Right—a woman's man should conceal
passion in a familiar air of indifference. Now there's
Mr. Clerimont; I can't allow him the least freedom,
but the unfashionable fool grows so fond of me, he
cannot hide it in public.

Fain. Aye, madam, have often wondered at your
ladyship's choice of one who seems to have so little of
the Beau Monde in his carriage, but just what you
force him to———while there were so many pretty
gentlemen.——— [*Dancing.*

Mrs. Cler. O young gentleman you are mightily
mistaken, if you think such animals as you, and pretty
beau Titmouse, and pert Billy Butterfly, tho' I suffer
you to come in, and play about my rooms, are any
ways in competition with a man whose name one
would wear.

Fain. Oh, madam! then I find we are———

Mrs. Cler. A woman of sense must have respect for
a man of that character; but, alas! respect——is respect! respect is not the thing——respect has something too solemn for soft moments——You things are
more proper for hours of dalliance.

Cler. Sen. [*Peeping.*] How have I wronged this fine
lady!——I find I am to be a cuckold out of her pure
esteem for me.

Mrs. Cler. Besides, those fellows for whom we have respect, have none for us; I warrant on such an occasion Clerimont would have ruffled a woman out of all form, while you————

Cler. Sen. A good hint————now my cause comes on. . [*Aside.*

Fain. Since, then, you allow us fitter for soft moments, why do we misemploy 'em. Let me kiss that beauteous hand, and clasp that graceful frame.

Mrs. Cler. How, Fainlove! What, you don't design to be impertinent————but my lips have a certain roughness on 'em to day, han't they?

Fain. [*Kissing.*] No————they are all softness———— their delicious sweetness is inexpressible————here language fails—let me applaud thy lips not by the utterance, but by the touch of mine.

Enter CLERIMONT, *Sen. drawing his sword.*

Cler. Sen. Ha, villain! ravisher! invader of my bed and honour! draw.

Mrs. Cler. What means this insolence, this intrusion into my privacy? What, do you come into my very closet without knocking? Who put this into your head?

Cler. Sen. My injuries have alarm'd me, and I'll bear no longer, but sacrifice your bravado, the author of 'em.

Mrs. Cler. O poor Mr. Fainlove————Must he die for his complaisance, and innocent freedoms with me? How could you, if you might? Oh! the sweet youth!

What, fight Mr. Fainlove ? What will the ladies say ?

Fain. Let me come at the intruder on ladies private hours———the unfashionable monster———I'll pre- vent all future interruption from him———let me come——— [*Drawing his sword.*

Mrs. Cler. O the brave pretty creature ! Look at his youth and innocence———He is not made for such rough encounters———Stand behind me———Poor Fain- love ?—There is not a visit in town, sir, where you shall not be displayed at fool length for this intru- sion———I banish you for ever from my sight and bed.

Cler. Sen. I obey you, madam, for distance is be- coming in no man but an husband———[*Giving her the letter, which she reads, and falls into a swoon.*] I've gone too far—[*Kissing her.*] The impertinent was guilty of nothing but what my indiscretion led her to———This is the first kiss I've had these six weeks—but she awakes.———Well, Jenny, you topp'd your part, in- deed———Come to my arms thou ready willing fair one———Thou hast no vanities, no niceties; but art thankful for every instance of love that I bestow on thee——— [*Embracing her.*

Mrs. Cler. What, am I then abused ? Is it a wench then of his ? Oh me ! Was ever poor abused wife, poor innocent lady thus injured !
[*Runs and seizes* Fainlove's *sword.*

Cler. Sen. Oh the brave pretty creature !———Hurt Mr. Fainlove ! Look at his youth, his innocence——— Ha, ha ! [*Interposing.*

G iij

Fain. Have a care, have a care, dear sir—I know myself she'll have no mercy.

Mrs. Cler. I'll be the death of her——let me come on——Stand from between us, Mr. Clerimont—— I would not hurt you. [*Pushing and crying.*

Cler. Sen. Run, run, Jenny. [*Exit* Jenny.

[*Looks at her upbraidingly before he speaks.*

Well, madam, are these the innocent freedoms you claim'd of me? Have I deserv'd this? How has there been a moment of yours ever interrupted with the real pangs I suffer? The daily importunities of cre- ditors, who become so by serving your profuse va- nities : did I ever murmur at supplying any of your diversions, while I believed 'em (as you call'd 'em) harmless? must, then, those eyes, that used to glad my heart with their familiar brightness, hang down with guilt? guilt has transform'd thy whole person; nay the very memory of it——Fly from my growing passion.

Mrs. Cler. I cannot fly, nor bear it—Oh! look not——

Cler. Sen. What can you say? speak quickly.

[*Offering to draw.*

Mrs. Cler. I never saw you moved before—Don't murder me, impenitent; I'm wholly in your power as a criminal, but remember I have been so in a tender regard.

Cler. Sen. But how have you consider'd that regard?

Mrs. Cler. Is't possible you can forgive what you ensnared me into?—Oh! look at me kindly——You

know I have only err'd in my intention, nor saw my
danger, till, by this honest art, you had shown me
what 'tis to venture to the utmost limit of what is
lawful. You laid that train, I'm sure, to alarm, not
to betray, my innocence——Mr. Clerimont scorns
such baseness! therefore I kneel—I weep—I am
convinced.   [*Kneels.*
                 [Cler. Sen. *takes her up embracing her.*

Cler. Sen. Then kneel, and weep no more——my
fairest——my reconciled!——Be so in a moment, for
know I cannot (without wringing my own heart,)
give you the least compunction—— Be in humour—
It shall be your own fault, if ever there's a serious
word more on this subject.

Mrs. Cler. I must correct every idea that rises in
my mind, and learn every gesture of my body a-new
——I detest the thing I was.

Cler. Sen. No, no—You must not do so—Our joy
and grief, honour and reproach, are the same; you
must slide out of your foppery by degrees, so that it
may appear your own act.

Mrs. Cler. But this wench!——

Cler. Sen. She is already out of your way——You
shall see the catastrophe of her fate yourself——But
still keep up the fine lady till we go out of town——
You may return to it with as decent airs as you please
——And now I have shown you your error, I'm in
so good humour as to repeat you a couplet on the occasion——

" They only who gain minds, true laurels wear,
" 'Tis less to conquer, than convince the fair."

[*Exeunt.*

SCENE II.

A Room.   Enter POUNCE, *with papers.*

[*A table, chairs, pen, ink, and paper.*]

Pounce. 'Tis a delight to gall these old rascals, and set 'em at variance about stakes, which I know neither of 'em will ever have possession of.

Enter TIPKIN, *and Sir* HARRY.

Tip. Do you design, Sir Harry, that they shall have an estate in their own hands, and keep house themselves, poor things ?

Sir Har. No, no, sir, I know better ; they shall go down into the country, and live with me, nor touch a farthing of money, but having all things necessary provided, they shall go tame about the house, and breed.

Tip. Well, Sir Harry, then considering that all human things are subject to change, it behoves every man that has a just sense of mortality, to take care of his money.

Sir Har. I don't know what you mean, brother— What do you drive at, brother ?

Tip. This instrument is executed by you, your son,

and my niece, which discharges me of all retrospects.

Sir Har. It is confest, brother; but what then?—

Tip. All that remains is, that you pay me for the
young lady's twelve years board, as also all other
charges, as wearing apparel, *&c.*

Sir Har. What is this you say? Did I give you my
discharge from all retrospects, as you call it, and after
all do you come with this and t'other, and all that?
I find you are, I tell you, sir, to your face, I find
you are——

Tip. I find, too, what you are, Sir Harry.

Sir Har. What am I, sir? What am I?

Tip. Why, sir, you are angry.

Sir Har. Sir I scorn your words, I am not angry—
Mr. Pounce is my witness, I am gentle as a lamb—
Would it not make any flesh alive angry, to see a
close hunks come after all with a demand of——

Tip. Mr. Pounce, pray inform Sir Harry in this
point.

Pounce. Indeed, Sir Harry, I must tell you plainly,
that Mr. Tipkin, in this, demands nothing but what
he may recover—For tho' this case may be consider'd
multifariam; that is to say, as 'tis usually, commonly,
vicatim, or vulgarly exprest——Yet, I say, when we
only observe, that the power is settled as the law requires, *assensu patris*, by the consent of the father—
That circumstance imports you are well acquainted
with the advantages which accrue to your family
by this alliance, which corroborates Mr. Tipkin's

demand, and avoids all objections that can be made.

Sir Har. Why then I find you are his adviser in all this—

Pounce. Look ye, Sir Harry, to show you I love to promote among my clients a good understanding; tho' Mr. Tipkin may claim four thousand pounds, I'll engage for him, and I know him so well, that he shall take three thousand nine hundred and ninety-eight pounds, four shillings, and eight-pence farthing.

Tip. Indeed, Mr. Pounce, you are too hard upon me.

Pounce. You must consider a little, Sir Harry is your brother.

Sir Har. Three thousand nine hundred and ninety-eight pounds, four shillings, and eight-pence farthing! for what, I say? for what, sir?

Pounce. For what, sir! for what she wanted, sir, a fine lady is always in want, sir—Her very clothes would come to that money in half the time.

Sir Har. Three thousand nine hundred and ninety-eight pounds, four shillings and eight-pence farthing for clothes! pray how many suits does she wear out in a year?

Pounce. Oh, dear sir, a fine lady's clothes are not old by being worn, but by being seen.

Sir Har. Well, I'll save her clothes for the future, after I have got her into the country—I'll warrant her she shall not appear more in this wicked town, where clothes are worn out by sight——And as to what you demand, I tell you, sir, 'tis extortion.

Tip. Sir Harry, do you accuse me of extortion?

Sir Har. Yes, I say extortion.

Tip. Mr. Pounce, write down that——There are very good laws provided against scandal and calumny —Loss of reputation may tend to loss of money——

Pounce. Item, For having accused Mr. Tipkin of extortion.

Sir Har. Nay, if you come to your *Items*—Look ye, Mr. Tipkin, this is an inventory of such goods as were left to my Niece Bridget by her deceased father, and which I expect shall be forth-coming at her marriage to my son——

Imprimis, A golden locket of her mother's, with something very ingenious in Latin on the inside of it.

Item, A couple of musquets, with two shoulder-belts and bandeliers.

Item, A large silver caudle-cup, with a true story engraven on it.

Pounce. But, Sir Harry——

Sir Har. Item, A base viol, with almost all the strings to it, and only a small hole on the back.

Pounce. But nevertheless, sir——

Sir Har. This is the furniture of my brother's bed-chamber that follows—A suit of tapestry hangings, with the story of Judith and Holofernes, torn only where the head should have been off—an old bed-stead curiously wrought about the posts, consisting of two load of timber—a hone, a bason, three razors, and a comb-case——Look ye, sir, you see I can *Item* it.

Pounce. Alas! Sir Harry, if you had ten quire of *Items*, 'tis all answer'd in the word retrospect.

Sir Har. Why then, Mr. Pounce and Mr. Tipkin, you are both rascals.

Tip. Do you call me rascal, sir Harry?

Sir Har. Yes, sir.

Tip. Write it down, Mr. Pounce——at the end of the leaf.

Sir Har. If you have room; Mr. Pounce—put down villain, son of a whore, curmudgeon, hunks, and scoundrel.

Tip. Not so fast, Sir Harry, he cannot write so fast, you are at the word villain—Son of a whore, I take it, was next——You may make the account as large as you please, Sir Harry.

Sir Har. Come, come, I won't be used thus—— Hark ye, sirrah, draw—What do you do at this end of the town without a sword?—Draw, I say—

Tip. Sir Harry, you are a military man, a colonel of the militia.

Sir Har. I am so, sirrah, and will run such an extorting dog as you through the guts, to show the militia is useful.

Pounce. Oh dear, oh dear!—How am I concern'd to see persons of your figure thus moved—The wedding is coming in—We'll settle these things afterwards.

Tip. I am calm.

Sir Har. Tipkin, live these two hours—but expect—

Enter HUMPHRY *leading* NIECE, *Mrs.* CLERIMONT *led by* FAINLOVE, *Capt.* CLERIMONT, *and* CLERIMONT, Sen.

Pounce. Who are these? Hey-day, who are these, sir Harry? Ha!

Sir Har. Some frolic, 'tis wedding-day—no matter.

Hump. Haw, haw; father—master, uncle—Come, you must stir your stumps, you must dance—Come, old lads, kiss the ladies—

Mrs. Cler. Mr. Tipkin, sir Harry,—I beg pardon for an introduction so mal-a-propos——I know sudden familiarity is not the English way——Alas, Mr. Gubbin, this father and uncle of yours must be new modell'd—How they stare both of them!

Sir Har. Hark ye, Numps, who is this you have brought hither? is it not the famous fine lady Mrs. Clerimont—What a pox did you let her come near your wife—

Hump. Look ye, don't expose yourself, and play some mad country prank to disgrace me before her—I shall be laught at, because she knows I understand better.

Mrs. Cler. I congratulate, madam, your coming out of the bondage of a virgin state—A woman can't do what she will properly 'till she's married.

Sir Har. Did you hear what she said to your wife?

Enter AUNT *before a service of dishes.*

Aunt. So, Mr. Bridegroom, pray take that nap-

H

kin, and serve your spouse to-day, according to custom.

Hump. Mrs. Clerimont, pray know my aunt.

Mrs. Cler. Madam, I must beg your pardon; I can't possibly like all that vast load of meat that you are sending in to table—besides, 'tis so offensively sweet, it wants that haut-goût we are so delighted with in France.

Aunt. You'll pardon it, since we did not expect you. Who is this?   [*Aside.*

Mrs. Cler. Oh, madam, I only speak for the future, little saucers are so much more polite———Look ye, I'm perfectly for the French way, whene'er I'm admitted, I take the whole upon me.

Sir Har. The French, madam,——I'd have you to know——

Mrs. Cler. You'll not like it at first, out of a natural English sullenness, but that will come upon you by degrees——When I first went into France, I was mortally afraid of a frog, but in a little time I could eat nothing else, except sallads.

Aunt. Eat frogs! have I kist one that has eat frogs —paw! paw!

Mrs. Cler. Oh, madam—A frog and a sallad are delicious fare—" 'tis not long come up in France it-
" self, but their glorious monarch has introduced
" the diet which makes 'em so spiritual——He era-
" dicated all gross food by taxes, and for the glory
" of the monarch sent the subject a grazing; but I fear
" I defer the entertainment and diversion of the day."

Hump. Now, father, uncle——before we go any further, I think 'tis necessary we know who and who's together—then I give either of you two hours to guess which is my wife——And 'tis not my cousin——so far I'll tell you.

Sir Har. How ! What do you say ? But oh !—you mean she is not your cousin now—she's nearer a-kin; that's well enough—Well said, Numps—Ha, ha, ha !

Hump. No, I don't mean so, I tell you I don't mean so—My wife hides her face under her hat.

[*All looking at* Fainlove.

Tip. What does the puppy mean : his wife under a hat !

Hump. Aye, aye, that's she, that's she——a good jest, 'faith.——

Sir Har. Hark ye, Numps,—what dost mean, child ? —Is that a woman, and are you really married to her ?

Hump. I am sure of both.

Sir Har. Are you so, sirrah ? then, sirrah, this is your wedding dinner, sirrah——Do you see, sirrah, here's roast meat.   [*Shakes his cane at* Humphry.

Hump. Oh, ho ! what, beat a married man ! hold him, Mr. Clerimont, brother Pounce, Mr. Wife ; no body stand by a young married man !

[*Runs behind* Fainlove.

Sir Har. Did not the dog say, brother Pounce ? What, is this Mrs. Ragoût—This madam Clerimont ! Who the devil are you all, but especially who the devil are you too ?

[*Beats* Humphry *and* Fainlove *off the stage, following.*

H ij

Tip. [*Aside.*] Master Pounce, all my niece's fortune will be demanded now—for I suppose that redcoat has her—Don't you think that you and I had better break?

Pounce. You may as soon as you please, but 'tis my interest to be honest a little longer.

Tip. Well, Biddy, since you would not accept of your cousin, I hope you han't disposed of yourself elsewhere.

Niece. If you'll for a little while suspend your curiosity, you shall have the whole history of my amour to this my nuptial day, under the title of the loves of Clerimont and Parthenissa.

Tip. Then, madam, your portion is in safe hands—

Capt. Come, come, old gentleman, 'tis in vain to contend; here's honest Mr. Pounce shall be my engineer, and I warrant you we beat you out of all your holds.

Aunt. What, then, is Mr. Pounce a rogue? he must have some trick, brother; it cannot be; he must have cheated t'other side, for I'm sure he's honest. [*Apart to* Tipkin.

Cler. Sen. Mr. Pounce, all your sister has won of this lady, she has honestly put into my hands, and I'll return it her, at this lady's particular request.
[*To* Pounce.

Pounce. And the thousand pounds you promised in your brother's behalf, I'm willing should be her's also.

" *Capt.* Then go in, and bring 'em all back to make

" the best of an ill game; we'll eat the dinner and
" have a dance together, or we shall transgress all
" form."

Re-enter FAINLOVE, HUMPHRY, *and Sir* HARRY.

Sir Har. Well, since you say you are worth something, and the boy has set his heart upon you, I'll
have patience till I see further.

Pounce. Come, come, Sir Harry, you shall find my
alliance more considerable than you imagine; the
Pounces are a family that will always have money, if
there's any in the world—Come, fiddlers.

DANCE *here.*

Capt. *You've seen th' extremes of the domestic life.*
A son too much confined—too free a wife ;
By generous bonds you either should restrain;
And only on their inclinations gain ;
Wives to obey must love, children revere,
While only slaves are govern'd by their fear.

[*Exeunt omnes.*

EPILOGUE.

BRITONS, who constant war, with factious rage,
For liberty against each other wage,
From Foreign insult save this English Stage.
No more th' Italian squalling tribe admit,
In tongues unknown; 'tis Popery in wit.
The songs, (their selves confess,) from Rome they bring,
And 'tis High Mass, for aught you know, they sing.
Husbands take care, the danger may come nigher,
The women say their eunuch is a friar.

But is it not a serious ill, to see
Europe's great arbiters so mean can be;
Passive, with an affected joy to sit,
Suspend their native taste of manly wit;
Neglect their Comic humour, Tragic rage,
For known defects of Nature, and of age:
Arise, from shame, ye conquering Britons rise;
Suck unadorn'd effeminacy despise;
Admire, (if you will doat on foreign wit,)
Not what Italians sing, but Romans writ.
So shall less work, such as to-night's slight Play,
At your command with justice die away;
'Till then forgive your writers, that can't bear
You should such very Tramontanes appear,
The nation, which contemns you, to revere.

Let *Anna's soil be known for all its charms*;
As *fam'd for liberal sciences, as arms* :
Let *those derision meet, who would advance*
Manners, or speech, from Italy or France.
Let *them learn you, who would your favour find,*
And English be the language of mankind.

De Wilde pinx.   Thornthwaite s:

M.ʳ ROCK as TEAGUE

—A poor Irishman, Heaven save me.

London, Printed for J. Bell, British Library, Strand, July 28. 1792

THE COMMITTEE.

A

COMEDY,

BY THE HON. SIR R. HOWARD.

ADAPTED FOR

THEATRICAL REPRESENTATION,

AS PERFORMED AT THE

THEATRES-ROYAL,

DRURY-LANE AND COVENT-GARDEN.

REGULATED FROM THE PROMPT-BOOKS,
By Permission of the Managers.

" The Lines distinguished by inverted Commas, are omitted in the representation."

LONDON:

Printed for the Proprietors, under the Direction of
JOHN BELL, British-Library, STRAND,
Bookseller to His Royal Highness the PRINCE of WALES.

MDCCXCII.

THE COMMITTEE.

Although the days of fanaticism are past, and we have even difficulty to imagine, how in the minds of our ancestors

" So much hypocrisy and nonsense,
" Obtain'd th' advowson of their conscience;"

yet this play, unadorned with any brilliancy of either thought or language, gives very much pleasure from the excellence of one character it possesses——— The stiff Puritans as disfigured humanity may be dismissed, but the truth and nature of *Teague* will be admitted and admired, until time shall have changed our impression received of the natives of Ireland.

The honest Irishman of the Sir R. Howard, we are told, is no creature of the invention, he was copied from an original, as faithful, and as inconsiderate as himself;—warmly attached to an interest which his very nature incapacitated him from serving:——And when he was sent with intelligence to gladden the heart of a *Parent*, transported himself with joy, he vented it among his own friends in noisy intemperance, and delayed for some days the happiness he was distracted by having to communicate.

PROLOGUE.

TO cheat the most judicious eyes, there be
Ways in all trades, but this of poetry;
Your tradesman shews his ware by some false light,
To hide the faults and slightness from your sight:
Nay, though 'tis full of bracks, he'll boldly swear
'T's excellent, and so help off his ware.
He'll rule your judgment by his confidence,
Which in a poet you'd call impudence;
Nay, if the world afford the like again,
He swears he'll give it you for nothing then.
Those are words too a poet dares not say;
Let it be good or bad, you're sure to pay.
—Wou'd 'twere a penn'worth;——but in this you are
Abler to judge than he that made the ware;
However, his design was well enough,
He try'd to shew some newer-fashion'd stuff.
Not that the name Committee can be new,
That has been too well known to most of you:
  But you may smile, for you have past your doom;
  The poet dares not, his is still to come.

A iij

Dramatis Personae.

DRURY-LANE.

Men.

Colonel CARELESS, - - -	- Mr. Brereton.
Colonel BLUNT, - - -	- Mr. Aickin.
Lieutenant STORY, - - -	- Mr. Fawcet.
NEHEMIAH CATCH,	
JOSEPH BLEMISH, *Committee*	- Mr. Waldron,&c.
JONATHAN HEADSTRONG, *Men.*	
EZEKIEL SCRAP,	
Mr. DAY, *Chairman to the Committee,* -	- Mr. Baddeley.
ABEL, *Son to Mr.* Day, - - -	- Mr. Burton.
OBADIAH, *Clerk to the Committee,* -	- Mr. Parsons.
TEAGUE, - - - -	- Mr. Moody.
Tavern boy, - - -	- Mr. Everaid.
Bailiff, - - - -	- Mr. Griffith.
Soldier, - - - -	- Mr. Blanchard,
Two Chairmen, - - -	- Mr. Heath, &c.
Gaol keeper, - - -	- Mr. Kear.
A Servant *to Mr.* Day,	
A Stage Coachman,	
Book seller, - - - -	- Mr. Carpenter.
Porter, - - - -	- Mr. Wrighten.

Women.

Mrs. RUTH, - - -	- Miss Pope.
Mrs. DAY, - - -	- Mrs Bradshaw.
Mrs. ARBELLA, - - -	- Miss Jarrat.
Mrs. CHAT, - - -	- Mrs. Cartwright.

SCENE, *London.*

THE COMMITTEE.

ACT I. SCENE I.

Enter Mrs. DAY, *brushing her hoods and scarfs, Mrs.*
ARBELLA, *Mrs* RUTH, *Colonel* BLUNT, *and a*
Stage-Coachman.

Mrs. Day.

Now, out upon't, how dusty 'tis! All things consider'd, 'tis better travelling in the winter; especially
for us of the better sort, that ride in coaches. And
yet, to say truth, warm weather is both pleasant and
comfortable: 'tis a thousand pities that fair weather
should do any hurt.—Well said, honest coachman,
thou hast done thy part! My son Abel paid for my
place at Reading, did he not?

Coach. Yes, an't please you.

Mrs. Day. Well, there's something extraordinary
to make thee drink.

Coach. By my whip, 'tis a groat of more than ordinary thinness.—Plague on this new gentry, how liberal they are. [*Aside.*] Farewell, young mistress; fare-

well, gentlemen. Pray when you come by Reading,
let Toby carry you.   [*Exit.*

Mrs. Day. Why how now, Mrs. Arbella? What,
sad! Why, what's the matter?

Arb. I am not very sad.

Mrs. Day. Nay, by my honour, you need not, if you
knew as much as I.   Well——I'll tell you one thing;
you are well enough; you need not fear, whoever
does; say I told you so—if you do not hurt yourself;
for as cunning as he is, and let him be as cunning as
he will, I can see with half an eye, that my son Abel
means to take care of you in your composition, and
will needs have you his guest. Ruth and you shall
be bedfellows. I warrant, that same Abel many and
many a time will wish his sister's place; or else
his father ne'er got him.——Though I say it, that
should not say it, yet I do say it———'tis a notable
fellow———

Arb. I am fallen into strange hands, if they prove
as busy as her tongue———   [*Aside.*

Mrs. Day. And now you talk of this same Abel, I
tell you but one thing :——I wonder that neither he
nor my husband's honour's chief clerk, Obadiah, is
not here ready to attend me. I dare warrant my son
Abel has been here two hours before us; 'Tis the
veriest Princox; he will ever be gallopping, and yet
he is not full one and twenty, for all his appearances.
He never stole this trick of gallopping; his father was
just such another before him, and would gallop with
the best of 'em : he, and Mrs. Busie's husband, were

counted the best horsemen in Reading——ay, and
Berkshire to boot. I have rode formerly behind Mr.
Busie, but in truth I cannot now endure to travel
but in a coach ; my own is at present, in disorder,
and so I was fain to shift in this ;——but I warrant
you, if his honour, Mr. Day, chairman of the honourable committee of sequestrations, should know
that his wife rode in a stage-coach, he would make
the house too hot for some.——Why, how is't with
you, sir ? What, weary of your journey ?

[*To the Colonel.*

Blunt. Her tongue will never tire. [*Aside.*]——So
many, mistress, riding in the coach, has a little distemper'd me with heat.

Mrs. Day. So many, sir ! why there were but six—
What would you say if I should tell you that I was
one of the eleven that travell'd at one time in one
coach?

Blunt. O, the devil; I have given her a new theme.

[*Aside.*

Mrs. Day. Why, I'll tell you—Can you guess how
'twas ?

Blunt. Not I, truly. But 'tis no matter, I do believe it.

Mrs. Day. Look you, thus it was ; there was, in the
first place, myself, and my husband—I should have
said first, but his honour would have pardon'd me if
he had heard me ; Mr. Busie that I told you of, and
his wife ; the mayor of Reading and his wife ; and

this Ruth that you see there, in one of our laps—but
now, where do you think the rest were?

Blunt. A top o' th' coach, sure.

Mrs. Day. Nay, I durst swear you would never
guess—why—would you think it; I had two growing
in my belly, Mrs. Busie one in hers, and Mrs. May-
oress of Reading a chopping boy, as it proved afterwards, in hers, as like the father as if it had been spit
out of his mouth; and if he had come out of his
mouth, he had come out of as honest a man's mouth
as any in forty miles of the head of him: for, would
you think it? at the very same time, when this same
Ruth was sick, it being the first time the girl was
ever coach'd, the good man, Mr. Mayor, I mean,
that I spoke of, held his hat for the girl to ease her
stomach in.————

Enter ABEL, *and* OBADIAH.

—O, are you come? Long look'd for comes at last.
" What—you have a slow set pace, as well as your
" hasty scribble, sometimes:" . Did you not think it
fit, that I should have found attendance ready for me
when I alighted?

Ob. I ask your honour's pardon; for I do profess
unto your ladyship, I had attended sooner, but that
his young honour, Mr. Abel, demurr'd me by his
delays.

Mrs. Day. Well, son Abel, you must be obey'd,
and I partly, if not quite, guess your business; pro-

viding for the entertainment of one I have in my eye.
Read her and take her:——Ah, is't not so?

Abel. I have not been deficient in my care, forsooth.

Mrs Day. Will you never leave your forsooths?
Art thou not ashamed to let the clerk carry himself
better, and shew more breeding, than his master's
son?

Abel. If it please your honour, I have some business
for your more private ear.

Mrs Day. Very well.

Ruth. What a lamentable condition has that gentleman been in! faith I pity him.

Arb. Are you so apt to pity men?

Ruth. Yes, men that are humoursome, as I would
children that are froward; I would not make them
cry on purpose.

Arb. Well, I like his humour, I dare swear he's
plain and honest.

Ruth. Plain enough of all conscience; faith, I'll
speak to him.

Arb. Nay, pr'ythee don't: he'll think thee rude.

Ruth. Why then I'll think him an ass.——How is't
after your journey, sir?

Blunt. Why, I am worse after it.

Ruth. Do you love riding in a coach, sir?

Blunt. No, forsooth, nor talking after riding in a
coach.

Ruth. I should be loath to interrupt your medita-
tions, sir: we may have the fruits hereafter.

Blunt. If you have, they shall break loose spite of my teeth.—This spawn is as bad as the great pike.

[*Aside.*

Arb. Pr'ythee peace!———Sir, we wish you all happiness.

Blunt. And quiet, good sweet ladies——I like her well enough.——Now would not I have her say any more, for fear she should jeer too, and spoil my good opinion. If 'twere possible, I would think well of one woman.

Mrs. Day. Come, Mrs. Arbella, 'tis as I told you, Abel has done it; say no more. Take her by the hand, Abel; I profess, she may venture to take thee for better for worse. Come, Mistress, the honourable committee will sit suddenly. Come, let's along. Farewell, sir.   [*Exit all but* Blunt.

Blunt. How! the committee ready to sit! Plague on their honours; for so my honour'd lady, that was one of the eleven, was pleas'd to call 'em. I had like to have come a day after the fair. 'Tis pretty, that such as I have been must compound for their having been rascals. Well, I must go look a lodging, and a solicitor: I'll find the arrantest rogue I can, too: for, according to the old saying, set a thief to catch a thief.

Enter Colonel CARELESS, *and* Lieutenant.

Care. Dear Blunt, well met; when came you, man?

Blunt. Dear Careless, I did not think to have met

thee so suddenly. Lieutenant, your servant, I am
landed just now, man.

Care. Thou speak'st as if thou had'st been at sea.

Blunt. It's pretty well guess'd; I have been in a
storm.

Care. What business brought thee?

Blunt. May be the same with yours; I am come to
compound with their honours.

" *Care.* That's my business too. Why, the com-
" mittee sits suddenly.

" *Blunt.* Yes, I know it; I heard so in the storm I
" told thee of."

Care. What storm, man?

Blunt Why, a tempest, as high as ever blew from
woman's breath. I have rode in a stage coach, wedged
in with half a dozen; one of them was a committee-
man's wife; his name is Day; and she accordingly
will be call'd, your honour, and your ladyship;
" with a tongue that wags as much faster than all
" other women's, as in the several motions of a watch,
" the hand of the minute moves faster than that of
" the hour." There was her daughter, too; but a
bastard, without question: for she had no resemblance to the rest of the notch'd rascals, and very
pretty, and had wit enough to jeer a man in prospe-
rity to death.———There was another gentlewoman,
and she was handsome; nay, very handsome; but I
kept her from being as bad as the rest.

Care. Pr'ythee how, man?

Blunt. Why, she began with two or three good

words, and I desired her she would be quiet while she was well.

Care. Thou wert not so mad.

Blunt. I had been mad if I had not—But when we came to our journey's end, there met us two such formal and stately rascals, that yet pretended religion and open rebellion, ever painted : they were the hopes and guide of the honourable family, viz. the eldest son, and the chiefest clerk, rogues—and hereby hangs a tale.—This gentlewoman, I told thee, I kept civil, by desiring her to say nothing, is a rich heiress of one that died in the king's service, and left his estate under sequestration. This young chicken has this kite snatch'd up, and designs her for this her eldest rascal.

Care. What a dull fellow wert thou, not to make love, and rescue her.

Blunt. I'll woo no woman.

Care. Wouldst thou have them court thee? A soldier, and not love a siege!—How now, who art thou?

Enter TEAGUE.

Teague. A poor Irishman, Heav'n save me, and save all your three faces; give me a thirteen.

Care. I see thou wouldst not lose any thing for want of asking.

Teague. I cann't afford it.

Care. Here, I am pretty near; there's sixpence for thy confidence.

Teague. By my troth it is too little, give me another sixpence-halfpenny, and I'll drink your healths.

Care. How long hast thou been in England?

Teague. Ever since I came here, and longer too, faith.

Care. What hast thou done since thou cam'st into England?

Teague. Serv'd Heav'n, and St. Patrick, and my good sweet king, and my good sweet master; yes, indeed.

Care. And, what dost thou do now?

Teague. Cry for them every day, upon my soul.

Care. Why, where's thy master?

Teague. He's dead, mastero, and left poor Teague. Upon my soul, he never serv'd poor Teague so before in all his life.

Care. Who was thy master?

Teague. E'en the good colonel Danger.

Care. He was my dear and noble friend.

Teague. Yes, that he was, and poor Teague's too.

Care. What dost thou mean to do?

Teague. I will get a good master, if any good master will get me: I cannot tell what to do else, by my soul; for I went to one Lilly; he lives at that house, at the end of another house, by the maypole house; and tells every body by one star, and t'other star, what good look they shall have; but he could not tell nothing for poor Teague.

Care. Why, man?

Teague. Why, 'tis done by the stars and the plant-

B ij

ers; and he told me there were no stars for Irishmen. I told him there was as many stars in Ireland as in England, and more too; and if a good master cannot get me, I will run into Ireland, and see if the stars be not there still; and if they be, I will come back, and beat his pate, if he will not then tell me some good look, and some stars.

Care. Poor fellow! I pity him; I fancy's he's simply honest.—Hast thou any trade?

Teague. .Bo, bub bub bo! a trade, a trade! an Irishman with a trade! an Irishman scorns a trade; his blood is too thick for a trade. I will run for thee forty miles; but I scorn to have a trade.

Blunt. Alas, poor simple fellow!

Care. I pity him; nor can I endure to see any man miserable that can weep for my prince and friend. Well, Teague, what sayest thou if I will take thee?

Teague. Why, I say you could not do a better thing.

Care. Thy master was my dear friend; wert thou with him when he was kill'd?

Teague. Yes, upon my soul, that I was; and I did howl over him, and I ask'd him why he died, but the devil burn the word he said to me; and i'faith I staid kissing his sweet face, 'till the rogues came upon me, and took all away from me, and left me nothing but this mantle; I have never any victuals, neither, but a little snuff.

Care. Come, thou shalt live with me; love me as thou didst thy master.

Teague. That I will, if you will be good to poor Teague.

Care. Now, to our business; for I came but last night myself; and the lieutenant and I were just going to seek a solicitor.

Blunt. One may serve us all; what say you, lieutenant, can you furnish us?

Lieu. Yes, I think I can help you to plough with a heifer of their own.

Care. Now I think on't, Blunt, why didst thou not begin with the committee-man's cow.

Blunt. Plague on her, she lowbell'd me so, that I thought of nothing, but stood shrinking like a dar'd lark.

Lieu. But, hark you, gentlemen, there's an ill-tasting dose to be swallow'd first; there's a covenant to be taken.

Teague. Well, what is that covenant? By my soul I will take it for my new master.

Care. Thank thee, Teague.——A covenant, say'st thou?

Teague. Well, where is that covenant?

Care. We'll not swear, lieutenant.

Lieu. You must have no land, then.

Blunt. Then, farewell acres, and may the dirt choak 'em.

Care. 'Tis but being reduc'd to, Teague's equipage; 'twas a lucky thing to have a fellow that can teach one this cheap diet of snuff.

Teague. Oh, you shall have your bellyful of it.

Lieu. Come, gentlemen, we must lose no more time; I'll carry you to my poor house, where you shall lodge: for, know, I am married to a most illustrious person, that had a kindness for me.

Care. Pr'ythee, how didst thou light upon this good fortune?

Lieu. Why, you see there are stars in England, tho' none in Ireland. Come, gentlemen, time calls us; you shall have my story hereafter.

[*Exit* Blunt *and Lieutenant.*

Care. Come, Teague; however, I have a suit of clothes for thee; thou shalt lay by thy blanket for some time. It may be, thee and I may be reduc'd together to thy country fashion.

Teague. Upon my soul, joy, I will carry thee to my little estate in Ireland.

Care. Hast thou got an estate?

Teague. By my soul, and I have; but the land is of such a nature, that if you had it for nothing, you would scarce make your money of it.

Care. Why, there's the worst on't; the best will help itself. [*Exeunt.*

Enter Mr. DAY and Mrs. DAY.

Mr. Day. Welcome, sweet duck; I profess thou hast brought home good company, indeed; money and money's worth: if we can but now make sure of this heiress, Mrs. Arbella, for our son Abel.

Mrs. Day. If we can! you are ever at your *ifs*; you're afraid of your own shadow; I can tell you one

if more, that is, *if* I did not bear you up, your heart
would be down in your breeches at every turn. Well,
if I were gone—there's another *if* for you.

Mr. Day. I profess thou sayest true ; I should not
know what to do indeed. I am beholden to thy good
counsel for many a good thing ; I had ne'er got Ruth,
nor her estate, into my fingers else.

Mrs. Day. Nay, in that business too, you were at
your *ifs.* Now, you see she goes currently for our
own daughter; and this Arbella shall be our daughter too, or she shall have no estate.

Mr. Dav If we could but do that, wife!

Mrs Day. Yet again at your *ifs?*

Mr. Day. I have done, I have done; to your counsel, good duck ; you know I depend upon that.

Mrs. Day. You may, well enough; you find the
sweet on't ; and, to say truth, 'tis known too well
that you rely upon it. In truth, they are ready to
call me the committee-man ; they well perceive the
weight that lies upon me, husband.

Mr. Day. Nay, good duck, no chiding now, but to
your counsel.

Mrs Day. In the first place, (observe how I lay a
design in politics) d'ye mark ? counterfeit me a letter from the king, where he shall offer you great matters to serve him and his interest under-hand. Very
good; and in it let him remember his kind love and
service to me. This will make them look about 'em,
and think you somebody. Then promise them, if
they'll be true friends to you, to live and die with

them, and refuse all great öffers; then, whilst 'tis warm, get the composition of Arbella's estate into your own power, upon your design of marrying her to Abel.

Mr. Day. Excellent.

Mrs. Day. Mark the luck on't too, their names sound alike; Abel and Arbella, they are the same to a trifle, it seemeth a providence.

Mr. Day. Thou observest right, duck, thou canst see as far into a millstone as another.

Mrs. Day. Pish! do not interrupt me.

Mr. Day. I do not, good duck, I do not.

Mrs. Day. You do not, and yet you do; you put me off from the concatenation of my discourse. Then, as I was saying, you may intimate to your honourable fellows, that one good turn deserves another. That language is understood amongst you, I take it, ha?

Mr. Day. Yes, yes, we use those items often.

Mrs. Day. Well, interrupt me not.

Mr. Day. I do not, good wife.

Mrs. Day. You do not, and yet you do. By this means get her composition put wholly into your hands; and then, no Abel, no land—But, in the mean time, I would have Abel do his part too.

Mr. Day. Ay, ay, there's a want; I found it.

Mrs. Day. Yes, when I told you so before.

Mr. Day. Why, that's true, duck, he is too backward; if I were in his place, and as young as I have been———

Mrs. Day. O, you'd do wonders! But, now I think

on't, there may be some use made of Ruth; 'tis a
notable witty harlotry.

Mr. Day. Ay, and so she is, duck; I always
thought so.

Mrs. Day. You thought so, when I told you I had
thought on't first.——Let me see——It shall be so;
we'll set her to instruct Abel, in the first place; and
then to incline Arbella; they are hand and glove;
and women can do much with one another.

Mr. Day. Thou hast hit upon my own thoughts.

Mrs Day. Pray, call her in; you thought of that
too, did you not?

Mr. Day. I will, duck. Ruth! why, Ruth!

Enter RUTH.

Ruth. Your pleasure, sir?

Mr Day. Nay, 'tis my wife's desire, that——

Mrs. Day. Well, if it be your wife's, she can best
tell it herself, I suppose. D'ye hear, Ruth; you may
do a business that may not be the worse for you. You
know I use but few words.

Ruth. What does she call a few?   [*Aside.*

Mrs. Day. Look you now, as I said, to be short,
and to the matter; my husband and I do design this
Mrs. Arbella for our son Abel, and the young fellow is not forward enough. You conceive? Pr'ythee,
give him a little instructions how to demean himself,
and in what manner to speak, which we call address,
to her; " for women best know what will please wo-
" men." Then, work on Arbella on the other side;

work, I say, my poor girl ; no more, but so. You
know my custom is to use but few words. Much
may be said in a little; you sha'n't repent it.

Mr. Day. And I say something too, Ruth.

Mrs. Day. What need you ? Don't you see it all
said already to your hand ? What sayest thou, girl ?

Ruth. I shall do my best—— I would not lose the
sport for more than I'll speak of.   [*aside.*

Mrs. Day. Go, call Abel, good girl. [*Exit* Ruth.]
By bringing this to pass, husband, we shall secure
ourselves, if the king should come ; you'll be hanged
else.

Mr. Day. Oh, good wife, let's secure ourselves by
all means. There's a wise saying: 'Tis good to have
a shelter against every storm. I remember that.

Mrs. Day. You may well, when.you have heard
me say it so often.

Enter RUTH, *with* ABEL.

Mr. Day. O, son Abel, d'ye hear——

Mrs. Day. Pray hold your peace, and give every
body leave to tell their own tale—D'ye hear, son
Abel, I have formerly told you that Arbella would
be a good wife for you ; a word's enough to the wise ;
some endeavours must be used, and you must not be
deficient. I have spoken to your sister Ruth, to instruct you what to say, and how to carry yourself;
observe her directions, as you'll answer the contrary; be confident, and put home. Ha, boy, hadst
thou but thy mother's pate. Well, 'tis but a folly to

talk of that that cannot be. Be sure you follow your
sister's directions.

Mr. Day. Be sure, boy.—Well said, duck, I say.

[*Exeunt Mr. and Mrs. Day.*

Ruth. Now, brother Abel.

Abel. Now, sister Ruth.

Ruth. Hitherto he observes me punctually. [*Aside*]
Have you a month's mind to this gentlewoman, Mrs.
Arbella?

Abel. I have not known her a week yet.

Ruth. O, cry you mercy, good brother Abel. Well,
to begin then, you must alter your posture, " and by
" your grave and high demeanor, make yourself ap-
" pear a hole above Obadiah; lest your mistress
" should take you for such another scribble-scrabble
" as he is;" and always hold up your head as if it
were bolster'd up with high matters; your hands
join'd flat together, projecting a little beyond the rest
of your body, as ready to separate when you begin to
open.

Abel. Must I go apace, or softly?

Ruth. O, gravely, by all means, as if you were
loaded with weighty considerations—so—Very well.
Now, to apply our prescription. Suppose, now, that
I were your mistress, Arbella, and met you by accident—Keep your posture—so—and when you come
just to me, start like a horse that has spy'd something
on one side of him, and give a little gird out of the
way, declaring that you did not see her before,

bv reason of your deep contemplations. Then you
must speak.   Let's hear.

Abel. Save you, mistress.

Ryth. O, fie, man! you should begin thus: Pardon, mistress, my profound contemplations, in which
I was so buried that I did not see you :—— and then,
as she answers, proceed.   I know what she'll say, I
am so used to her.

Abel. This will do well, if I forget it not.

Ruth. Well, try once.

Abel. Pardon, mistress, my profound contemplations, in which I was so hid, that you could not see me.

Ruth. Better sport than I expected. [*Aside.*] Very
well done, you're perfect.   Then she will answer,
Sir, I suppose you are so busied with state affairs,
that it may well hinder you from taking notice of any
thing below them.

Abel. No, forsooth, I have some profound contemplations, but no state affairs.

Ruth. O, fie, man! you must confess that the
weighty affairs of state lie heavy upon you ; but 'tis a
burthen you must bear; and then shrug your shoulders.

Abel. Must I say so? I am afraid my mother will
be angry, for she takes all the state matters upon
herself.

Ruth. Pish! Did she not charge you to be ruled by
me? Why, man, Arbella will never have you, if she
be not made believe you can do great matters with

parliament-men, and committee-men: how should she hope for any good by you else in her composition?

Abel. I apprehend you now; I shall observe.

Ruth. 'Tis well; at this time I'll say no more: put yourself in your posture——so——Now go look your mistress; I'll warrant you the town's our own.

Abel. I go.　　　　　　　　　　　[*Exit* Abel.

Ruth. Now I have fixed him, not to go off till he discharges on his mistress. I could burst with laughing.

Enter ARBELLA.

Arb. What dost thou laugh at, Ruth?

Ruth. Didst thou meet my brother Abel.

Arb. No.

Ruth. If thou hadst met him right, he had played at hard head with thee.

Arb. What dost thou mean?

Ruth. Why, I have been teaching him to woo, by command of my superiors; and have instructed him to hold up his head so high, that of necessity he must run against every thing that comes in his way.

Arb. Who is he to woo?

Ruth. Even thy own sweet self.

Arb. Out upon him.

Ruth. Nay, thou wilt be rarely courted; I'll not spoil the sport by telling thee any thing before-hand. They have sent to Lilly; and his learning being built upon knowing what most people would have him say,

C

he has told them for a certain, that Abel shall have a rich heiress ; and that must be you.

Arb. Must be ?

Ruth. Yes, committee-men can compel more than stars.

Arb. I fear this too late. You are their daughter, Ruth.

Ruth. I deny that.

Arb. How !

Ruth. Wonder not that I begin thus freely with you; 'tis to invite your confidence in me.

Arb. You amaze me.

Ruth. Pray do not wonder, nor suspect——When my father, Sir Basil Thoroughgood, died, I was very young, " not above two years old :" 'tis too long to tell you how this rascal, being a trustee, catch'd me and my estate, " being the sole heiress unto my fa- " ther, into his gripes;" and now for some years has confirmed his unjust power by the unlawful power of the times. I fear they have designs as bad as this on you. You see I have no reserve, and endeavour to be thought worthy of your friendship.

Arb. I embrace it with as much clearness. Let us love and assist one another.——Would they marry me to this their first-born puppy ?

Ruth. No doubt, or keep your composition from you.

Arb. 'Twas my ill-fortune to fall into such hands, foolishly enticed by fair words and large promises of assistance.

Ruth. Peace !

Enter OBADIAH.

Ob. Mrs. Ruth, my master is demanding your company, together, and not singly, with Mrs. Arbella ; you will find them in the parlour. The Committee being ready to sit, calls upon my care and circumspeftion to set in order the weighty matters of state for their wise and honourable inspeftion. [*Exit.*

Ruth. We come. Come, dear Arbella, never be perplex'd ; cheerful spirits are the best bladders to swim with : if thou art sad, the weight will sink thee. Be secret, and still know me for no other than what I seem to be, their daughter. Ancther time thou shalt know all particulars of my strange story.

Arb. Come, wench, they cannot bring us to compound for our humours ; they shall be free still.

[*Exeunt.*

ACT II.   SCENE I.

Enter TEAGUE.

Teague.

I'FAITH, my sweet master has sent me to a rascal ; I have a great mind to go back and tell him so. He asked me, why he could not send one that could speak English. Upon my soul, I was going to give him an Irish knock. The devil's in them all, they will not

C ij

talk with me. I will go near to knock this man's pate, and that man Lilly's pate too——that I will: I will teach them prate to me. [*One cries books within.*] How now, what noises aré that ?——

Enter Bookseller.

Book. New books, new books! A desperate plot and engagement of the bloody cavaliers! Mr. Salt-marsh's alarum to the nation, after having been three days dead! Mercurius Britannicus, &c.

Teague. How's that? They cannot live in Ireland after they are dead three days!

Book. Mercurius Britannicus, or the Weekly Post; or, The Solemn League and Covenant.

Teague. What is that you say? Is it the covenant you have?

Book. Yes; what then, sir?

Teague. Which is that covenant?

Book. Why, this is the covenant.

Teague. Well, I must take that covenant.

Book. You take my commodities?

Teague. I must take that covenant, upon my soul now.

Book. Stand off, sir, or I'll set you further.

Teague. Well, upon my soul now, I will take that covenant for my master.

Book. Your master must pay me for't then?

Teague. I must take it first, and my master will pay you afterwards.

Book. You must pay me now——

Teague. Oh, that I will—[*Knocks him down.*] Now you're paid, you thief o' the world. Here's covenants enough to poison the whole nation. [*Exit.*

Book. What a devil ails this fellow? [*Crying.*] He did not come to rob me certainly, for he has not taken above two pennyworth of lamentable ware away; but I feel the rascal's fingers. I may light upon my wild Irishman again, and if I do, I will fix him with some catchpoles that shall be worse than his own country bogs. [*Exit.*

Enter Colonel CARELESS, *Colonel* BLUNT, *and Lieutenant* STORY.

Lieu. And what say you, noble colonels? How, and how d'ye like my lady? I gave her the title of Illustrious, from those illustrious commodities which she deals in, hot water and tobacco.

Care. Pr'ythee, how cam'st thou to think of marrying?

Lieu. Why, that which hinders other men " from " those venereal conditions," prompted me to matrimony, hunger and cold, colonel.

" *Care.* Which you destroyed with a fat woman, " strong water, and stinking tobacco.

" *Lieu.* No, faith, the woman conduced but little; " but the rest could not be purchased without.

" *Care.* She's beholden to you.

" *Lieu.* For all your mocking, she had been ruined " if it had not been for me.

" *Care.* Pr'ythee, make but that good.

" *Lieu.* With ease, sir——Why, look you, you
" must know she was always a most violent cavalier,
" and of a most ready and large faith; abundance of
" rascals had found her soft place, and perpetually
" would bring her news, news of all prices; they
" would tell her news from half-a-crown to a gill of
" hot water, or a pipe of the worst mundungus.
" I have observ'd their usual rates; they would bor-
" row half-a-crown upon a story of five thousand men
" up in the north; a shilling upon a town's revolting;
" sixpence upon a small castle, and consume hot wa-
" ter and tobacco, whilst they were telling news of
" arms conveyed into several parts, and ammunition
" hid in cellars; that at the last, if I had not mar-
" ried, and blown off these flies, she had been abso-
" lutely consumed.

" *Care.* Well, lieutenant, we are beholden to you
" for these hints; we may be reduced to as bad."
See where Teague comes. Goodness, how he smiles.
Why so merry, Teague?

Enter TEAGUE *smiling:*

Teague. I have done a thing for you indeed.
Care. What hast thou done, man?
Teague. Guess.
Care. I cann't.
Teague. Why, then, guess again—I have taken the
covenant.
Care. How came you by it?

Teague. Very honestly; I knocked a fellow down in the street, and took it from him.

Care. Was there ever such a fancy? Why, didst thou think this was the way to take the covenant?

Teague. I am sure it is the shortest, and the cheapest way to take it.

Blunt. I am pleased yet with the poor fellow's mistaken kindness; I dare warrant him honest, to the best of his understanding.

Care. This fellow, I prophesy, will bring me into many troubles by his mistakes: I must send him on no errand but, How d'ye: and to such as I would have no answer from again.—Yet his simple honesty prevails with me, I cannot part with him.

Lieu. Come, gentlemen, time calls——How now, who's this?

Enter OBADIAH, *and four persons more with papers.*

Care. I am a rogue if I have not seen a picture in hangings walk as fast.

Blunt. 'Slife, man, this is that good man of the committee family that I told thee of, the very clerk; how the rogue's loaded with papers!—Those are the winding-sheets to many a poor gentleman's estate. 'Twere a good deed to burn them all.

Car. Why, thou art not mad?——Well met, sir; pray do not you belong to the committee of sequestrations?

Ob. I do belong to that honourable committee, who are now ready to sit for the bringing on the work.

Blunt. Oh, plague! what work, ras——

Car. Pr'ythee be quiet, man—Are they to sit presently?

Ob. As soon as I can get ready, my presence being material.   [*Exit.*

Car. What, wert thou mad? Wouldst thou have beaten the clerk, when thou wert going to compound with the rascals, his masters?

Blunt. The sight of any of the villains stirs me.

Lieu. Come, colonels, there's no trifling, let's make haste, and prepare your business; let's not lose this sitting. Come along, Teague.   [*Exeunt.*

Enter ARBELLA *at one door,* ABEL *at another, as if he saw her not, and starts when he comes to her, as* Ruth *had taught him.*

Arb. What's the meaning of this? I'll try to steal by him.

Abel. Pardon, mistress, my profound contemplations, in which I was so hid that you could not see me.

Arb. This is a set form——they allow it in every thing, but their prayers.

Abel. Now you should speak, forsooth.

Arb. " Ruth, I have found you; but I'll spoil the " dialogue." [*Aside.*]——What should I say, sir?

Abel. What you please, forsooth.

Arb. Why, truly, sir, 'tis as you say; I did not see you.

Enter RUTH, *as over-hearing them, and peeps.*

Ruth. This is lucky.

Abeʹ. No, forsooth, 'twas I that was not to see you.

Arb Why, sir, would your mother be angry if you
should ?

Abel. No, no, quite contrary——I'll tell you that
presently ; but first I must say, that the weighty affairs lie heavy upon my neck and shoulder. [*Shrugs.*

Arb. Would he were tied neck and heels.———
This is a notable wench : look where the rascal peeps
too ; if I should beckon to her she'd take no notice ;
she is resolved not to relieve me.   [*Aside.*

Abel. Something I can do, and that with somebody ;
that is, with those that are somebodies.

Arb. Whist, whist, [*Beckons to* Ruth, *and she shakes
her head.*] Pr'ythee, have some pity. O, unmerciful
girl !

Abel. I know parliament-men, and sequestrators ;
I know committee-men, and committee men know
me.

Arb. You have great acquaintance, sir ?

Abel. Yes, they ask my opinion, sometimes——

Arb. What weather 'twill be. Have you any skill,
sir ?

Abel. When the weather is not good, we hold a
fast.

Arb. And then it alters ?

Abeʹ. Assuredly.

Arb. In good time——No mercy, wench ?

Abel. Our profound contemplations are caused by the consternation of our spirits for the nation's good; we are in labour.

Arb. And I want a deliverance.—Hark ye, Ruth, take off your dog, or I'll turn bear indeed.

Ruth. I dare not ; my mother will be angry.

Arb. O, hang you.

Abel. You shall perceive that I have some power, if you please to——

Arb O, I am pleased, sir, that you should have power ; I must look out my hoods and scarfs, sir ; 'tis almost time to go.

Abel. If it were not for the weighty matters of state which lie upon my shoulders, myself would look them.

Arb. O, by no means, sir ; 'tis below your greatness——Some luck yet ; she never came seasonably before.

Enter Mrs. DAY.

Mrs. Day. Why, how now, Abel ? Got so close to Mrs. Arbella ; so close indeed ! nay, then I smell something. Well, Mr. Abel, you have been so us'd to secresy in counsel and weighty matters, that you have it at your fingers' ends. Nay, look ye, mistress, look ye, look ye; mark Abel's eyes : ah, there he looks. Ruth, thou art a good girl; I find Abel has got ground.

Ruth. I forbore to come in, till I saw your honour first enter : but I have overheard all.

Mrs. Day. And how has Abel behaved himself, wench, ha ?

Ruth. O, beyond expeɕtation ! " If it were lawful, " I'd undertake he'd make nothing to get as many " women's good-wills as he speaks to ;" he'll not need much teaching ; you may turn him loose.

Arb. O, this plaguy wench !

Mrs. Day. Say'st thou so, girl ? It shall be something in thy way ; a new gown, or so ; it may be a better penny. Well said, Abel, I say ; I did think thou wouldst come out with a piece of thy mother's at last :——But I had forgot, the committee are near upon sitting. Ha, Mistress, you are crafty ; you have made your composition beforehand. Ah, this Abel's as bad as a whole committee ; take that item from me. Come, make haste, call the coach, Abel. Well said, Abel, I say.   [*Exeunt Mrs.* Day *and* Abel.

" *Arb.* We'll fetch our things and follow you.

" Now, wench, canst thou ever hope to be forgiven ?

" *Ruth.* Why, what's the matter ?

" *Arb.* The matter ! Couldst thou be so unmerci-" ful, to see me praɕtised on, and pelted at, by a " blunderbuss charged with nothing but proofs, " weighty affairs, spirit, profound contemplation, and " such like ?

" *Ruth.* Why, I was afraid to interrupt you ; I " thought it convenient to give you what time I " could, to make his young honour your friend.

" *Arb.* I am beholden to you : I may cry quittance.

" *Ruth.* But did you mark Abel's eyes ? Ah, there
" were looks !

" *Arb.* Nay, pr'ythee give off; my hour's ap-
" proaching, and I cann't be heartily merry till it be
" past.   Come, let's fetch our things ; her ladyship's
" honour will stay for us.

" *Ruth.* I'll warrant ye, my brother Abel is not in
" order yet ; he's brushing a hat almost a quarter of
" an hour, and as long a driving the lint from his
" black clothes, with his wet thumb,

" *Arb.* Come, pr'ythee hold thy peace, I shall
" laugh in's face else, when I see him come along.
" Now for an old shoe.   [*Exeunt.*

A Table set out.   The Committee, and OBADIAH *order-
ing books and papers.*

Ob. Shall I read your honours' last order, and give
you the account of what you last debated ?

Mr. Day. I first crave your favours, to communicate an important matter to this honourable board,
in which I shall discover unto you my own sincerity,
and zeal to the good cause.

1 *Com.* Proceed, sir.

Mr. Day. The business is contained in this letter :
'tis from no less a man than the king ; and 'tis to me,
as simple as I sit here.   Is it your pleasures that our
clerk should read it ?

2 *Com.* Yes, pray give it him.

Ob. [*Reads.*] ' Mr. Day, *we have received good intelligence of your great worth and ability, especially in state-*

matters; and therefore thought fit to offer you any prefer- ·
ment, or honour, that you shall desire, if you will become
my intire friend. Pray remember my love and service to
your discreet wife, and acquaint her with this ; whose wis-
dom, I hear, is great. So recommending this to her and
your wise consideration, I remain,

Your friend, C. K.

2 *Com.* C. K. !

Mr. Day. Ay, that's for the king.

2 Com. I suspeĉt—[*Aside.*] Who brought you this
letter ?

Mr. Day. Oh, fie upon't ! my wife forgot that particular. [*Aside.*]——Why, a fellow left it for me,
and shrunk away when he had done.. I warrant you,
he was afraid I should have laid hold on him. You
see, brethren, what I rejeĉt ; but I doubt not but to
receive my reward ; and I have now a business to
offer, which in some measure may afford you an occasion.

2 Com. This letter was counterfeited certainly.

[*Aside.*

Mr. Day. But first be pleased to read your last
order.

2 Com. What does he mean ? That concerns me.

[*Aside.*

Ob. The order is, that the composition arising out
of Mr. Lashley's estate be and hereby is invested and
allowed to the honourable Mr. Nathaniel Catch, for
and in respeĉt of his sufferings and good service.

D

Mr. Day. It is meet, very meet; we are bound in duty to strengthen ourselves against the day of trouble, when the common enemy shall endeavour to raise commotions in the land, and disturb our new-built Zion.

" *2 Com.* Then I'll say nothing, but close with " him: we must wink at one another.—I receive " your sense of my services with a zealous kindness. " Now, Mr. Day, I pray you propose your business."

Mr. Day. I desire this honourable board to understand, that my wife being at Reading, and to come up in the stage-coach; it happened that one Mrs. Arbella, a rich heiress of one of the cavalier party, came up also in the same coach. Her father being newly dead, and her estate before being under sequestration, my wife, who has a notable pate of her own, (you all know her) presently cast about to get her for my son Abel; and accordingly invited her to my house; where, though time was but short, yet my son Abel made use of it. They are without, " as I " suppose : but before we call them in, I pray let us " handle such other matters as are before us.

" *1 Com.* Let us hear then what estates besides lie " before us, that we may see how large a field we " have to walk in.

" *2 Com.* Read.

" *Ob.* One of your last debates was upon the plea " of an infant, whose estate is under sequestration.

" *Mr. Day.* And fit to be kept so till he comes of " age, and may answer for himself; that he may not

" be in possession of the land till he can promise he
" will not turn to the enemy.

" *Ob.* Here is another of almost the like nature ;
" an estate before your honours under sequestration.
" The plea is, that the party died without any offer
" of taking up arms ; but in his opinion he was for
" the king. He has left his widow with child, which
" will be the heir ; and his trustees complain of
" wrong, and claim the estate.

" 2 *Com.* Well, the father, in his opinion, was a
" cavalier ?

" *Ob.* So it is given in.

" 2 *Com.* Nay, 'twas so, I warrant you ; and there's
" a young cavalier in his widow's belly ; I warrant
" you that too ; for the perverse generation in-
" creaseth. I move, therefore, that their two estates
" may remain in the hands of our brethren here, and
" fellow-labourers, Mr. Joseph Blemish, and Mr.
" Jonathan Headstrong, and Mr. Ezekiel Scrape,
" and they to be accountable at our pleasures ; where-
" by they may have a godly opportunity of doing
" good for themselves.

" *Mr. Day.* Order it, order it.

" 3 *Com.* Since it is your pleasures, we are content
" to take the burthen upon us, and be stewards to
" the nation.

" 2 *Com.* Now verily it seemeth to me that the
" work goeth forward, when brethren hold together
" in unity.

" *Mr. Day.* Well, if we have now finished, give

D ij

" me leave to tell you my wife is without," together
with the gentlewoman that is to compound. She will
needs have a finger in the pie.

"3 *Com.* I profess we are to blame to let Mrs.
" Day wait so long."

Mr. Day. We may not neglect the public for private respects. I hope, brethren, that you will please
to cast the favour of your countenances upon Abel.

2, 3 *Com.* You wrong us to doubt it, brother Day.
Call in the compounders.

Ob. Call in the compounders.

Por. Come in the compounders.

Enter Mrs. DAY, ABEL, ARBELLA, RUTH; *and
after them the* Colonels *and* TEAGUE; *they give the
Door-keeper something, who seems to scrape.*

Mr. Day. Come, duck, I have told the honourable
committee that you are one that will needs endeavour
to do good for this gentlewoman.

2 *Com.* We are glad, Mrs. Day, that any occasion
brings you hither.

Mrs. Day. I thank your honours. I am desirous
of doing good, which I know is always acceptable in
your eyes.

Mr. Day. Come on, son Abel, what have you to
say?

Abel. I come unto your honours full of profound
contemplations for this gentlewoman.

Arb. 'Slife, he's at's lesson, wench.

[*Aside to* Ruth.

Ruth. Peace—Which whelp opens next? Oh, the
wolf is going to bark.   [*Aside.*

Mrs. Day. May it please your honours, I shall presume to inform you, that my son Abel has settled
his affections on this gentlewoman, and desires your
honours' favour to be shewn unto him in her composition.

2 Com. Say you so, Mrs. Day? Why the Committee have taken it into their serious and pious consideration; together with Mr. Day's good service upon
some knowledge that is not fit to communicate.

Mrs. Day. That was the letter I invented. [*Aside.*

2 Com. And the composition of this gentlewoman is
consigned to Mr. Day; that is, I suppose, to Mr.
Abel, and so consequently to the gentlewoman. You
may be thankful, mistress, for such good fortune;
your estate's discharged, Mr. Day shall have the discharge.

Blunt. O, damn the vultures!   [*Aside.*

Care. Peace, man.   [*Aside.*

Arb. I am willing to be thankful when I understand the benefit. I have no reason to compound for
what's my own; but if I must, if a woman can be a
delinquent, I desire to know my public censure, not
to be left in private hands.

2 Com. Be contented, gentlewoman; the Committee does this in favour of you. We understand how
easily you can satisfy Mr. Abel; you may, if you
please, be Mrs. Day.

Ruth. And then, good night to all.   [*Aside.*

Arb. How, gentlemen! Are you private marriage-jobbers? D'ye make markets for one another?

2 Com. How's this, gentlewoman?

Blunt. A brave, noble creature!　　[*Aside.*

Care. Thou art smitten, Blunt; that other female too, methinks, shoots fire this way.　　[*Aside.*

Teague. Take care she don't burn your wig.

Mrs. Day. I desire your honours to pardon her incessant words; perhaps she doth not imagine the good that is intended her.

2 Com. Gentlewoman, the Committee, for Mrs. Day's sake, passes by your expressions; " you may " spare your pains, you have the Committee's reso- " lution;" you may be your own enemy, if you will.

Arb. My own enemy!

Ruth. Pr'ythee, peace, 'tis to no purpose to wrangle here; we must use other ways.　　[*Aside.*

2 Com. Come on, gentlemen! What's your case?
　　　　　　　　　　　[*To the colonels.*

Ruth. Arbella, there's the downright cavalier that came up in the coach with us.——On my life, there's a sprightly gentleman with him.

　　[*While they speak, the colonels pull the papers out,
　　　　and deliver 'em.*

Care. Our business is to compound for our estates; of which here are the particulars, which will agree with your own survey.

Teague. And here's the particulars of Teague's estate, forty cows, and the devil a bull amongst them.

Ob. The particulars are right.

Mr. Day. Well, gentlemen, the rule is two years purchase; the first payment down, the other at six months end, and the estate to secure it.

Care. Can you afford it no cheaper?

2 Com. 'Tis our rule.

Care. Very well; 'tis but selling the rest to pay this, and our more lawful debts.

2 Com. But, gentlemen,, before you are admitted, you are to take the covenant. You have not taken it yet, have you?

Care. No. .

Teague. Upon my shoul, but he has now : I took it for him, and he has taken it from me, " that he " has."

" *Ruth.* What sport are we now like to have?"

2 Com. What fellow's that?

Care. A poor simple fellow, that serves me. Peace, Teague.

Teague. Why, did not I knock the fellow down?

2 Com. Well, gentlemen, it remains whether you'll take the covenant?

Teague. Why he has taken it.

Care. This is strange, and differs from your own principle, to impose on other men's consciences.

Mr. Day. Pish, we are not here to dispute ; we act according to our instructions, and we cannot admit any to compound without taking it; therefore your answer.

Teague. Was it for nothing I took the——

Care. Hold your tongue. No, we will not take it.

Much good may it do them that have swallows large
enough; 'twill work one day in their stomachs.

Blunt. The day may come, when those that suffer
for their consciences and honour may be rewarded.

Mr. Day. Ay, ay, you make an idol of that honour.

Blunt. Our worships then are different : you make
that your idol which brings you interest; we can
obey that which bids us lose it.

Arb. Brave gentlemen!   [*Aside.*

Ruth. I stare at 'em till my eyes ache.   [*Aside.*

2 *Com.* Gentlemen, you are men of dangerous spirits. Know, we must keep our rules and instructions, lest we lose what Providence hath put into our
hands.

Care. Providence! such as thieves rob by.

2 *Com.* What's that, sir? Sir, you are too bold.

Care. Why, in good sooth, you may give losers
leave to speak; I hope your honours, out of your
bowels of compassion, will permit us to talk over our
departing acres.

Mr. Day. It is well you are so merry.

Care. O, ever whilst you live, clear souls make
light hearts? faith, would I might ask one question?

2 *Com.* Swear not then.

Care. Thou shalt not covet thy neighbours' goods,
there's a Rowland for your Oliver.

Teague. There's an Oliver for your Rowland, take
that till the pot boils.

Care. My question is only, which of all you is to

have our estates : or will you make traitors of them, draw 'em, and quarter 'em ?

2 Com. You grow abusive.

Blunt. No, no, 'tis only to intreat the honourable persons that will be pleased to be our house-keepers, to keep them in good reparations ; we may take possession again without the help of the covenant.

2 Com. You'll think better on't, and take this covenant.

- Care. We will be as rotten first as their hearts that invented it.

Ruth. 'Slife, Arbella, we'll have these two men ; there are not two such again to be had for love nor money.

Mr. Day. Well, gentlemen, your follies light upon your own heads ; we have no more to say.

Care. Why then hoist sails for a new world——

Teague. Ay, for old Ireland.

Care. D'ye hear, Blunt, what gentlewoman is that ?

Blunt. 'Tis their witty daughter I told thee of.

Care. I'll go speak to 'em ; I'd fain convert that pretty covenanter.

Blunt. Nay, pr'ythee let's go.

Care. Lady, I hope you'll have that good fortune not to be troubled with the covenant.

Arb. If they do, I'll not take it.

Blunt. Brave lady ! I must love her against my will—

Care. For you, pretty one, I hope your portion will be enlarged by our misfortunes. Remember your benefactors. .

Ruth. If I had all your estates, I could afford you as good a thing.

Care. Without taking the covenant ?

Ruth. Yes, but I would invent another oath.

Care. Upon your lips ?

Ruth. Nay, I am not bound to discover.

Blunt. Pr'ythee, come ! Is this a time to spend in fooling ?

Care. Now have I forgot every thing.

Blunt. Come, let's go.

2 Com. Gentlemen, void the room.

Care. Sure, 'tis impossible that kite should get that pretty merlin. •

Blunt. Come, pr'ythee let's go ; these muck-worms will have earth enough to stop their mouths with one day.

Care. Pray use our estates husband-like, and so our most honourable bailiffs, farewell.   [*Exit.*

Teague. Ay, bumbaily rascals——

Mr. Day. You are rude. Door-keeper, put 'em forth there.

Por. Come forth, ye there ; this is not a place or such as you.

Teague. Devil burn me, but ye are a rascal, that you are.

Por. And, please your honours, this profane Irish-man swore an oath at the door, even now, when I would have put him out.

2 Com. Let him pay for't.

Por. Here, you must pay, or lie by the heels.

Teague. What, must I pay by the heels? I will not pay by the heels. Master, ubbub boo!

Enter CARELESS.

Care. What's the matter?

Teague. This gander-fac'd gag says I must pay by the heels.

Care. What have you done?

Teague. Only swore a bit of an oath.

Care. Here's a shilling, pay for't, and come along.

Teague. Well, I have not curs'd, how much had that been?

Por. That had been but sixpence.

Teague. Och, If I had but one sixpence halfpenny in the world, but I would give it for a curse to ease my stomach on you. My money is like a wild colt, I am oblig'd to drive it up in a corner to catch it. I have hold of it by the scruff of the neck. Here Mister, there's the shilling for the oath. And there's the sixpence halfpenny for you, for the curse, before-hand; and now, my curse, and the curse of Cromwell, light upon you all, you thieves, you.

[*Knocks down the Porter, and exit.*

" *Ruth.* Hark ye, Arbella; 'twere a sin not to love " these men.

" *Arb.* I am not guilty, Ruth."

Mrs. Day. Has this honourable board any other command?

2 *Com.* Nothing farther, good Mrs. Day.—Gentle-

woman, you have nothing to care for, but be grateful
and kind to Mr. Abel.

Arb. I desire to know what I must directly trust
to, or I will complain.

Mrs. Day. The gentlewoman needeth no doubt,
she shall suddenly perceive the good that is intended
her, if she does not interpose in her own light.

Mr. Day. I pray withdraw; the Committee has
pass'd their order, and they must now be private.

2 *Com.* Nay, pray, mistress, withdraw. [*Exeunt all
but the Committee.*] "So, brethren, we have finished
" this day's work; and let us always keep the bonds
" of unity unbroken, walking hand in hand, and
" scattering the enemy.

" *Mr. Day.* You may perceive they have spirits ne-
" ver to be reconcil'd; they walk according to na-
" ture, and are full of inward darkness.

" 2 *Com.* It is well, truly, for the good people, that
" they are so obstinate, whereby their estates may of
" right fall into the hands of the chosen, which truly
" is a mercy."

Mr. Day. I think there remaineth nothing farther,
but to adjourn till Monday. " Take up the papers
" there, and bring home to me their honours order
" for Mrs. Arbella's estate. So, brethren, we sepa-
" rate ourselves to our particular endeavours, 'till we
" join in public on Monday, two of the clock;" and
so peace remain with you.   [*Exeunt.*

ACT III.   SCENE I.

Enter Colonel CARELESS, *Colonel* BLUNT, *and Lieute-*
nant STORY.

Lieutenant.

BY my faith, a sad story. I did apprehend this covenant would be the trap.

Care. Never did any rebels fish with such cormo-
rants; no stoppage about their throats; the rascals
are all swallow.

" *Blunt.* Now am I ready for any plot: I'll go find
" some of those agitants, and fill up a blank commis-
" sion with my name.   And if I can but find two or
" three gather'd together, they are sure of me; I
" will please myself, however, with endeavouring to
" cut their throats.

" *Care.* Or do something to make them hang us,
" that we may but part on any terms."

Enter TEAGUE.

How now, Teague ! what says the learned——

Teague. Well then, upon my shoul, the man in
the great cloak, with the long sleeves, is mad, that
he is.

Care. Mad, Teague !

Teague. Yes i' faith is he; he said, I was sent to
make game of him.

Care. Why, what didst thou say to him ?

E

Teague. I ask'd him if he would take any counsel.

Care. 'Slife, he might well enough think thou mock'dst him. Why, thou shouldst have ask'd him when we might have come for counsel.

Teague. Well, that is all one, is it not? If he would take any counsel, or you would take any counsel, is not that all one then?

Care. Was there ever such a mistake?

Blunt. Pr'ythee never be troubled at this; we are past counsel. If we had but a friend amongst them, that could but slide us by this covenant.

Care. Nothing anger'd me so, as that my old kitchen-stuff acquaintance turn'd her head another way, and seem'd not to know me.

Blunt. How! kitchen-stuff acquaintance!

Care. Mrs. Day, that commanded the party in the stage-coach, was my father's kitchen-maid, and in days of yore was called Gillian.

Lieu. Hark ye, colonel; what if you did visit this translated kitchen-maid?

Teague. Well, how is that? a kitchen-maid! where is she now?

Blunt. The lieutenant advises well.

Care. Nay, stay, stay; in the first place, I'll send Teague to her, to tell her I have a little business with her, and desire to know when I may have leave to wait on her.

Blunt. We shall have Teague mistake again.

Teague. I will not mistake the kitchen-maid. Whither must I go now, to mistake that kitchen-maid?

Care. But, d'ye hear, Teague ? you must take no notice of that, upon thy life ; but, on the contrary, at every word you must say, your ladyship, and your honour. As for example, when you have made a leg, you must begin thus : My master presents his service to your ladyship, and having some business with your honour, desires to know when'he may have leave to wait upon your ladyship. [Teague *turns his back on the Colonel.*] Blockhead, you must not turn your back.

Teague. Oh, no, sir, I always turn my face to a lady——But was she your father's kitchen-maid ?

Care. Why, what then ?

Teague. Upon my shoul, I shall laugh upon her face, for all I would not have a mind to do it.

Care. Not for a hundred pounds, Teague ; you must be sure to set your countenance, and look very soberly, before you begin.

Teague. If I should think then of any kettles, spits, or any thing that will put a mind into my head of a kitchen, I should laugh then, should I not ?

Care. Not for a thousand pounds, Teague ; thou may'st undo us all.

Teague. Well, I will hope I will not laugh then : I I will keep my mouth if I can, that I will, from running to one side, and t'other side. Well, now, where does this Mrs. Tay live.

Lieu. Come, Teague, I'll walk along with thee, and shew thee the house, that thou may'st not mistake that, however.

E ij

Teague. Shew me the door, and I'll find the house myself.

Care. Pr'ythee do, lieutenant.

Teague. O, sir, what is Mrs. Tay's name?

" *Care.* Have a care, Teague; thou shalt find us in
" the Temple." [*Exeunt Lieut. and* Teague.] " Now,
" Blunt, have I another design.

" *Blunt.* What further design canst thou have?

" *Care.* Why, by this means I may chance to see
" these women again, and get into their acquaintance.

" *Blunt.* With both, man?

" *Care.* 'Slife, thou art jealous; dost love either of
" 'em?

" *Blunt.* Nay, I cann't tell; all is not as 'twas.

" *Care.* Like a man that is not well, and yet knows
" not what ails him.

" *Blunt.* Thou art something near the matter: but
" I'll cure myself with considering, that no woman
" can ever care for me.

" *Care.* And why, pr'ythee?

" *Blunt.* Because I can say nothing to them.

" *Care.* The less thou canst say, they'll like thee
" the better; she'll think 'tis love that has ham-
" string'd thy tongue. Besides, man, a woman cann't
" abide any thing in the house should talk, but she
" and her parrot. What, is it the cavalier girl thou
" lik'st?

" *Blunt.* Canst thou love any of the other breed?

" *Care.* Not honestly—yet I confess that ill-begot-
" ten, pretty rascal never look'd towards me, but she

" scatter'd sparks as fast as kindling charcoal ; thine's
" grown already to an honest flame. Come, Blunt,
" when Teague comes we will resolve on something.

                           [*Exeunt.*

         Enter ARABELLA *and* RUTH.

" *Arb.* Come, now, a word of our own matters.
" How dost thou hope to get thy estate again ?

" *Ruth.* You shall drink first ; I was just going to
" ask you how you would get yours again. You are
" as fast, as if you were under covert-baron.

" *Arb.* But I have more hopes than thou hast.

" *Ruth.* Not a scruple more, if there were but
" scales that could weigh hopes; for these rascals
" must be hang'd, before either of us shall get
" our own. You may eat and drink out of yours, as
" I do, and be a sojourner with Abel.

" *Arb.* I am hamper'd ; but I'll not entangle my-
" self with Mr. Abel's conjugal cords—Nay, I am
" more hamper'd than thou thinkest ; for if thou art
" in as bad a case as I, (you understand me) hold up
" thy finger.

" *Ruth.* Behold ! Nay, I'll ne'er forsake thee. [Ruth
" *holds up her finger.*] If I were not smitten, I would
" persuade myself to be in love, if 'twere but to bear
" thee company.

" *Arb.* Dear girl ! Hark ye, Ruth, the composition-
" day made an end of all ; all's gone.

" *Ruth.* Nay, that fatal day put me into the condi-

                    E iij

" tion of a compounder too ; there was my heart
" brought under sequestration.

" *Arb.* That day, wench !

" *Ruth.* Yes, that very day, with two or three.for-
" cible looks, 'twas driven an inch, at least, out of
" its old place. Sense or reason cann't find the way
" to't now.

" *Arb.* That day, that very day! If you and I
" should like the same man ?

" *Ruth.* Fie upon't! as I live thou mak'st me start.
" Now dare not I ask which thou lik'st.

" *Arb.* Would they were now to come in, that we
" might watch one another's eyes, and discover by
" signs. I am not able to ask thee, neither.

" *Ruth.* Nor I to tell thee. Shall we go ask Lilly
" which it is?

" *Arb.* Out upon him ! Nay, there's no need of
" stars; we know ourselves, if we durst speak.

" *Ruth.* Pish! I'll speak; if it be the same, we'll
" draw cuts.

" *Arb.* No: hark ye, Ruth, do you act them both,
" for you saw their several humours, and then watch
" my eyes where I appear most concern'd. I cann't
" dissemble, for my heart.

" *Ruth.* I dare swear that will hinder thee to dis-
" semble, indeed—Come, have at you, then; I'll
" speak as if I were before the honourable rascals.
" And first, for my brave, blunt colonel, who, hating
" to take the oath, cry'd out, with a brave scorn
" (such as made thee in love, I hope) hang yourselves,

" rascals; the time will come, when those that dare
" be honest, will be rewarded. Don't I act him
" bravely ? Don't I act him bravely ?

 " *Arb.* O, admirably well ! Dear wench, do it once
" more.

 " *Ruth.* Nay, nay, I must do the other now.

 " *Arb.* No, no; this once more, dear girl, and I'll
" act the other for thee.

 " *Ruth.* No, forsooth, I'll spare your pains; we are
" right; no need of cuts; send thee good luck with
" him I acted; and wish me well with my merry co-
" lonel, that shall act his own part.

 " *Arb.* And a thousand good lucks attend thee. We
" have sav'd our blushes admirably well, and reliev'd
" our hearts from hard duty—But mum, see where
" the mother comes, and with her, her son, a true
" exemplification or duplicate of the original Day.
" Now for a charge.

Enter Mrs. DAY, *and* ABEL.

 " *Ruth.* Stand fair; the enemy draws up."

Mrs. Day. Well, Mrs. Arbella, I hope you have
consider'd enough by this time; you need not use so
much consideration for your own good; you may
have your estate, and you may have Abel, and you
may be worse offer'd—Abel, tell her your mind ?
ne'er stand, shilly, shally—Ruth, does she incline, or
is she wilful ?

 Ruth. I was just about the point, when your honour interrupted us—One word in your ladyship's ear.

" *Abel.* You see, forsooth, that I am somebody, though you make nobody of me; you see I can prevail ; therefore, pray, say what I shall trust to ; for. I must not stand shilly, shally.

Arb. You are hasty, sir.

Abel. I am called upon by important affairs; and therefore 'I must be bold, in a fair way, to tell you that it lies upon my spirits exceedingly.

Arb. Saffron-posset drink is very good against the heaviness of the spirit.

Abel. Nay, forsooth, you do not understand my meaning.

Arb. You do, I hope, sir ; and 'tis no matter, sir, if one of us know it.

Enter TEAGUE.

Teague. Well now, who are all you ?

Arb. What's here, an Irish elder, come to examine us all ?

Teague. Well, now, what is your names, every one ?

Ruth. Arbella, this is a servant to one of the colonels ; upon my life, 'tis the Irishman that took the covenant the right way.

Arb. Peace, what should it mean ?

Teague. Well, cannot some of you all say nothing, without speaking ?

Mrs. Day. Why, how now, sauce-box ! what would you have ? What, have you left your manners without ? Go out, and fetch 'em in.

Teague. What should I fetch, now ?

Mrs. Day. D' you know who you speak to, sirrah ?

Teague. Yes, I do; and it is little my own mother thought I should speak to the like of you.

Abel. You must not be so saucy unto her honour.

Teague. Well, I will knock you down, if you be saucy, with my hammer.

Ruth. This is miraculous.

Teague. Is there none of you that I must speak to, now ?

Arb. Now, wench, if he should be sent to us,   [*Aside.*

Teague. Well, I would have one Mrs. Tay speak unto me.

Mrs. Day. Well, sirrah, I am she; what's your business ?

Teague. O, are you there ? With yourself, Mrs. Tay —Well, I will look well first, and I will set my face, and tell her my message.   [*Aside.*

" *Ruth.* How the fellow begins to mould himself.

" *Arb.* And tempers his chops, like a hound that " has lapp'd before his meat was cold enough.

" *Ruth.* He looks as if he had some gifts to pour " forth; those are Mr. Day's own white eyes, before " he begins to say grace. Now for a speech rattling " in his kecher, as if his words stumbled in their way.

Teague. " Well, now I will tell thee, i'faith." My master, the good colonel Careless, bid me ask thy good ladyship——Upon my soul, now, the laugh will come upon my mouth, in spite of me.

[*He laughs always when he says ladyship, or honour.*

Mrs. Day. Sirrah, sirrah! What, were you sent to abuse me?

Ruth. As sure as can be.   [*Aside.*

Teague. I do not abuse thy good honour—I cannot help my laugh now. I will try again, now; I will not think of a kitchen, nor a dripping-pan, nor a mustard-pot—My master would know of your lady-ship——

Mrs. Day. Did your master send you to abuse me, you rascal? By my honour, sirrah——

Teague. Why do you abuse yourself, now, joy?

Mrs. Day How, sirrah! Do I mock myself? This is some Irish traitor.

Teague. I am no traitor, that I am not; I am an Irish rebel. You are cozen'd now.

Mrs. Day. Sirrah, sirrah, I will make you know who I am—An impudent Irish rascal!

Abel. He seemeth a dangerous fellow, and of a bold, seditious sp'rit

Mrs. Day. You are a bloody rascal, I warrant ye.

Teague. You are a foolish, brabble-bribble woman, that you are.

Abel. Sirrah, we that are at the head of affairs, must punish your sauciness.

Teague. And we that are at the tail of affairs will punish your sauciness.

Mrs. Day. Ye rascally varlet, get out of my doors.

Teague. Will not I give you my message, then?

Mrs. Day. Get you out, rascal.

Teague. I pr'ythee let me tell my message.

Mrs. Day. Get you out, I say.

Teague. The devil burn your ladyship, and honour-
ship, and kitchenship.   [*Exit.*

" *Arb.* Was there ever such a scene? 'Tis impos-
" sible to guess any thing.

" *Ruth.* Our colonels have don't, as sure as thou
" livest, to make themselves sport; being all the re-
" venge that is in their power. Look, look, how her
" honour struts about, like a beast stung with flies."

Mrs. Day. How the villain has distemper'd me!
Out upon't too, that I have let the rascal go unpu-
nish'd. And you [*To* Abel.] can stand by, like a
sheep; run after him then, and stop him. I'll have
him laid by the heels, and make him confess who sent
him to abuse me. Call help as you go. Make haste,
I say.   [*Exit* Abel.

Ruth. 'Slid, Arbella, run after him, and save the
poor fellow for sake's sake; stop Abel, by any means,
that he may 'scape.

Arb. Keep his dam off, and let me alone with the
puppy.   [*Exit.*

Ruth. Fear not.

Mrs Day. 'Uds my life, the rascal has heated me!
—Now I think on't, I'll go myself, and see it done—
A saucy villain!

Ruth. But I must needs acquaint your honour with
one thing first, concerning Mrs. Arbella.

Mrs. Day. As soon as ever I have done. Is't good
news, wench?

Ruth. Most excellent! If you go out, you may

spoil all. Such a discovery I have made, that you will bless the accident that anger'd you.

Mrs. Day. Quickly then, girl.

Ruth. When you sent Abel after the Irishman, Mrs. Arbella's colour came and went in her face; and at last, not able to stay, she slunk away after him, for fear the Irishman should hurt him; she stole away, and blush'd the prettiest.

Mrs. Day. I protest he may be hurt indeed. I'll run myself too.

Ruth. By no means, forsooth, " nor is there any
" need on't; for she resolv'd to stop him before he
" could get near the Irishman. She has done it, upon
" my life; and if you should go out, you might spoil
" the kindest encounter that the loving Abel is ever
" like to have.

" *Mrs. Day.* Art sure of this?"

Ruth. If you do not find she has stopt him, let me ever have your hatred. Pray, credit me.

" *Mrs. Day.* I do, I do believe thee. Come, we'll
" go in, where I use to read; there thou shalt tell
" me all the particulars, and the manner of it. I
" warrant 'twas pretty to observe.

" *Ruth.* O, 'twas a thousand pities you did not
" see't: when Abel walk'd away so bravely, and
" foolishly, after this wild Irishman, she stole such
" kind looks from her own eyes; and having robb'd
" herself, sent them after her own Abel; and then"—

Mrs. Day. Come, good wench; I'll go in, and hear all at large. It shall be the best tale thou hast

told these two days.   Come, come, I long to hear all.
Abel, for his part, needs no help by this time.   Come,
good wench.   [*Exit.*

" *Ruth.* So far I am right.   Fortune, take care for
" future things."   [*Exit.*

Enter Colonel BLUNT, *as taken by Bailiffs.*

Blunt. At whose suit, rascals ?

1 *Bail.* You shall know that time enough.

Blunt. Time enough, dogs ! Must I wait your lei-
sures ?

1 *Bail.* O, you are a dangerous man ! 'Tis such
traitors as you that disturb the peace of the nation.

Blunt. Take that, rascal. [*Kicking him.*] If I had
any thing at liberty, besides my foot, I would bestow it on you.

1 *Bail.* You shall pay dearly for this kick before
you are let loose, and give good special bail.   Mark
that, my surly companion ; we have you fast.

Blunt. 'Tis well, rogues ; you caught me conve-
niently.   Had I been aware, I would have made some
of your scurvy souls my special bail.

" 1 *Bail.* O, 'tis a bloody-minded man ! I'll war-
" rant ye, this vile cavalier has eat many a child.

" *Blunt.* I could gnaw a piece or two of you,
" rascals."

Enter Colonel CARELESS.

Care. How is this ! Blunt in hold ! You catchpole,

F

let go your prey, or——·[*Draws, and* Blunt, *in the scuffle, throws up one of their heels, gets a sword, and helps to drive them off.*

1 *Bail.* Murder, murder!

Blunt. Faith, Careless, this was worth thanks. I was fairly going.

Care. What was the matter, man?

Blunt. Why, an action or two for free quarter, now made trover and conversion. Nay, I believe we shall be sued with an action of trespass for every field we have marched over; and be indicted for riots, for going at unseasonable hours, above two in a company.

Enter TEAGUE, *running.*

Care. Well, come, let's away.

Teague. Now, upon my shoul, run as I do; the men in red coats are running too, and they cry murder, murder! I never heard such a noise in Ireland in all my life.

Care. 'Slife, we must shift several ways. Farewell. If we 'scape, we meet at night; I shall take heed now.

Teague. Shall I tell Mrs. Tay's message.

Care. O, good Teague, no time for messages.

[*Exeunt several ways.*

A Noise within. Enter Bailiffs and Soldiers.

1 *Bail.* This way, this way! Oh, villains! My neighbour Swash is hurt dangerously. Come, good soldiers, follow, follow.

Enter CARELESS *and* TEAGUE *again.*

Care. I am quite out of breath, and the blood-hounds are in a full cry upon a burning scent : plague on 'em, what a noise the kennels make ! What door's this, that graciously stands a little open ? What an ass am I to ask ? Teague, scout abroad ; if any thing happens extraordinary, observe this door, there you shall find me. Now, by your favour, landlord, as unknown.   [*Exeunt severally.*

Enter Mrs. DAY *and* OBADIAH.

Mrs. Day. It was well observed, Obadiah, to bring the parties to me first. 'Tis your master's will that I should, as I may say, prepare matters for him. In truth, in truth, I have too great a burthen upon me ; yet, for the public good, I am content to undergo it.

Ob. I shall, with sincere care, present unto your honour, from time to time, such negociations as I may discreetly presume may be material for your honour's inspection.

Mrs. Day. It will become you so to do. You have the present that came last ?

Ob. Yes, and please your honour ; the gentlewoman, concerning her brother's release, hath also sent in a piece of plate.

Mrs. Day. It's very well.

Ob. But the man without, about a bargain of the king's land, is come empty.

Mrs. Day. Bid him begone; I'll not speak with him. He does not understand himself.

Ob. I shall intimate so much to him.

[*As* Obadiah *goes out,* Col. Careless *meets him, and tumbles him back.*

Mrs. Day. Why, how now? What rude companion's this? What would you have? What's your business? What's the matter? Who sent you? Who d'you belong to? Who——

Care. Hold, hold, if you mean to be answer'd to all these interrogatories. You see I resolve to be your companion. I am a man; there's no great matter; nobody sent me; nor I belong to nobody. I think I have answer'd to the chief heads.

Mrs. Day. Thou hast committed murder for aught I know. How is't, Obadiah?

Care. Ha! what luck have I, to fall into the territories of my old kitchen acquaintance. I'll proceed upon the strength of Teague's message, tho' I had no answer.   [*Aside.*

Ob. Truly he came forcibly upon me, and I fear has bruised some intellectuals within my stomach.

Mrs. Day. Go in, and take some Irish slat, by way of prevention, and keep yourself warm. [*Exit* Ob.] Now, sir, have you any business, that you came in so rudely, as if you did not know who you came to? How came you in, Sir Royster? Was not the porter at the gate?

Care. No, truly; the gate kept itself, and stood

gaping, as if it had a mind to speak, and say, I pray come in.

Mrs. Day. Did it so, sir? And what have you to say?

Care. Ay, there's the point. Either she does not, or will not know me. What should I say? How dull am I? Pox on't, this wit is like a common friend, when one has need of him, he won't come near one.
            [*Aside.*

Mrs. Day. Sir, are you studying for an invention? For aught I know you have done some mischief, and '.were fit to secure you.

Care. So, that's well; 'twas pretty to fall into the head quarters of the enemy.   [*Aside.*

Mrs. Day. Nay, 'tis e'en so; I'll fetch those that shall examine you.

Care. Stay, thou mighty states-woman; I did but give you time to see if your memory would but be so honest as to tell you who I am.

Mrs. Day. What do you mean, sauce-box?

Care. There's a word yet of thy former employ-ments; that sauce. You and I have been acquainted.

Mrs. Day. I do not use to have acquaintance with cavaliers.

Care. Nor I with committee-men's utensils; " but " in *diebus illis*, you were not honourable, nor I a ma- " lignant." Lord, lord, you are horribly forgetful. " Pride comes with godliness and good clothes." What, you think I should not know you because you are disguised with curled hair and white gloves?

Alas! I know you as well as if you were in your sab-
bath-day's cinnamon waistcoat, " with a silver edging
" round the skirt.".

Mrs. Day. How, sirrah?

Care. And with your fair hands bath'd in lather;
or with your fragrant breath driving the fleeting am-
bergrease off from the waving kitchen-stuff.

Mrs. Day. Oh, you are an impudent cavalier! I remember you now indeed; but I'll————

Care. Nay, but hark you, the now-honourable, non
obstante past conditions; did I not send my footman,
an Irishman, with a civil message to you? Why all
this strangeness, then?

Mrs. Day. How, how, how's this! Was't you that
sent that rascal to abuse me, was't so?

Care. How now! What, matters grow worse and
worse!

Mrs. Day. I'll teach you to abuse those that are in
authority. Within, there! who's within?

Care. 'Slife, I'll stop your mouth, if you raise an
alarm. [*She cries out, he stops her mouth.*

Mrs. Day. Stop my mouth, sirrah! whoo, whoo,
ho!

Care. Yes, stop your mouth. What, are you good
at a who-bub, ha?

Enter RUTH.

Ruth. What's the matter, forsooth?

Mrs. Day. The matter! Why, here's a rude cavalier has broke into my house; 'twas he too, that

sent the Irish rascal to abuse me too, within my own walls. Call your father, that he may grant order to secure him. 'Tis a dangerous fellow.

Care. Nay, good, pretty gentlewoman, spare your motion.——What must become of me? Teague has made some strange mistake. [*Aside.*

Ruth. 'Tis he! what shall I do? Now, invention be equal to my love. [*Aside.*] Why, your ladyship will spoil all. I sent for this gentleman, and enjoin'd him secresy, even to you yourself, till I had made his way. O, fie upon't, I am to blame; but, in truth, I did not think he would have come these two hours.

Care. I dare swear she did not; I might very probably not have come at all.

Ruth. How came you to come so soon, sir? 'Twas three hours before you appointed.

Care. Hey-day! I shall be made believe I came hither on purpose presently. [*Aside.*

Ruth. 'Twas upon a message of his to me, and please your honour, to make his desires known to your ladyship that he had consider'd on it, and was resolv'd to take the covenant, and give you five hundred pounds to make his peace, and bring his business about again, that he may be admitted in his first condition.

Care. What's this?——D'ye hear, pretty gentlewoman?

Ruth. Well, well, I know your mind; I have done your business.

Mrs. Day. Oh, his stomach's come down.

1

Ruth. Sweeten him again, and leave him to me; I warrant the five hundred pounds, and— [*Whispers.*

Care. Now I have found it; this pretty wench has a mind to be left alone with me, at her peril. [*Aside.*

Mrs. Day. I understand thee—Well, sir, I can pass by rudeness, when I am.inform'd there was no intention of it. I leave you and my daughter to beget a right understanding. [*Exit Mrs. Day.*

Care. We should beget sons and daughters sooner. What does all this mean? [*Aside.*

Ruth. I am sorry, sir, that your love for me should make you thus rash.

Care. That's more than you know; but you had a mind to be left alone with me, that's certain.

Ruth. 'Tis too plain, sir; you'd ne'er have run yourself into this danger else.

Care. Nay, now you're out; the danger run after me.

Ruth. You may dissemble.

Care. Why, 'tis the proper business here; but we lose time; you and I are left to beget a right understanding. Come, which way?

Ruth. Whither?

Care. To your chamber or closet.

Ruth. But I am engaged you shall take the covenant.

Care. No, I never swear when I am bid.

Ruth. But you would do as bad.

Care. That's not against my principles.

Ruth. Thank you for your fair opinion, good Signior Principle. There lies your way, sir. However, I will own so much kindness for you, that I repent not the civility I have done, to free you from the trouble you were like to fall into ; make me a leg, if you please, and cry, thank you ; and so the gentle-woman that desired to be left alone with you, desires to be left alone with herself, she being taught a right understanding of you.

Care. No: I am rivetted ; nor shall you march off thus with flying colours. My pretty commander in chief, let us parley a little farther, and but lay down ingenuously the true state of our treaty. The busi-ness in short is this : we differ seemingly upon two evils, and mine the least ; and therefore to be chosen. You had better take me, than I take the covenant.

Ruth. We'll excuse one another.

Care. You would not have me take the covenant, then ?

Ruth. No; I did but try you. I forgive your idle looseness for that firm virtue. Be constant to your fair principles, in spite of fortune.

Care. What's this got into petticoats?——" But, " d'ye hear : I'll not excuse you from my proposi-" tion, notwithstanding my release. Come, we are " half way to a right understanding—Nay, I do love " thee.

" *Ruth.* Love Virtue : you have but here and there " a patch of it ; y'are ragged still.

,"*Care.* Are you not the Committee Day's daugh-
" ter ?"

Ruth. Yes. What then?

Care. Then am I thankful. I had no defence against thee and matrimony, but thy own father and mother, which are a perfect committee to my own nature.

" *Ruth.* Why, are you sure I would have match'd
" with a malignant, not a compounder neither?

" *Care.* Nay, I have made thee a jointure against
" my will. Methinks it were but as reasonable, that
" I should do something for my jointure; but by the
" way of matrimony, honestly to increase your gene-
" ration, this, to tell you truth, is against my con-
" science.

" *Ruth.* Yet you would beget right understand-
" ings.

" *Care.* Yes, I would have 'em all bastards.

" *Ruth.* And me a whore.

" *Care.* That's a coarse name; but 'tis not fit a
" Committee-man's daughter should be too honest,
" to the reproach of her father and mother."

Ruth. When the quarrel of the nation is reconciled, you and I shall agree : 'till when, sir———

Enter TEAGUE.

Teague. Are you here then? Upon my shoul, the good colonel Blunt is overtaken again now, and carried to the devil, " that he is, i'faith now."

Care. How, taken and carried to the devil!

Teague. He desired to go to the devil, I wonder of my shoul he was not afraid.

Care. I understand it now. What mischief's this?

Ruth. You seem troubled, sir.

Care. I have but a life to lose, that I am weary of. Come, Teague.

Ruth. Hold, you shan't go before I know the business. What d'ye talk of?

Care. My friend, my dearest friend, is caught up by rascally bailiffs, and carried to the Devil-tavern. Pray let me go.

Ruth. Stay but a minute, if you have any kindness for me.

Care. Yes, I do love you.

Ruth. Perhaps I may serve your friend.

Enter ARBELLA.

O Arbella, I was going to see you.

Arb. What's the matter?

Ruth. The colonel which thou lik'st is taken by bailiffs; there's his friend too, almost distracted. You know the mercy of these times.

Arb. What dost thou tell me? I am ready to sink down!

Ruth. Compose yourself, and help him nobly; you have no way, but to smile upon Abel, and get him to bail him.

Enter ABEL *and* OBADIAH.

Arb. Look where he and Obadiah come ; sent hither by Providence——Oh, Mr. Abel, where have you been this long time ? Can you find of your heart to keep thus out of my sight ?

Abel. Assuredly some important affairs constrained my absence, as Obadiah can testify, bona fide.

Teague. The devil brake your bones a Friday.

Ob. I can do so, verily, myself being a material party.

Care. Pox on 'em, how slow they speak.

Teague. Speak faster.

Arb. Well, well, you shall go no more out of my sight ; I'll not be satisfied with your bona fide's. I have some occasions that call me to go a little way ; you shall e'en go with me, and good Obadiah too. You shall not deny me any thing.

Abel. It is not meet I should. I am exceedingly exalted. Obadiah, thou shalt have the best bargain of all my tenants.

Ob. I am thankful.

" *Care.* What may this mean ?" · [*Aside.*

Arb. Ruth, how shall we do to keep thy swift mother from pursuing us ?

Ruth. Let me alone : as I go to the parlour, where she sits, big with expectation, I'll give her a whisper, that we are going to fetch the very five hundred pounds.

Arb. How can that be ?

Ruth. No question now. Will you march, sir?

Care. Whither?

Ruth. Lord, how dull these men in love are!—
Why, to your friend. No more words.

" *Care.* I will stare upon thee, though."

ACT IV. SCENE I.

Colonel BLUNT *brought in by Bailiffs.*

1 *Bailiff.*

Ay, ay, we thought how well you'd get bail.

Blunt. Why, you unconscionable rascal, are you
angry that I am unlucky, or do you want some fees?
I'll perish in a dungeon, before I'll give you a farthing.

1 *Bail.* Choose, choose. Come, along with him.

Blunt. I'll not go your pace neither, rascals; I'll
go softly, if it be but to hinder you from taking up
some other honest gentleman.

" 1 *Bail.* Very well, surly sir; we will carry you
" where you shall not be troubled what pace to walk;
" you'll find a large bill. Blood is dear.

" *Blunt.* Not yours, is it?—a farthing a pint were
" very dear for the best blood you have."

Enter ARBELLA, RUTH, ABEL, *Colonel* CARELESS,
and OBADIAH.

1 *Bail.* How now! are these any of your friends?

Blunt. Never; if you see women; that's a rule.

G

Arb. [*To* Abel.] Nay, you need have no scruple, 'tis a near kinsman of mine. You do not think, I hope, that I would let you suffer—You—that must be nearer than a kinsman to me.

Abel. But my mother doth not know it.

Arb. If that be all, leave to me and Ruth, we'll save you harmless : besides, I cannot marry, if my kinsman be in prison; he must convey my estate, as you appoint; for 'tis all in him. We must please him.

Abel. The consideration of that doth convince me, Obadiah, 'tis necessary for us to set at liberty this gentleman, being a trustee for Mrs. Arbella's estate. Tell 'em, therefore, that you and I will bail this gentleman—and—d'ye héar, tell them who I am.

Ob. I shall.—Gentlemen, this is the honourable Mr. Abel Day, the first-born of the honourable Mr. Day, chairman of the committee of sequestrations; and I myself by name Obadiah, and clerk to the said honourable committee.

1 *Bail.* Well, sir, we know Mr. Day, and Mr. Abel.

Abel. Yes, that's I; and I will bail this gentleman. I believe you dare not except against the bail : nay, you shall have Obadiah's too, one that the state trusts.

1 *Bail.* With all our hearts, sir.———But there are charges to be paid.

Arb. Here, Obadiah, take this purse and discharge them, and give the bailiffs twenty shillings to drink.

Care. This is miraculous !

1 *Bail.* A brave lady !—I'faith, mistress, we'll drink your health.

Abel. She's to be my wife, as sure as you are here: what say you to that now?

1 *Bail.* [*Aside.*] That's impossible: here's something more in this.—Honourable Mr. Abel, the sheriff's deputy is hard by in another room, if you please to go thither, and give your bail, sir.

Abel. Well, shew us the way, and let him know who I am.   [*Exeunt* ABEL, OBADIAH, *and Bailiffs.*

Care. Hark ye, pretty Mrs. Ruth, if you were not a committee-man's daughter, and so consequently against monarchy, two princes should have you and that gentlewoman.

Ruth. No, no, you'll serve my turn; I am not ambitious.

Care. Do but swear then, that thou art not the issue of Mr. Day; and, though I know 'tis a lie, I'll be content to be cozened, and believe.

Ruth. Fie, fie; you cann't abide taking of oaths. Look, look, how your friend and mine take aim at one another. Is he smitten?

Care. Cupid has not such another wounded subject; nay, and is vex'd he is in love too. Troth, 'tis partly my own case.

Ruth. Peace! she begins, as need requires.

Arb. You are free, sir.

Blunt. Not so free as you think.

Arb. What hinders it?

Blunt. Nothing, that I'll tell you.

Arb. Why, sir?

Blunt. You'll laugh at me.

Arb. Have you perceived me apt to commit such a rudeness? Pray let me know it.

Blunt. Upon two conditions you shall know it.

Arb. Well! make your own laws.

Blunt. First, I thank ye, y'have freed me nobly; pray believe it; you have this acknowledgment from an honest heart, one that would crack a string for you; that's one thing.

Arb. Well! the other.

Blunt. The other is only, that I may stand so ready, that I may be gone just as I have told it you; together with your promise, not to call me back: and upon these terms, I give you leave to laugh when I am gone. Careless, come, stand ready, that, at the sign given, we may vanish together.

Ruth. If you please, sir, when you are ready to start, I'll cry one, two, three, and away.

Blunt. Be pleased to forbear, good smart gentlewoman: you have leave to jeer when I am gone, and I am just going; by your spleen's leave, a little patience.

Arb. Pr'ythee, peace.

Ruth. I shall contain, sir.

Blunt. That's much for a woman to do.

Arb. Now, sir, perform your promise.

Blunt. Careless, have you done with your woman?

Care. Madam——

Blunt. Nay, I have thanked her already: pr'ythee no more of that dull way of gratitude. Stand ready, man; yet nearer the door. So, now my misfortune that I promised to discover is, that I love you above my sense or reason. So, farewell, and laugh. Come, Careless.

Care. Ladies, our lives are yours; " be but so " kind as to believe it, till you have something to " command." [*Exeunt.*

Ruth. Was there ever such humour?

Arb. As I live, his confession shews nobly.   ⸜

Ruth. It shews madly, I am sure. An ill-bred fellow! not endure a woman to laugh at him!

Arb. He's honest, I dare swear.

Ruth. That's more than I dare swear for my colonel.

Arb. Out upon him.

Ruth. Nay, 'tis but want of a good example; I'll make him so.

Arb. But, d'ye hear, Ruth, we were horribly to blame, that we did not enquire where they lodged, under pretence of sending to them about their own business.

Ruth. " Why, thy whimsical colonel discharged " himself off like a gun: there was no time between " the flashing in the pan, and the going off, to ask a " question. But, hark ye," I have an invention upon the old account of the five hundred pounds, which shall make Abel send Obadiah to look 'em.

Arb. Excellent! the trout Abel will bite immediately at that bait. " The message shall be as from " his master Day, senior, to come and speak with " him; they'll think presently 'tis about their com-

" position, and come certainly. In the mean time,
" we'll prepare them with counter expectations."

Enter Abel *and* Obadiah.

Ruth. Peace I see where Abel and the gentle 'squire
of low degree, Obadiah, approach, having newly entered themselves into bonds.

Arb. Which I'll be sure to tell his mother, if he
be ever more troublesome.

Ruth. And that he's turned an errant cavalier, by
bailing one of the brood.

Abel. I have, according to your desires, given freedom to your kinsman and trustee. I suppose he doth
perceive that you may have power in right of me.

Arb. Good, Mr. Abel, I am sincerely beholden to
you, and your authority.

Ruth. O, fie upon't, brother, I did forget to acquaint you with a business before the gentlemen
went. O me, what a sieve-like memory have I I
'Twas an important affair too.

Abel. If you discover it to me, I shall render you
my opinion upon the whole.

Ruth. The two gentlemen have repented of their
obstinacy, and would now present five hundred
pounds to your good honourable mother to stand
their friend, that they may be permitted to take the
covenant; and we, negligent we, have let them go,
before we knew where to send to them.

Abel. That was the want of being us'd to important

affairs. It is ill to neglect the accepting of their cōnversion, together with their money.

Ruth. Well, there is but one way; " do you send
" Obadiah, in your father's name, to desire 'them
" both to come to his house about some business that
" will be fur their good, but no more; for then they'll
" take it ill; for they enjoined us secresy; and when
" they come, let us alone:" Obadiah may enquire
them out.

Ob. The bailiffs did say they were gone to the
Devil.

Abel. Hasten thither, good Obadiah, as if you had
met my honourable father, and desire them to come
unto his house, about an important affair that is for
their good.

Ob. I shall use expedition.　　　　　*[Exit.*

Abel. And we will hasten " home, lést the gentle-
" men should be before us, and not know how to ad-
" dress their offers; and then we will hasten" our
being united in the bonds of matrimony.

Arb. Soft and fair goes far.　　　　*[Exeunt.*

Enter the two Colonels, *and* TEAGUE, *as at the Tavern.*

Care. Did ever man get away so craftily from the
thing he lik'd ? Terrible business ! afraid to tell a
woman what she desired to hear. " I pray heartily
" that the boys do not come to the knowledge of thy
" famous retreat; we shall be followed by those
" small birds, as you have seen an owl pursued.

" *Blunt.* I shall break some of their wings then."

Care. To leave a handsome woman; a woman that came to be bound body for body for thee; one that does that which no woman will hardly do again.

Blunt. What's that?

Care. Love thee, and thy blunt humour; a mere chance, man. Come, Teague, give us a song.

Teague. I am a cup too low.

Care. Here, then.   [*Gives him a glass.*

Teague. I should like to wet 'tother eye.

Care. Here.

SONG by TEAGUE.

Last Patrick-mass night, 'bove all days in the year,
I set out for London before I got there :
But when I took leave of my own natural shore,
O, whillil-a-lu, I did screech, bawl, and roar.

I did wake in the morning, while yet it was night,
And cou'd not see one bit of land, but was quite out of sight;
So, with tumbling and tossing, and jolting poor Teague,
My stomach was sea-sick in less than a league.

'At Chester, to show my high birth, and great mind,
I took a place in the coach, but walk'd in it behind;
The seas they did roar, and the winds were uncivil,
And, upon my soul, I thought we were all blown to the
*   devil.*

At Coventry next, where you see peeping Tom,
Who was kill'd for a look at the Duchess's bum;

But when her grace rid on her saddle all bare,
Devil burn me, no wonder that old Snob did stare.

" *Blunt.* You practise your wit to no purpose; I
" am not to be persuaded to lie still, like a jack-a-
" lent, to be cast at; I had rather be a whisp hung
" up for a woman to scold at, than a fix'd lover for
" 'em to point at. Your squib began to hiss."

Enter OBADIAH.

Care. Peace, man, here's Jupiter's Mercury. Is
his message to us, trow?

Ob. Gentlemen, you are opportunely overtaken
and found out.

Blunt. How's this?

Ob. I come unto you in the name of the honourable
Mr Day, who desires to speak with you both about
some important affair, which is conducing for your
good.

Blunt. What train is this?

Care. Peace, let us not be rash.——Teague!

Teague. Eh!

Care. Were it not possible that you could entertain
this fellow in the next room till he were pretty
drunk?   [*Aside.*

Teague. I warrant you, I will make him and myself too drunk, for thy sweet sake.

Care. Be sure, Teague.——Some business, that
will take us up a very little time to finish, makes us
desire your patience till we dispatch it. In the mean

time, sir, do us the favour as to call for a glass of
sack in the next room : Teague shall wait upon you,
and drink your master's health.

Ob. It needeth not; nor do I use to drink healths.

Care. None but your master's, sir, and that by way
of remembrance.

Ob. We, that have the affairs of state under our
tuition, cannot long delay ; my presence may be re-
quired for carrying on the work.

Care. Nay, sir, it shall not exceed above a quarter
of an hour; perhaps we'll wait upon you to Mr. Day
presently. Pray, sir, drink but one glass or two; we
would wait upon you ourselves, but that would hinder us from going with you.

Ob. Upon that consideration I shall attend a little.

Care. Go wait upon him—Now, Teague, or never.

Teague. I will make him so drunk as can be, upon
my shoul. 　　　　[*Exeunt* Teague *and* Obadiah.

Blunt. What a devil should this message mean ?

Care. 'Tis too plain ; this cream of committee rascals, who has better intelligence than a state-secre-
tary, has heard of his son Abel's being hamper'd in
the cause of the wicked, and in revenge would en-
tice us to perdition.

Blunt. If Teague could be so fortunate as to make
him drunk, we might know all.

" *Care.* If the close-hearted rogue will not be open-
" mouth'd, we'll leave him pawn'd for all our scores,
" and stuff his pockets with blank commissions.

" *Blunt.* Only fill up one with his master's name.

" *Care.* And another with his wife's name for ad-
" jutant-general, together with a bill of ammunition
" hid under Day's house, and make it be digged down
" with scandal of delinquency. A rascal, to think to
" invite us into Newgate !

" *Blunt.* Well, we must resolve what to do.

" *Care.* I have a fancy come into my head, that
" may produce an admirable scene.

" *Blunt.* Come, let's hear ?

" *Care.* 'Tis upon supposition that Teague makes
" him drunk ; and, by the way, 'tis a good omen that
" we have no sober apparition in that wavering pos-
" ture of frailty ; we'll send him home in a sedan,
" and cause him to be delivered in that good-natured
" condition to the ill-natured rascal his master.

" *Blunt.* It will be excellent. How I pray for
" Teague to be victorious !"

Enter Musician.

Mus. Gentlemen, will you have any music ?

Blunt. Pr'ythee, no ; we are out of tune.

Care. Pish, we never will be out of humour.

Enter TEAGUE *and* OBADIAH *drunk.*

" See and rejoice where Teague with laurel comes."

Blunt. And the vanquished Obadiah, with nothing
fixed about him but his eyes.

Teague. Well now, upon my shoul, Mr. Obadiah
sings as well as the man now. Come then, will you
sing an Irish song after me ?

Ob. I will sing Irish for the king now.

Teague. I will sing for the king as well as you. Hark you now!

[*He sings an Irish song, and* Obadiah *tries.*

SONG.

Oh, Teady-foley, you are my darling,
You are my looking-glass, both night and morning ;
I had rather have you without a farthing,
Than Bryan Gaulichar, with his house and garden.

La, ral, lidy.

O, Norah, agra, I do not doubt you,
And for that reason I kiss and mouth you ;
And if there was ten and twenty about you,
Devil burn me, if I wou'd go without you.

La, ral, lidy.

Ob. That is too hard stuff; I cannot do these and these material matters.

Teague. Here now, we will take some snuff for the king——So, there, lay it upon your hand; put one of your noses to it now; so, snuff now. Upon my shoul, Mr. Obad. Commit. will make a brave Irishman. Put this in your other nose.

Ob. I will snuff for the king no more. Good Mr. Teague, give me some more sack, and sing English, for my money.

Teague. I will tell you that Irish is as good and better too. Come, now, we will dance. Can you play an Irish tune? [*Dance,* Obadiah *tumbles down.*

Teague. Obid, Obid! upon my soul I believe he's dead.

Care. Dead!

Teague. Dead drunk. Poor Obid is sick, and I will mull him some wine—I will put some spice in't. [*Puts some snuff into the funnel.*] Now I will howl over him as they do in Ireland : Oh, oh, oh.

Care. Peace, Teague, you'll alarm the enemy.—— Here's a shilling, call a chair, and let them carry him in this condition to his kind master. If you meet the ladies, say we would speak with them at the Lieu- tenant's.

Teague. Give me the thirteen, and I will give him an Irish sedan.

Care. How's that?

Teague. This way.,
　　　　　[*Takes him by the keels, and draws him off.*
　　　　　　　　　　　　　　　　　[*Exeunt.*

Enter Mr. DAY and Mrs. DAY.

Mrs. Day. Dispatch quickly, I say, and say I said it; many things fall between the lip and the cup.

Mr. Day. Nay, duck, let thee alone for counsel. Ah, if thou hadst been a man!

Mrs. Day. Why then you would have wanted a woman, and a helper too.

Mr. Day. I profess so I should, and a notable one too, though I say't before thy face, and that's no ill one,

Mrs. Day. Come, come, you are wand'ring from the matter; dispatch the marriage, I say, whilst she is thus taken with our Abel.   Women are uncertain.

Mr. Day. How if she should be coy?

Mrs. Day. You are at your *ifs* again; if she be foolish, tell her plainly what she must trust to: no Abel, no land.   Plain dealing's a jewel.   Have you the writings drawn, as I advised you, which she must sign?

Mr. Day. Ay, I warrant you, duck; here, here they be.   Oh, she has a brave estate!

Mrs. Day. What news you have!

Mr. Day. Look you, wife————

[Day *pulls out writings, and lays out his keys.*

Mrs. Day. Pish, teach your grannum to spin; let me see.

Enter a Servant.

Serv. May it please your honour, your good neighbour Zachariah is departing this troublesome life: he has made your honour his executor, but cannot depart till he has seen your honours.

Mr. Day. Alas! alas! a good man will leave us. Come, good duck, let us hasten.   Where is Obadiah, to usher you?

Mrs. Day. Why, Obadiah!—A varlet, to be out of the way at such a time; truly he moveth my wrath. Come, husband, along; I'll take Abel in his place.

[*Exeunt.*

Enter RUTH *and* ARBELLA.

Ruth. What's the meaning of this alarm? There's some carrion discover'd; the crows are all gone upon a sudden.

Arb. The she Day call'd most fiercely for Obadiah. Look here, Ruth, what have they left behind?

Ruth. As I live, it is the Day's bunch of keys, which he always keeps so closely:——well——if thou hast any mettle, now's the time.

Arb. To do what.

Ruth. To fly out of Egypt.

Enter ABEL.

Arb. Peace, we are betray'd else; as sure as can be, wench, he's come back for the keys.

Ruth. We'll forswear 'em in confident words, and no less confident countenances.

Abel. An important affair hath call'd my honourable father and mother forth, and in the absence of Obadiah I am enforced to attend their honours; "and " therefore I conceiv'd it right and meet to acquaint " you with it, lest, in my absence, you might have " apprehended that some mischance had befallen my " person: therefore I desire you to receive consola- " tion:" and so I bid you heartily farewell.   [*Exit.*

Arb. Given from his mouth this 1ᴏth of April. —He put me in a cruel fright.

" *Ruth.* As I live, I'm all over in such a dew as " hangs about a still when 'tis first set a going; but

" this is better and be'ter: there never was such an
" opportunity to break prison. I know the very
" places, the holes in his closet, where the compo-
" sition of your estate lies, and where the deeds of
" my own estate lie. I have cast my eye upon them
" often, when I have gone up to him on errands, and
" to call him to dinner."—If I miss, hang me.

Arb. But whither shall we go?

Ruth. To a friend of mine, and of my father's,
that lives near the Temple, and will harbour us,
fear not; and so set up for ourselves, and get our
colonels.

Arb. Nay, the mischief that I have done, and the
condition we are in, makes me as ready as thou art.
Come, let's about it.

Ruth. Stay; do you stand centinel here. That's
the closet window; I'll call for thee, if I need thee;
and be sure to give notice of any news of the enemy.

                                   [*Exit.*

Arb. I warrant thee.—" May but this departing
" brother have so much string of life left him, as
" may tie this expecting Day to his bed-side, till we
" have committed this honest robbery"————Hark!
what's that——this apprehension can make a noise
when there is none.

Ruth. I have 'em, I have 'em; nay the whole co-
vey, and his seal at arms bearing a dog's leg. [*Above.*

Arb. Come, make haste then.

" *Ruth* As I live, here's a letter counterfeited
" from the king, to the rascal his rebellious subject

" Day; with a remembrance to his discreet wife.
" Nay, what dost thou think these are ? I'll but cast
" my eye upon these papers, that were schismatical,
" and lay in separation : What dost think they are ?
- " *Arb.* I can't tell. Nay, pr'ythee come away.

" *Ruth.* Out upon the precise baboon I they are
" letters from two wenches; one for an increase of
" salary to maintain his unlawful issue; another
" from a wench that had more conscience than he,'
" and refus'd to take the physic that he prescrib'd to
" take away a natural tympany.

" *Arb.* Nay, pr'ythee dispatch.

" *Ruth.* Here be abundance more. Come, run
" up, and help me carry 'em. We'll take the whole
" index of his rogueries : we shall be furnish'd with
" such arms, offensive and defensive, that we shall
" never need sue to him for a league. Come, make
" haste.

" *Arb.* I come."

Enter TEAGUE, *with* OBADIAH *on his back.*

Teague. Long life to you, madam; my master is at
Lieutenant Story's, and wants to speak to you, and
that dear creature too.

Arb. and Ruth. Conduct us to him.

Teague. Oh, that I will—Come along, and I will
follow you.   [*Exeunt all but* Obadiah.

Ob. Some small beer, good Mr. Teague.

Enter as return'd, Mr. DAY, *Mrs.* DAY, *and* ABEL.

Mr. Day. He made a good end, and departed as unto sleep.

Mrs. Day. I'll assure you his wife took on grievously; I do not believe she'll marrry this half year.

Mr. Day. He died full of exhortation. Ha, duck, shouldst be sorry to lose me?

Mrs. Day. Lose you! I warrant you you'll live as long as a better thing——Ah, Lord, what's that?

[Obadiah *sings.*

Mr. Day. How now! what's this? How!——Obadiah——and in a drunken distemper assuredly!

Mrs. Day. O, fie upon't! who would have believ'd that we should have liv'd to have seen Obadiah overcome with the creature.——Where have you been, sirrah?

Ob. D—d—drinking the ki—ki—king's health.

Mr. Day. O terrible! some disgrace put upon us, and shame brought within our walls. I'll go lock up my neighbour's will, and come down and shew him a reproof.——How——how——I cannot feel my keys——nor——[*He feels in his pockets, and leaps up.*]——I hear 'em jingle.——Didst thou see my keys, duck?

Mrs. Day. Duck me no ducks.——I see your keys! see a fool's head of your own! Had I kept them, I warrant they had been forth coming. You are so slappish, you throw 'em up and down at your tail.

Why don't you go look if you have not left them in the door ?

Mr. Day. I go, I go, duck.　　　　　　　　[*Exit.*

Mrs. Day. Here, Abel, take up this fallen crea‑ture, who has left his uprightness; carry him to a bed, and when he is return'd to himself, I will exhort him.

Abel. He is exceedingly overwhelmed.

　　　　　　　　　　[*Goes to lift him up.*

Ob. Stand away, I say, and give me some sack, that I may drink a health to the king. [*Sings Teady Foley.*] Where's Mr. Teague !

Enter Mr. DAY.

Mr. Day. Undone, undone ! robb'd, robb'd ! the doors left open, and all my writings and papers stolen ! Undone, undone !——Ruth, Ruth !

Mrs. Day. Why Ruth, I say ! Thieves, thieves !

Enter Servant.

Serv. What's the matter, forsooth ? Here has been no thieves : I have not been a minute out of the house.

Mrs. Day. Where's Ruth, and Mrs. Arbella ?

Serv. I have not seen them a pretty while.

Mr. Day. 'Tis they have robb'd me, and taken away the writings of both their estates. Undone, un‑done !

Mrs. Day. This came with staying for you, [*To* Abel.] coxcomb, we had come back sooner else :

you slow drone, we must be undone for your dullness.

Ob. Be not in wrath.

Mrs. Day. I'll wrath you, ye rascal you. I'll teach you, you drunken rascal, and you sober dull man.

Ob. Your feet are swift and violent; their motion will make them fume.

Mrs. Day. D'ye lie too, ye drunken rascal?

Mr. Day. Nay, patience, good duck, and let's lay out for these women; they are the thieves.

Mrs. Day. 'Twas you that left your keys upon the table to tempt them : ye need cry, good duck, be patient. Bring in the drunken rascal, ye booby : when he is sober, he may discover something. Come, take him up; I'll have 'em hunted.

·[*Exeunt Mr. and Mrs.* Day.

Abel. I rejoice yet, in the midst of my sufferings, that my mistress saw not my rebukes. Come, Obadiah, I pray raise yourself upon your feet, and walk.

Ob. Have you taken the covenant? That's the question.

Abel. Yea.

Ob. And will you drink a health to the king? That's t'other question.

Abel. Make not thyself a scorn.

Ob. Scorn in my face! Void, young Satan.

Abel. I pray you walk in, I shall be assisting.

Ob. Stand off, and you shall perceive by my steadfast going, that I am not drunk. Look ye now—so, softly, softly; gently, good Obadiah, gently and steadily, for fear it should be said that thou art in drink. So, gently and uprightly, Obadiah.

　　　　　　　　[*He moves his legs, but stands still.*

Abel. You do not move.

Ob. Then do I stand still, as fast you go.

　　　　　　　Enter Mrs. DAY.

Mrs. Day. What, stay all day! There's for you, sir; [*To* Abel.] you are a sweet youth to leave in trust. Along, you drunken rascal; [*To* Obadiah.] I'll set you both forward.

Ob. The Philistines are upon us, and Day has broke loose from darkness; high keeping has made her fierce. 　　　　　　　　[*She beats them off.*

Mrs. Day. Out, you drunken rascal: I'll make you move, you beast. 　　　　　　　　[*Exeunt.*

ACT V.　SCENE I.

" *Enter Bookseller and Bailiffs, having laid hold on* TEAGUE.

" *Bookseller.*

" COME along, sir; I'll teach you to take cove" nants.

" *Teague.* Will you teach me then? Did not I take " it then? Why will you teach me now?

" *Book.* You shall pay dearly for the blows you

" struck me, my wild Irish; by St. Patrick, you
" shall.

" *Teague.* What have you now to do with St. Pa-
" trick ? he will scorn your covenant.

" *Book.* I'll put you, sir, where you shall have
" worse liquor than your bonny-clabber.

" *Teague.* Bonny-clabber! By my gossip's hand
" now, you are a rascal if you do not love bonny-
" clabber; and I will break your pate if you will not
" let me go to my master.

" *Book.* O, you are an impudent rascal. Come,
" away with him.

" *Enter Colonel* CARELESS.

" *Care.* How now !—hold, my friend ; whither do
" you carry my servant ?

" *Book.* I have arrested him, sir, for striking me,
" and taking away my books.

" *Care.* What has he taken away ?

" *Book.* Nay, the value of the thing is not much ;
" 'twas the covenant, sir.

" *Teague.* Well, I did take the covenant, and my
" master took it from me ; and we have taken the co-
" venant then, have we not ?

" *Care.* Here, honest fellow ; here's more than thy
" covenant's worth; here, bailiffs, here's for you to
" drink.

" *Book.* Well, sir, you seem an honest gentleman ;
" for your sake, and in hopes of your custom, I re-
" lease him.

" 1 *Bail.* Thank ye, noble sir.

[" *Exeunt Book. and Bailiffs.*

Care. " Farewell, my noble friends——so——d'ye
" hear, Teague, pray take no more covenants."——
Have you paid the money I sent you with ?·

Teague. Yes, but I will carry no more, look you
there, now.

Care. Why, Teague ?

Teague. God sa' my shoul now, I shall run away
with it.

Care. Pish, thou art too honest.

Teague. That I am too upon my shoul now ; but
the devil is not honest, that he is not ; he would not
let me alone when I was going ; but he made me go
to this little long place, and t'other little long place ;
and upon my shoul was carrying me to Ireland, for
he made me go by a dirty place like a lough now ;
and therefore I know now it was the way to Ireland.
Then I would stand still, and then he would make
me go on ; and then I would go to one side, and he
would make me go to t'other side ; and then I got a
little farther, and did run then ; and upon my shoul
the devil could not catch me ; and then I did pay
the money : but I will carry no money, that I will
not.

Care. 'But thou sha't, Teague, when I have more to
send ; thou art proof now against temptation.

Teague. Well then, if you send me with money
again, and if I do not come to thee upon the time,

the devil will make me begone then with the money. Here's a paper for thee, 'tis a quit way indeed.

Care. That's well said, Teague——— [*Reads.*

Enter Mr. DAY, OBADIAH, *and Soldiers.*

Ob. See, sir, providence hath directed us; there is one of them that clothed me with shame, and the most malignant amongst the wicked.

Mr. Day. Soldiers, seize him. I charge him with treason! Here's a warrant to the keeper, as I told you.

" 1 *Sold* Nay, no resistance."

Care. What's the matter, rascals?

Mr. Day. You shall know that, to your cost, here-after. Away with him.

Care. Teague, tell 'em I shall not come home to-night. I am engag'd.

Teague. I pr'ythee ben't engag'd.

Care. Gentlemen, I am guilty of nothing, that I know of.

Mr. Day. That will appear, sir.———Away with him.

Teague. What will you do with my master, now?

Mr. Day. Be quiet, sir, or you shall go with him.

Teague. That I will, for all you, you old fool.

Care. Teague, come hither.

Teague. Sir?

Care. Here, take this key, open my bureau, and

burn all the papers you find there; and here, burn this letter.

Teague. Pray, give me that pretty clean letter, to send to my mother.

Care. No, no; be sure to do as I tell you.

Mr. Day. Away with him.   We will be aveng'd on the scorner; and I'll go home, and tell my duck this part of my good fortune.   [*Exeunt.*

Enter Chairmen with Sedans, Women come out.

" *Ruth.* So far we are right.—Now, honest fellow,
" step over, and tell the two gentlemen, that we two
" women desire to speak with them.

Enter Colonel BLUNT, *and Lieutenant.*

" *Chair.* See, mistress, here's one of them."

Ruth. That's thy colonel, Arbella; catch him quickly, or he'll fly again.

Arb. What should I do?

Ruth. Put forth some good words, " as they use to
" shake oats, when they go to catch a skittish jade."
Advance.

Arb. Sir.

Blunt Lady?———'Tis she.

Arb. I wish, sir, that my friend and I had some conveniency of speaking to you; we now want the assistance of some noble friend.

Blunt. Then I am happy:——Bring me but to do something for you.   I would have my actions talk, not I.   My friend will be here immediately; I dare speak

I

for him too—Pardon my last confusion; but what I told you, was as true as if I had staid—

Ruth. To make affidavit of it.

Blunt. Good, over-charg'd gentlewoman, spare me but a little.

Arb. Pr'ythee, peace. Canst thou be merry, and we in this condition ?—Sir, I do believe you noble, truly worthy. If we might withdraw any whither out of sight, I would acquaint you with the business.

Lieu. My house, ladies, is at that door, where both the colonels lodge. Pray, command it. Colonel Careless will immediately be here.

Enter TEAGUE.

Teague. He will not come; that commit rogue Tay has got him with men in red coats, and he is gone to prison here below this street. He would not let me go with him, i'faith, but made me come till thee now.

Ruth. O, my heart !—Tears, by your leave, a while. —[*Wipes her eyes.*] D'ye hear, Arbella, here, take all the trinkets, only the bait that I'll' use; " accept of " this gentleman's house, there let me find thee; I'll " try my skill—Nay, talk not. [*Exit.*

Blunt. Careless in prison ! Pardon me, madam; I must leave you for a little while; pray be confident; " this honest friend of mine will use you with all re- " spects till I return."

Arb. What do you mean to do, sir ?

Blunt. I cannot tell: yet I must attempt something.

You shall have a sudden account of all things. You
say you dare believe : pray be as good as your word :
and whatever accident befals me, know I love you
dearly. " Why do you weep ?

" *Arb.* Do not run yourself into a needless danger.

" *Blunt.* How ! d'ye weep for me ? Pray let me
" see. Never woman did so before, that I know of.
" I am ravish'd with it. The round gaping earth
" ne'er suck'd showers so greedily as my heart drinks
" these. ‥ Pray, if you love me, be but so good and
" kind as to confess it.

" *Arb.* Do not ask what you may tell yourself.

" *Blunt.* I must go ; honour and friendship call me.
" Here, dear lieutenant, I never had a jewel but this ;
" use it as right ones should be used ; do not breathe
" upon it, but gaze as I do—hold—one word more.
" The soldier that you often talk'd of to me is still
" honest ?

" *Lieu.* Most perfeſtly.

" *Blunt.* And I may trust him ?

" *Lieu.* With your life.

" *Blunt.* Enough—Pray let me leave my last looks
" fix'd upon you——So ; I love you, and am honest.
" Be careful, good lieutenant, of this treasure—she
" weeps still—I cannot go, and yet I must." [*Exit.*

Lieu. Madam, pray let my house be honour'd with
you. Be confident of all respeſt and faith.

" *Arb.* What uncertainties pursue my love and for-
" tune !"   [*Exeunt.*

Enter RUTH, *with a Soldier.*

Ruth. Come, give me the bundle; so, now the habit. 'Tis well; there's for your pains. Be secret, and wait where I appointed you.

Sold. If I fail, may I die in a ditch.   [*Exit.*

Ruth. Now for my wild colonel. " First, here's a
" note, with my Lady Day's seal to it, for his re-
" lease; if that fails (as he that shoots at these ras-
" cals must have two strings to his bow), then here's
" my red coat's skin to disguise him, and a string to
" draw up a ladder of cords, which I have prepared
" against it grows dark. One of them will hit sure.
" I must have him out; and I must have him, when
" he is out. I have no patience to expect." Within
there—ho !—

Enter Keeper.

Ruth. Have not you a prisoner, sir, in your custody, one Colonel Careless ?

Keep. Yes, mistress; and committed by your father, Mr. Day.

" *Ruth.* I know it; but there was a mistake in it.
" Here's a warrant for his delivery, under his hand
" and seal.

" *Keep.* I would willingly obey it, mistress; but
" there's a general order come from above, that all
" the king's party should be kept close, and none re-
" leas'd, but by the state's order.

" *Ruth.* This goes ill."—May I speak with him, sir ?

Keep. Very freely, mistress: there's no order to forbid any to come to him. To say truth, 'tis the most pleasant'st gentleman—I'll call him forth. [*Exit.*

Ruth. O' my conscience, every thing must be in love with him. Now for my last hopes; if this fail, I'll use the ropes myself.

Enter Keeper *and* CARELESS.

Care. Mr. Day's daughter speak with me ?

Keep. Ay, sir, there she is. [*Exit.*

Ruth. O, sir, does the name of Mr. Day's daughter trouble you ? You love the gentlewoman, but hate his daughter.

Care. Yes, I do love the gentlewoman you speak of most exceedingly.

Ruth. And the gentlewoman loves you. But what luck this is, that Day's daughter should ever be with her, to spoil all !

Care. Not a whit, one way; I have a pretty room within, dark, and convenient.

Ruth. For what ?

Care. For you and I to give counter-security for our kindness to one another.

Ruth. But Mr. Day's daughter will be there, too.

Care. 'Tis dark; we'll ne'er see her.

Ruth. You care not who you are wicked with. Methinks a prison should tame you.

" *Care.* Why, d'ye think a prison takes away blood

l iij

" and sight? As long as I am so qualified, I am
" touch-wood; and whenever you bring fire, I shall
" fall a burning.

. " *Ruth.* And you would quench it.

" *Care.* And you shall kindle it again.

" *Ruth.* No, you will be burnt out at last, burnt to
" a coal, black as dishonest love."

Care. Is this your business? Did you come to disturb my contemplations with a sermon? Is this all?

Ruth. One thing more—I love you, it's true; but
I love you honestly. If you know how to love me
virtuously, I'll free you from prison, and run all for-
tunes with you.

Care. Yes, I could love thee all manner of ways;
" if I could not, freedom were no bait; were it from
" death, I should despise your offer, to bargain for a
" lie"—But——

Ruth. " Oh noble!"—But what?

Care. The name of that rascal that got thee. Yet
I lie too; he ne'er got a limb of thee. Pox on't,
thy mother was as unlucky to bear thee. But how
shall we salve that? Take off but these incumbrances,
and I'll purchase thee in thy smock; but to have such
a flaw in my title——

Ruth. Can I help nature?

Care. Or I honour? Why, hark you, now; do but
swear me into a pretence; do but betray me with an
oath, that thou wert not begot on the body of Gillian,
my father's kitchen-maid.

Ruth. Who's that?

Care. Why, the honourable Mrs. Day, that now is.

Ruth. Will you believe me, if I swear?

Care. Ay, that I will, though I know all the while 'tis not true.

Ruth. I swear, then, by all that's good, I am not their daughter.

Care. Poor, kind, perjur'd, pretty one, I am beholden to thee. Wouldst damn thyself for me?

Ruth. You are mistaken. I have try'd you fully. " You are noble, and I hope you love me. Be ever " firm to virtuous principles." My name is not so godly a one as Ruth, but plain Anne, daughter to Sir Basil Thorowgood; " one, perhaps, that you have " heard of, since in the world he has still had so loud " and fair a character." 'Tis too long to tell you how this Day got me, an infant, and my estate into his power, and made me pass for his own daughter, " my " father dying when I was but two years old. This " I knew but lately, by an unexpected meeting of an " ancient servant of my father's." But two hours since, Arbella and I found an opportunity of stealing away all the writings that belong'd to my estate, and her composition. In our flight we met your friend, with whom I left her, as soon as I had intelligence of your misfortune, to try to get your liberty; which if I can do, you have your estate, for I have mine.

Care. Thou more than——

Ruth. No, no, no raptures at this time. Here's your disguise, purchas'd from a true-hearted redcoat. " Here's a bundle." Let this line down when

'tis almost dark, and you shall draw up a ladder of
ropes. " If the ladder of ropes be done sooner, I'll
" send it by a soldier that I dare trust, and you may.
" Your window's large enough." As soon as you receive it, come down; " if not, when 'tis dark, let
" down your line," and at the bottom of the window you shall find yours, more than her own, not
Ruth, but Anne.

Care. I'll leap into thy arms——

Ruth. So you may break your neck. If you do,
I'll jump too. But time steals on our words—Observe
all I have told you. So, farewell.

Care. Nay, as the good fellows use to say, let us not
part with dry lips——One kiss.

Ruth. Not a bit of me, 'till I am all yours.

Care. Your hand, then, to shew I am grown reasonable. A poor compounder.

Ruth. Pish! there's a dirty glove upon't.——

" *Care.* Give me but any naked part, and I'll kiss
" it as a snail creeps, and leave sign where my lips
" slid along——

" *Ruth.* Good snail, get out of your hole first:
" think of your business. So, fare——"

Care. Nay, pr'ythee be not asham'd that thou art
loth to leave me. 'Slid, I am a man; but I'm as arrant a rogue as thy quondam father Day, if I could
not cry to leave thee a brace of minutes.

Ruth. Away; we grow foolish—farewell—yet, be
careful——Nay, go in.

Care. Do you go first.

Ruth. Nay, fie, go in.

Care. We'll fairly then divide the victory, and draw off together.—So—I will have the last look.

[Exeunt severally, looking at one another.

Enter Colonel BLUNT, *and Soldier.*

Blunt. No more words. I do believe, nay, I know thou art honest. I may live to thank thee better.

Sol. I scorn any encouragement to love my king, or those that serve him. I took pay under these people with a design to do him service. The lieutenant knows it.

Blunt. He has told me so. No more words. Thou art a noble fellow. Thou art sure his window's large enough ?

Sol. Fear it not.

Blunt. Here, then, carry him this ladder of ropes. So ; now, give me the coat. Say not a word to him, but bid him dispatch when he sees the coast clear. He shall be waited for at the bottom of his window. Give him thy sword too, if he desires it.

Sol. I'll dispatch it instantly ; therefore get to your place.   *[Exit.*

Blunt. I warrant ye.

Enter TEAGUE.

Teague. Have you done every thing then ? By my shoul, now, yonder is the man with the hard name ; that man, now, that I made drunk for thee ; Mr. Tay's rascal. He is coming along there behind ; now, upon my shoul, that he is.

Blunt. The rascal comes for some mischief. Teague, now or never play the man.

Teague. How should I be a man, then?

Blunt. Thy master is never to be got out, if this rogue gets hither; meet him therefore, Teague, in the most winning manner thou canst, and make him once more drunk, and it shall be called the Second Edition of Obadiah, put forth with Irish notes upon him; and if he will not go drink with thee——

Teague. I will carry him upon my back, if he will not go; and if he will not be drunk, I will cut his throat then, that I will, for my sweet master now, that I will.

Blunt. Dispatch, good Teague; and dispatch him too, if he will not be conformable; and if thou canst but once more be victorious, bring him in triumph to Lieutenant Story's, there shall be the general rendezvous. Now or never, Teague.

Teague. I warrant you I will get drink into his pate, or I will break it for him, that I will, I warrant you. He shall not come after you now.

" *Blunt.* Good luck go with thee! [*Exit* Teague.]
" The fellow's faithful and stout; that fear's over.
" Now to my station.   [*Exit.*

" *Colonel* CARELESS, *as in Prison.*

" *Care.* The time's almost come : how slow it flut-
" ters. My desires are better winged. How I long
" to counterfeit a faintness when I come to the bot-

" tom, and sink into the arms of this dear witty fair!
" ——Ha, who's this?

" *Enter Soldier.*

" *Sol.* Here, sir, here's a ladder of ropes, fasten it
" to your window, and descend: you shall be wait-
" ed for.

" *Care.* The careful creature has sent it—but, d'ye
" hear, sir, could you not spare that implement by
" your side? it might serve to keep off small curs.

" *Sol.* You'll have no need on't, but there it is;
" make haste, the coast is clear. [*Exit.*

" *Care.* O this pretty she captain-general over my
" soul and body; the thought of her musters every
" faculty I have: she has sent the ropes, and stays
" for me; no dancer of the ropes ever slid down with
" that swiftness, or desire of haste, that I will make
" to thee. [*Exit.*

" *Enter* BLUNT *in his Soldier's Coat.*

" *Blunt.* All's quiet, and the coast clear; so far it
" goes well; that is the window; in this nook I'll
" stand, 'till I see him coming down. [*Steps in.*

" *Colonel* CARELESS *above, in his Soldier's Habit, lets*
" *down the Ladder of Ropes, and speaks.*

" *Care.* I cannot see my north star that I must sail
" by; 'tis clouded: perhaps she stands close in some
" corner; I'll not trifle time: all's clear. Fortune,
" forbear thy tricks, but for this small occasion."

Enter BLUNT *and* CARELESS.

Blunt. What's this! a soldier in the place of Careless? I am betray'd, but I'll end this rascal's duty.

Care. How, a soldier!—betray'd! this rascal sha'n't
laugh at me.   [*Both draw.*

Blunt. Dog.

Care. How, Blunt!

Blunt. Careless!

Care. You guess shrewdly. Plague, what contrivance hath set you and I a tilting at one another?

Blunt. How the devil got you a soldier's habit?

Care. The same friend, for aught I know, that furnish'd you—This kind gentlewoman is Ruth still.
Ha, here she is! I was just ready to be suspicious.

Enter RUTH.

Ruth. Who's there?

Care. Two notable charging red-coats.

Ruth. As I live, my heart is at my mouth.

Care. Pr'ythee, let it come to thy lips, that I may
kiss it. "What have you in your lap?"

Ruth. "The ladder of ropes:" how in the name
of wonder got you hither?

Care. Why, I had the ladder of ropes, and came
down by it.

Blunt. Then the mistake is plainer; 'twas I that
sent the soldier with the ropes.

Ruth. What an escape was this! Come, let's lose
no time; here's no place to explain matters in.

Care. I will stay to tell thee I shall never deserve thee.

Ruth. Tell me so when you have had me a little while. Come, follow me; " put on your plainest " garb; not like a dancing master, with your toes " out. Come along. [Ruth *pulls their hats over their* " *eyes.*] Hang down your head, as if you wanted " pay.——So." [*Exeunt.*

Enter Mr. DAY, *Mrs.* DAY, *and Mrs.* CHAT.

Mrs. Day. Are you sure of this, neighbour Chat?

Mrs. Chat. I'm as sure of it as I am that I have a nose to my face.

Mrs. Day. Is my————

Mr. Day. Ay! is my————

Mrs. Day. You may give one leave, methinks, to ask out one question. Is my daughter Ruth with her?

Mrs. Chat. She was not when I saw Mrs. Arbella last. I have not been so often at your honour's house, but that I know Mrs. Arbella, the rich heiress, that Mr. Abel was to have had, good gentleman, if he has his due. They never suspected me; for I used to buy things of my neighbour Story before she married the lieutenant; and stepping in to see Mrs. Story that now is, my neighbour Wish-well that was; I saw, as I told you, this very Mrs. Arbella; and I warrant Mrs. Ruth is not far off.

Mrs. Day. Let me advise then, husband.

Mr. Day. Do, good duck; I'll warrant 'em———

K

Mrs. Day. You'll warrant, when I have done the business.

Mr. Day. I mean so, duck.

Mrs. Day. Well! pray spare your meaning too. First, then, we'll go ourselves in person to this Story's house, and in the mean time send Abel for soldiers; and when he has brought the soldiers, let them stay at the door, and come up himself; and then, if fair means will not do, foul shall.

Mr. Day. Excellent well advised, sweet duck. Ah! let thee alone. Begone, Abel, and observe thy mother's directions. Remember the place. We'll be reveng'd for robbing us, and for all their tricks.

Abel. I shall perform it.

Mrs. Day. Come along, neighbour, and shew us the best way; " and by and by we shall have news " from Obadiah, who is gone to give the other co- " lonel's gaoler a double charge, to keep the wild " youth close. Come, husband, let's hasten." Mrs. Chat, the state shall know what good service you have done.

Mrs. Chat. I thank your honour.   [*Exeunt.*

Enter ARBELLA *and* Lieutenant.

Lieu. Pray, madam, weep no more! spare your tears till you know they have miscarried.

" *Arb.* 'Tis a woman, sir, that weeps: we want " men's reasons, and their courage to practise with.

" *Lieu.* Look up, madam, and meet your unex- " pected joys!"
.1

Enter RUTH, *Colonel* CARELESS, *and Colonel* BLUNT.

Arb. Oh, my dear friend! my dear, dear Ruth!

Care. Pray, none of these phlegmatic hugs. There, take your colonel; my captain and I can hug afresh, every minute.

Ruth. When did we hug last, good soldier?

Care. I have done nothing but hug thee in fancy, ever since you, Ruth, turn'd Annice.

Arb. You are welcome, sir: "I cannot deny I shar'd in all your danger.

"*Lieu.* If she had deny'd it, colonel, I would have
"betrayed her."

Blunt. I know not what to say, nor how to tell, how dearly, how well—I love you.

"*Arb.* Now, cann't I say I love him; yet I have
"a mind to tell him too.

"*Ruth.* Keep't in and choke yourself, or get the
"rising of the lights.

"*Arb.* What shall I say?

"*Ruth.* Say something, or he'll vanish.

"*Blunt.* D'ye not believe I love you? or cann't
"you love me? Not a word.——Could you——
"but"——

Arb. No more; I'll save you the labour of courtship, which should be too tedious to all plain and honest natures. It is enough; I know you love me.

Blunt. Or may I perish whilst I am swearing it.

K ij

Enter 'Prentice.

Lieu. How now, Jack?

'Pren. O master, undone! Here's Mr. Day the
Committee-man, and his fierce wife, come into the
shop. Mrs. Chat brought them in, and they say they
will come up; they know that Mrs. Arbella, and
their daughter Ruth, are here. Deny 'em if you dare,
they say.

Lieu. Go down, boy, and tell 'em I am coming to
'em. [*Exit 'Prentice.*] " This pure jade, my neighbour
" Chat, has betray'd us. What shall I do? I warrant
" the rascal has soldiers at his heels. I think I could
" help the colonels out at a back door.

" *Blunt* I'd die rather by my Arbella. Now, you
" shall see I love you.

" *Care.* Nor will I, Charles, forsake you, Annice."

Ruth. Come, be cheerful; I'll defend you all
against the assaults of captain Day, and major-general
Day, his new drawn-up wife. Give me my ammunition, [*To* Arbella.] the papers, woman. So, if I do
not rout 'em, fall on; let's all die together, and make
no more graves but one.

Blunt. 'Slife, I love her now, for all she has jeer'd
me so.

Ruth. " Go fetch him in, lieutenant. [*Exit Lieutenant.*"] Stand you all drawn up as my reserve—so—
I for the forlorn hope.

" *Care.* That we had Teague here! to quarrel with
" the female triumphing Day, whilst I threw the male

" Day out of the window. Hark, I hear the troop
" marching; I know the she Day's stamp, among the
" tramples of a regiment."

Arb. They come, wench; charge 'em bravely; I'll
second thee with a volley.

Ruth. They'll not stand the first charge, fear not;
now the Day breaks.

Care. Would 'twere his neck were broke.

Enter Mr. DAY *and Mrs.* DAY.

Mrs. Day. Ah, ha! my fine run-aways, have I
found you? What, you think my husband's honour
lives without intelligence. Marry, come up.

Mr. Day. My duck tells you how 'tis—We—

Mrs. Day. Why then let your duck tell 'em how
'tis; yet, as I was saying, you shall perceive we
abound in intelligence: else 'twere not for us to go
about to keep the nation quiet; but if you, Mrs.
Arbella, will deliver up what you have stolen, and
submit, and return with us, and this ungracious
Ruth.

Ruth. Anne, if you please.

Mrs. Day. Who gave you that name, pray?

Ruth. My godfathers and godmothers; on, forsooth,
I can answer a leaf farther.

Mr. Day. Duck, good duck, a word: I do not like
this name Annice.

Mrs. Day. You are ever in a fright, with a shri-
vell'd heart of your own.—Well, gentlewoman, you
are merry.

Arb. As newly come out of our wardships. I hope Mr. Abel is well.

Mrs. Day. Yes, he is well: you shall see him presently; yes, you shall see him.

Care. That is, with myrmidons. Come, good Anne, no more delay, fa l on.

Ruth. Then, before the furious Abel approaches with his red-coats, who, perbaps, are now marching under the conduct of that expert captain in weighty matters, know, the articles of our treaty are only these: this Arbella will keep her estate, and not marry Abel, but this gentleman; and I, Anne, daughter to Sir Basil Thorowgood, and not Ruth, as has been thought, have taken my own estate, together with this gentleman, for better for worse. We were modest, though thieves; only plundered our own.

Mrs. Day. Yes, gentlewoman, you took something else, and that my husband can prove; it may cost you your necks, if you do not submit.

Ruth. Truth on't is, we did take something else.

Mrs. Day. Oh, did you so?

Ruth. Pray give me leave to speak one word in private with my father Day?

Mr. Day. Do so, do so; are you going to compound? Oh, 'tis father Day, now!

Ruth. D'ye hear, sir; how long is it since you have practis'd physic?   [*Takes him aside.*

Mr. Day. Physic! what d'ye mean?

Ruth. I mean physic.——Look ye, here's a small

prescription of yours. D'ye know this hand-writing ?

Mr. Day. I am undone.

Ruth. Here's another upon the same subject. This young one, I believe, came into this wicked world for want of your preventing dose ; it will not be taken now neither. It seems your wenches are wilful: nay, I do not wonder to see 'em have more conscience than you have.

Mr. Day. Peace, good Mrs. Anne ! I am undone, if you betray me.

Enter ABEL, *goes to his Father.*

Abel. The soldiers are come.

Mr. Day. Go and send 'em away, Abel; here's no need, no need, now.

Mrs. Day. Are the soldiers come, Abel ?

Abel. Yes, but my father biddeth me send them away.

Mr. Day. No, not without your opinion, duck ; but since they have but their own, I think, duck, if we were all friends——

Mrs. Day. O, are you at your *ifs* again ; D'you think they shall make a fool of me, though they make an ass of you ? Call 'em up, Abel, if they will not submit ; call up the soldiers, Abel.

Ruth. Why, your fierce honour shall know the business that makes the wise Mr. Day inclinable to friendship.

Mr. Day. Nay, good sweetheart, come, I pray let us be friends.

Mrs. Day. How's this! what, am I not fit to be trusted now? Have you built your credit and reputation upon my counsel and labours, and am I not fit now to be trusted?

Mr. Day. Nay, good sweet duck, I confess I owe all to thy wisdom. Good gentlemen, persuade my duck that we may be all friends.

Care. Hark you, good Gillian Day, be not so fierce upon the husband of thy bosom; 'twas but a small start of frailty: say it were a wench, or so?

Ruth. As I live, he has hit upon't by chance. Now we shall have sport.   [*Aside.*

Mrs. Day. How, a wench, a wench! out upon the hypocrite. A wench! was not I sufficient? a wench! I'll be reveng'd, let him be ashamed if he will: call the soldiers, Abel.

" *Care.* Stay, good Abel; march not off so hastily."

Arb. Soft, gentle Abel, or I'll discover you are in bonds; you shall never be releas'd if you move a step.

Ruth. D'ye hear, Mrs. Day, be not so furious, hold your peace; you may divulge your husband's shame, if you are so simple, and cast him out of authority, nay, and have him tried for his life: read this. Remember too, I know of your bribery and cheating, and something else: you guess. Be friends, and forgive one another. Here's a letter counterfeited from the king, to bestow preferment upon Mr.

Day if he would turn honest; by which means, I suppose, you cozen'd your brother cheats; in which he was to remember his service to you. I believe 'twas your inditing. You are the committee-man. 'Tis your best way, (nay, never demur) to kiss and be friends. Now, if you can contrive handsomely to cozen those that cozen all the world, and get these, gentlemen to come by their estates easily, and without taking the covenant, the old sum of five hundred pounds, that I used to talk of, shall be yours yet.

Mrs. Day. We will endeavour.

Ruth. Come, Mrs. Arbella, pray let's all be friends.

Arb. With all my heart.

Ruth. Brother Abel, the bird is flown; but you shall be released from your bonds.

Abel. I bear my afflictions as I may.

Enter TEAGUE, *leading* OBADIAH *in a Halter, and a*
         Musician.

Teague. What is this now? Who are you? Well, are not you Mrs. Tay? Well, I will tell her what I should say now! Shall I then? I will try if I cannot laugh too, as I did, or think of the mustard-pot.

Care. No, good Teague, there's no need of thy message now; but why dost thou lead Obadiah thus?

Teague. Well, I will hang him presently, that I will. Look you here, Mrs. Tay, here's your man, Obadiah, do you see? he would not let me make

him drunk, so I did take him in this string, and I am
going to choke him by the throat.

Blunt. Honest Teague, thy master is beholden to
thee, in some measure, for his liberty.

Care. Teague, I shall requite thy honesty.

Teague. Well, shall I hang him then? It is a rogue
now, who would not be drunk for the king.

Ob. I do beseech you, gentlemen; let me not be
brought unto death.

Teague. You shall be brought to the gallows, you
thief 'o' the world.

Care. No, poor Teague, 'tis enough; we are all
friends. Come, let him go.

Teague. Are you all friends? Then here, little
Obid, take the string, and go and hang yourself.

" *Care.* D'ye hear, my friend, [*To the Musician.*]
" is any of your companions with you?

" *Mus.* Yes, sir.

" *Care.* As I live, we'll all dance; it shall be the
" celebration of our weddings. Nay, Mr. Day, as
" we hope to continue friends, you and your uck
" shall trip it too.

" *Teague.* Ay, by my shoul will we; Obadiah shall
" be my woman too, and you shall dance for the
" king, that you shall.

" *Care.* Go, and strike up then: no chiding now,
" Mrs. Day. Come, you must not be refractory for
" once.

" *Mrs. Day.* Well, husband, since these gentlemen

" will have it so, and that they may perceive we are
" friends, dance.

" *Blunt.*   Now, Mr. Day, to your business; get it
" done as soon as you will, the five hundred pounds
" shall be ready.

Care.   " So, friends;" thanks, honest Teague;
thou shalt flourish in a new livery for this.   Now,
Mrs. Annice, I hope you and I may agree about
kissing, and compound every way.   Now, Mr. Day,

If you will have good luck in every thing,
Turn cavalier, and cry, God bless the king.

[Exeunt omnes.

EPILOGUE.

BUT now the greatest thing is left to do,
More just Committee, to compound with you ;
For, till your equal censures shall be known,
The poet's under sequestration :
He has no title to his small estate
Of wit, unless you please to set the rate.
Accept this half year's purchase of his wit,
For in the compass of that time 'twas writ :
Not that this is enough ; he'll pay you more,
If you yourselves believe him not too poor :
For 'tis your judgments give him wealth ; in this,
He's just as rich as you believe he is.

 Would all Committees could have done like you,
 Made men more rich, and by their payments too.

THE END.

/

HE NATURAL SON.

A

COMEDY,

By RICHARD CUMBERLAND, Esq.

ADAPTED FOR

THEATRICAL REPRESENTATION,

AS PERFORMED AT THE

THEATRES-ROYAL,

DRURY-LANE AND COVENT-GARDEN.

REGULATED FROM THE PROMPT-BOOKS,

By Permission of the Managers.

" The Lines distinguished by inverted Commas, are omitted in the Representation."

LONDON :

Printed for the Proprietors, under the Direction of

JOHN BELL, British-Library, STRAND,

Bookseller to His Royal Highness the PRINCE OF WALES.

MDCCXCII.

PROLOGUE.

BY THE AUTHOR.

Spoken by Mr. BANNISTER.

THE Comic Muse, as Cyprian records prove,
Was Comus' daughter, by the Queen of Love,
A left-hand lineage—whilst the Tragic Dame
From legal loins of father Vulcan came ;
Therefore this Muse loves frolic, fun, and joke,
That bellows-blowing, blustering, puff, and smoke.
—Hence mother Nature's bye-begotten stock.
Are all but chips of the old comic block ;
For all derive their pedigrees in tail,
From fathers frolicsome, and mothers frail.
—Therefore, if in this brat of ours you trace
Some feature of his merry mother's face,
Sure, sons of Comus, sure you'll let him in
To your gay brotherhood, as founder's kin.

A married Muse !—no ; Muses are too wise
To take a poet's jointure in the skies,
Th' anticipation of an unborn play,
Or star-sown acres in the milky way :
So each lives single, like a cloyster'd nun,
But does sometimes as other nuns have done—

A ij

Prays with grave authors, with the giddy prates,
Or ogles a young poet thro' the grates.

Therefore our rule is, never to enquire,
Who begat whom, what dam, or which the sire ;
But, soon as e'er the babe breathes vital air,
Take him, and never ask how he got there.
Some are still-born ; some sent to mother Earth,
Strangled by critic midwives in their birth ;
And many an unacknowledg'd foundling lies
Without a parent's hand to close its eyes :
Thus are our bills with deaths dramatic cramm'd,
And, what is worse—to die is to be damn'd.

You, the Humane Society, who sit
To mitigate the casualties of wit,
Save a frail Muse's NATURAL SON from death !—
He lives on fame, and fame lives on your breath.

Dramatis Personae.

DRURY-LANE.

Men.

Sir JEFFERY LATIMER,	Mr. Baddely.
BLUSHENLY,	Mr. Palmer.
RUEFULL,	Mr. Bensley.
JACK HUSTINGS,	Mr. King.
Major O'FLAHERTY,	Mr. Moody.
DUMPS,	Mr. Parsons.
DAVID,	Mr. Wrighten.

Women.

Mrs. PHŒBE LATIMER,	Miss Pope.
Lady PARAGON,	Miss Farren.
PENELOPE,	Miss Tidswell.

Servants, &c.

Time, *that of the Representation.*

SCENE, Sir JEFFERY's *Country House.*

THE NATURAL SON.

ACT I. SCENE I.

A Library. Mrs. PHOEBE LATIMER *discovered at a Table with Books, reading.* Enter PENELOPE, *after gently tapping at the door.*

Mrs. Phœbe.

WHO's there ?——Come in, Mrs. Penelope !—Come in without ceremony.

Pen. I beg pardon for disturbing you, madam ; but my lady ordered me to bring her a book out of the library.

Phœbe. What book does Lady Paragon wish to have ?

Pen. Any that comes first to hand, French or English.

Phœbe. Is she fond of reading poems ?

Pen. If they are moving.

Phœbe. A lady's productions, I doubt, are not so apt to move, else I should recommend this collection.

Pen. A lady write poems ! I wonder any lady will

do such a thing, 'tis sure destruction to the com
plexion.——Doctor Calomel says, a lady, to preserv
her beauty, should not even think; he has wrote
book purposely to dissuade people from reading.

Phœbe. Every book he writes will do that. So fa
however I subscribe to his maxims, as cautiously to
engage in any work of intense hot thinking, lest the
fire of the imagination should force its way into the
face, and the flag of the rose be made to predominate
over the wreck of the lily.

Pen. Then, as sure as can be, that's my Lady Paragon's reason for employing Mr. Blushenly to read to
her.

Phœbe. So, so! she employs him, does she?

Pen. Oh yes, ma'am, Mr. Blushenly sits with my
lady, and reads to her by the hour.

Phœbe. Humph! then depend upon it 'tis not to save
her eyes that she employs Mr. Blushenly; I rather
think it is to satisfy them.

Pen. Mr. Blushenly is a very handsome man, to be
sure.

Phœbe. You think so; and you are generally of
your lady's way of thinking, are you not?

Pen. 'Twould be no disparagement to my taste, if
I were.

Phœbe. On the contrary, Mrs. Penelope, your lady
and my niece is a professed admirer of beauty, so
great a one, that she admires even herself;—she may
like to gratify her ears as well as her eyes by employing Mr. Blushenly: so, now that we have ac-

counted for two of her five senses in the interest of
the reader, we need not seek for other reasons, Mrs.
Penelope, why you should carry this book to the lady;
and why I should intercept the gentleman from following it.

Pen. A malicious thing I she's in love with him herself.   [*Aside and exit.*

Phœbe. These confidential *commies* of the toilette are
sure ·to talk the language of their principals. Not
that I suspect my niece of an attachment—that's not
her passion; vanity and variety is her game.   Then
the condition of poor Blushenly keeps him back; a
dependant, a foundling, destitute of every thing but
what the Graces have bestowed; Nature his only
parent, Charity his nurse, and the wide world his inheritance.   ·

Enter BLUSHENLY, *and bows.*

Mr. Blushenly, good day to you I

Blush. Your most obedient, Mrs. Phœbe; always
amongst your books I ever at the toilette of the
Muses I

Phœbe. Yes, Mr. Blushenly, my beauty-wash is
cull'd from the blossoms of Parnassus; Truth holds
the glass, Nature gives the grace.   The mind, the
mind, Mr. Blushenly, must be clothed, and here is
its wardrobe; 'tis with that we attract the regards of
the man of sense, with that we hold commerce with
the worthy: misconstrue not my expression; the soul,
young gentleman, the soul is of no sex,

Blush. I am sorry for it, Mrs. Phœbe; for I have been apt to think all its softer attributes were of your department. Admit your doctrine to be true, and what becomes of the good old proverb, ' Love begets love,' if there be no sex in the question ?

- *Phœbe.* I like your proverb, I admit your proverb, I admit it in its full force, Mr. Blushenly : there is not a postulatum in philosophy I had not rather give up, than have you think for a moment that these tender attentions can be bestowed upon an unthankful heart.

Blush. Oh the vengeance! what is coming now ?

[*Aside.*

Phœbe. They are not lost, believe me: not a tear that springs in your eye, not a sigh that escapes from your breast, but generates in mine a congenial affection.——I appeal to what pass'd last night whilst I was at the harpsichord: you may remember the cantata was Parthenia's encouraging address to her bashful lover: I noticed the looks you gave me whilst I was singing; I felt them, you might perceive I did : they gave a meaning, an expression to the cadence : it might not reach perhaps to barbarous ears, but I am persuaded, Mr. Blushenly, it came home to your's.

Blush. The ears, madam, are the most dangerous avenues to the heart; your sex, as well as mine, have found them such to their cost.

Phœbe. The human voice, Mr. Blushenly, was not bestowed as the mere organ of speech, but as the oral index of the soul.—— You have a sweet voice, Mr. Blushenly; and what a recreation to my ears, after

being tortured with the crack'd untuneable trumpet
of my brother, Sir Jeffery Latimer, the hoarse hunt-
ing-horn of Jack Hustings, and the quarter-sessions
yell of our neighbouring country squires, to hear you
speak !——Thanks be to the times! these indigenious
barbarians are in the way to be exterminated by taxes,
as the Indian savages have been by rum.

Blush. Upon my word, Mrs. Phœbe, your partiality
puts me to the blush.

Phœbe. And it becomes you; blushing becomes
you : not that I approve of diffidence in excess, the
least resemblance of despair; no, on the contrary, I
would encourage hope, I would cherish even ambi-
tion.——There is one in this family, Mr. Blushenly,
warmly impressed in your favour : let not distance of
condition, nor the inscrutable mysteriousness of your
birth, put you out of heart; you have qualities that
can counterbalance fortune ; and you have a friend at
hand, who bears you much good-will, more than you
are aware of; more than it becomes her to express——
more, perhaps, than she can express——Oh! I shall
blush to death !

Enter Lady PARAGON, *reading.*

Lady P. ' *O'er her soft cheek consenting blushes move,*
  ' *And with kind stealth her secret soul betray;*
 ' *Blushes, which usher in the morn of love,*
  ' *Sure as the redd'ning east foretels the day.*'

AIKIN.

——Thank you for your female poet! thus we women
·I

write.——Blushenly, have you aired my lap-dog?
that's all you men are fit for.

Phœbe. How long has Lady Paragon been of that
opinion?——Vexatious and perverse!   [*Aside.*

Lady P. Her ladyship has been of that opinion long
enough to change it—half an hour.

Phœbe. I thought it would not be your lasting
creed.

Lady P. Ah no, no, no! Woman's a riddle, my
good aunt, and so is love: to love and be a woman,
that's not well; to be a woman, and not love, that's
worse.——Here, Blushenly, put this book in your
pocket, and come and read to me whilst I dress myself.

Phœbe. Lady Paragon, are you aware of what you
say?

Lady P. Not always; but I think I bade him come
and read to me whilst I am at my toilette; by which
means I divide my attentions between mind and body,
and keep peace with both parties: out of two offices I
think I have civilly offered him the best.——She's in
a horrid humour.   [*Aside.*

Phœbe. Well, niece, these may be modern manners: for my own part, I should think you have
already bestowed pains enough upon your person for
one day.

Lady P. True; but I dress and undress myself as a
child does her doll, for amusement.

Phœbe. And do you invite young gentlemen to be
present on these occasions, for amusement too?

Lady P. No, I do it for his good: when he shall see what frippery a woman is made up with, what a pasticcio of gauzes, pins, and ribbons go to compound that multifarious thing a well-dress'd woman; why then—why then—what was I going to say?—he'll find that modern beauty is but haberdasher's ware; and if he ever had any gallantry (which I very much doubt) he'll be cur'd of it at once, and you may lead him up and down the house like a tame philosopher.—Isn't it so, Blushenly?

Blush. I hope I shall never forget myself, when I approach your ladyship or Miss Phœbe.

Lady P. Look you there, now; didn't I tell you he was fit for nothing but to air a lady's lap-dog?

Phœbe. I perceive you are in one of your rallying humours, and want to be rid of me.

Lady P. Not I, upon my life!—part not in that opinion: I talk nonsense only to drive away spleen; be assured I never was in a more melancholy mood in my life.

Phœbe. I am sorry, niece Paragon, your father's family is so dull to you.

Lady P. Misconceive me not; I have every thing I want but one, and without that I starve in the midst of plenty.

Phœbe. And what is that one thing wanting, pray now?

Lady P. Flattery: simply the food of flattery; not a full meal, that is nauseating, but evermore a little relish now and then: truth is the daily bread;

B

the staff of life, flattery the salt.—As for this moping
mortifying thing, I can make nothing of him; a way-
post has more conversation.—' I hope I shall never
forget myself, when I approach your ladyship or
Miss Phœbe.'——Oh, you unaccountable creature!
may I be further, if he has said one flattering thing
to me since in the house I have been.

Blush. Nor ever shall attempt it: fine men may
make fine speeches, a flattering beggar only shews his
mind is as mean as his condition.

Lady P. Nay, if you talk sentiment to me, Blushenly, you'll set me a crying; hands off from that
edg'd tool, if you love me. Sentiment in the country is clear another thing from sentiment in town: in
my box at the Opera I can take it as glibly as a dish
of tea, down it goes, and there's an end of it; but
in walks of willows, and by the side of rivulets,
there's no joke in it; I'm undone if I hear it by
moon-light.—Of all things in the creation, I hate
pity.

Phœbe. Did I ever hear the like? Pity is the cha-
racteristic of our sex.

Blush. Right, madam, it is the sister of Love.

Lady P. Well, and if it is, because I take one of
the family, is that a reason I should maintain all the
relations?—Heaven defend me from pitying any thing
above a lap-dog or a monkey!

Phœbe. Oh, for a shame! would you throw that
away upon a brute, which is due to your fellow-
creatures?—Believe me, Mr. Blushenly, I have a

heart for pity, and your misfortunes have a share in it.

Lady P. O lud, lud, lud! I would not pity him for the world; I would not do him such an injury; for as sure as can be, if I pitied I should love him; and if I lov'd him, all the world would pity him.

-Blush. Envy him, you should have said : how any man belov'd by Lady Paragon can be an object of pity, is a mystery past my finding out.

Lady P. That may well be, and no great mystery neither; as for my lovers, they are in general the merriest, gayest creatures in nature; for, as I seldom take a liking to any of them, I seldom torment 'em; but if ever that happens, wo betide 'em! no cat ever tortur'd a mouse as I persecute the poor, dear, miserable creature.——So, now you are fairly warn'd, Blushenly; and if you run into a trap, you run with your eyes open. [*Lady* Paragon *is going, and stops at the door.*] Well, I'm going—If you are discreet you will not go with me—but if you are determined to venture, here lies your way.—What say you? Will you venture?—Aunt Phœbe, your servant.   [*Exit.*

Phœbe. Mr. Blushenly, let me advise you—you see what a fantastical thing it is—I have something to impart to you.—Nay, if you are resolved—go—I renounce you—I commit you to your folly.—Oh! I could tear out her eyes! I am betrayed, abused, insulted.

> [Blushenly *during these speeches stands silent, and in apparent suspense; at length hastily escapes, and follows Lady* Paragon.

Enter Sir JEFFERY LATIMER.

You have a notable wise head of your own, have you
not ?—Cackling like an old gander with but one gos-
ling to your back, and then to set that fox, dropt in
a bag at your door, to keep it.

Sir Jeff. Why, what the plague's the meaning of
all this ?

Phœbe. The meaning is, that, not content with
what Nature did for you, you will be a fool of your
own making.—The meaning is, that you have reared,
educated, father'd this *Terræ-filius* to bring heirs to
the Latimers, children of nobody, and grandchildren
without a name.

Sir Jeff. What would you have me do in the matter ?

Phœbe. Send a herald to the moon, from whence
he dropt, and search the office there, before you let
this foundling quarter arms with a family as ancient
as the monarchy.

Sir Jeff. Here's an outcry about nothing !—Look
out, and satisfy yourself.—There they are in the garden, innocently plucking a little fruit.

Phœbe. Yes, o' my conscience, the forbidden fruit
—But I'll not look out ; I cann't endure to see them :
your daughter's danger brings the tears into' my eyes.

Sir Jeff. I believe you are in most danger of the
two yourself.—Never tell me ! 'tis all rank jealousy.

Phœbe. Rank folly, Jeffery Latimer !—But I will
be more moderate.—Why did you call him home

from the University?——Why did you send him thither?—I'll argue calmly with you——Is it not enough that she has made one unhappy match?

Sir Jeff. Yes; but I doubt that match was of our making, sister Phœbe.—Let her choose next for herself, and she will have nobody but herself to complain of.

Phœbe. Fine arguing!—Brother, brother, you are *ignoramus*, or, as the Poet sings——

Sir Jeff. Damn the Poet!

Phœbe. Oaths are no arguments, Jeffery Latimer; mere *brutum fulmen*, as the logicians have it.

Sir Jeff. Damn the logicians!

Phœbe. Now I am cool, you are hot!—How often, brother Latimer, have I talk'd to you on the subject of passion? Have not I told you that the wise ancients call anger a short madness? You had best abuse them too, had you not?

Sir Jeff. No, no, not in your company; I have too much manners to abuse the ancients to their faces.

Phœbe. You have no manners, Jeffery Latimer; no one component particle of a gentleman about you, but the pedigree of one: then you swear and talk so loud, and have contracted such a yell at turnpike meetings and election ordinaries, that, I protest to you, if I did not see you be-perriwig'd with the mane of a lion, I should think by your braying I was in company with an ass.

Sir Jeff. I wish I had the patience of an ass.—Talk of my perriwig indeed! look at your own.—What

are all those flags and streamers but Cupid's artillery
in ambuscade? Men-traps and marriage-guns in
every curl.

Phœbe. Don't be gross, Jeffery Latimer, don't be
gross.—I'll not be made the butt of your ribaldry,
nor the dupe of your avarice; I'll take my fortune
into my own hands, and not leave it as a nest-egg to
hatch cuckows of another feather than my own. You
are a barren bird, brother Jeffery; your line is run
out, and you are the worm at the end of it; you are
the last of the Latimers, an evanescent quantity, as
the schoolmen express it: you stand at the foot of a
noble pedigree, like a brass farthing in a collection
of rich medals.

Sir Jeff. And what will you do for my pedigree?—
A second deluge cannot stop it more effectually.

Phœbe. I'll tell you what I'll do—live to my own
liking: I've sacrificed the morning of my day to your
humours, noon and evening I'll dedicate to my own.
[*Exit.*

Sir Jeff. 'Fore Heaven you make a long day of it,
if it's only noon with you yet!—Well, David, what's
the best news with you?

Enter DAVID.

David. An' please your worship, Mr. Hustings is
come to dine with you.

Sir Jeff. My honest friend, Jack Hustings! where
is he?

David. In the steward's parlour, putting the fowling-pieces in order: he has brought a brace of trout of his own hooking, would do your heart good to see them.

Sir Jeff. That's well, that's well! fly-fishing is in season, and then my friend Jack never comes empty-handed.—But I must have a word in private with you—shut the door.—You and I, David, have kept this secret of young Blushenly, as we call him, now these twenty years and upwards; the neighbours think him a bye-brat of my own (for the old story of a foundling dropt at my door gets no credit with them), and the education I have given him, which has been such in all points as I would have given my own son, strengthens their suspicions: in all this time my cousin Frances Latimer, though she has liberally maintain'd him in secret, has never seen him.

David. And, if report says true, she is likely to go out of the world without it.

Sir Jeff. So she does but acknowledge him at her death, be it so! My last letters out of Flanders left her in a very dangerous way.—How long ago is it, David, since my daughter's husband, Lord Paragon, died?

David. A year and a half to a day, next Lammas.

Sir Jeff. 'Twas a happy riddance: and what the world would think a misfortune (that she had no children by him), I account a blessing; for I would fain have a grandson of my own name and family to inherit my estate.

David. I thought your worship was coming to that

point; there is no male living of the name of Latimer, unless you call Mr. Blushenly so, in right of his mother.

Sir Jeff. And what is he but a Latimer? Why have I brought him and Lady Paragon together, think you, but in this very hope?—I have the pleasure to see their attachment advance every hour.

David. I can readily believe it; and a lovely couple they will be as the sun ever saw; a fine gentleman he is, and a kind-hearted and a handsome; no flouter nor fleerer at poor folks, but always humble and obliging: all the neighbours love him, all the poor bless him; and, for my own part—but I say little; it does not become a servant to be prating—I ask your worship's pardon for my boldness.

Sir Jeff. David, you have no need to ask pardon; I consider you as a friend rather than a servant—but we'll talk of this at our leisure——Get you gone for the present; I hear Jack Hustings at the door.

[*Exit* David.

Enter JACK HUSTINGS.

Ah, Jack! how runs the world with thee?

Jack. Rubs as it runs. How is it, knight?—Give me thy fore-finger; I am come to rumple a napkin with thee.

Sir Jeff. And thou shalt be as welcome, my good friend, as to-day and to-morrow into the bargain.

Jack. I know it, I know it well, else I would not come.—I have brought thee a brace of trout, knight;

they are the first I've taken this season, and I'll warrant 'em as pink as a petticoat ;—shew'd noble play,
up the stream and down the stream :—a cloud in the
sky, a ripple on the water;—here stood I; you
know my old watch; snap's the word—never miss
my throw.—Hast got a good breed of birds on thy
manor this season ? ..

Sir Jeff. Tolerable, tolerable, a pretty fairish
parcel.

Jack. So much the better ; I'll come and brush the
stubbles for thee in a week or two's time. I have
been putting your fowling-pieces in order, for your
armoury was in sad trim.—How does my dainty little
widow and fair Phœbe ?—I've a little matter of business for thee, if I can bring it out.

Sir Jeff. What's the matter now, Jack ?

Jack. Burst it ! I don't know what to say to it,
though I came partly o' purpose to open a bit of my
mind to thee, only other things put it out of my head.
—By the way, don't let me forget to remind thee of
Tom Trueby's election for verdurer—it comes on
next Tuesday—Sir Roger's folks will be there.——
Tom's an honest fellow, and of the right kidney;
we shall want your voice at the poll.

Sir Jeff. Here's my hand ; never flinch my friends;
I am staunch for Trueby. —Now go on with your business.

Jack. Why, I don't know how it is ; sometimes I
think I am rather lonesome of an evening, when the
days are short, and the roads bad, so that my neigh-

bours cann't visit me; then the parson's dead, and there I'm out of backgammon; books, you know, books are but dull company; a body is soon tired of reading.

Sir Jeff. Certainly; any resource is better than that; it gives me the hip at once.

Jack. Besides, I have had a great loss amongst my greyhounds, and so, do you see—I sometimes think, by way of killing time, to take a wife; that's all.

Sir Jeff. Well said, Jack; and you have a mind to take fair Phœbe, as you call her; 'foregad you will have wife enough, and to spare.

Jack. Yes, yes, I am aware of all that; she's a bouncer, I confess: but then it is mostly in winter evenings I have occasion for such a companion; when fishing and shooting seasons set in I am generally from home.

Sir Jeff. She has the vengeance of a temper.

Jack. Never mind that, mine will serve for both.

Sir Jeff. Have you broke your mind to her?

Jack. No, no, that's to come yet; I shall be a little awkward and ungain at courting, but I've a recipe for that.

Sir Jeff. How so, Jack?

Jack. Why I've got a little somewhat by heart out of a book, and can say it pretty smoothly; if I can bring her to that, I shall come tolerably well off—but I hope I shall have your good word, knight: if it is not with your liking, do you see, I am off, and no harm done.

Sir Jeff. 'Tis a small compliment to say I had rather pay her fortune to you than to a stranger, for marry she will ; but as for my good word with her, I would not do you the injury to offer it.—There she is in her castle ; if thou hast the heart to attack it, march up boldly, the coast is clear ; but if thou thinkest it better to fortify with a good dinner, and a flask of wine, friend David shall give thee a bottle of his best, and we'll have a crash, my dear boy, to set thee on thy mettle.

Jack. With all my heart, I like your counsel well ; it is an old saying, ' Women and wine ;' but I say, wine and women.

Sir Jeff. Come thy ways with me, then, and we will have a batch at backgammon, to while away the time till David gives the signal on the buttery-door.

[*Exeunt.*

ACT II. SCENE I.

A Chamber. Enter BLUSHENLY, *and Lady* PARAGON.

Lady Paragon.

So, you've escaped from the bottle, but there's a worse danger in wait for you : my aunt Phœbe is out of port, and has set all sails in full chace ; ribbands and gauzes streaming at her top, signals of distrest virginity on its cruise for a consort.

Blush. Is there no looking-glass in this house that will speak a plain truth to her ?

Lady P. Hellebore cann't cure her : don't you know there is nothing so foolish as the follies of ge-nius, nothing so weak as the weaknesses of the wise ?

Blush. Truly observed I—and if she will take the promissory notes of that swindler Vanity, before the solid security of honest nature, who can help it ?

Lady P. Nobody ; for let Truth write ever so le-gibly, Love is blind, you know, and cann't read it : sad coufusion in the human intellects that little mis-chievous deity is apt to make ; and when he aims an arrow at my aunt, he must be a sorry archer, if he does not hit so broad a mark.—After all, Harry, what do you mean to do ? she is very rich.

Blush. And I am very poor, but that's no proof I am very mercenary.

Lady P. She has one strong feature in her favour.

Blush. Her strong box, I grant you. Your lady-ship seems to think money a tempting circumstance, and so it is in the world's opinion ; but I am interest-ed to know your real sentiments ; suffer me to ask, if for a moment you can put yourself in my situation, would you marry Mrs. Phœbe Latimer ?

Lady P. Humph I that's a home question, and be-fore I answer it, I must know what your situation is.

Blush. A thing without parents, and without a name ; a waife, a stray that your father has taken up upon his manor, and keeps upon the trespass till its beggarly owner perhaps shall reclaim it.

Lady P. Hold, hold, hold I you quite mistake me, you distress me ;—'tis not your circumstances, Harry, but your affections, that my question points at; and, sure I ought to know the state of that person's heart, for whom I am called upon to answer in such a case: resolve my question, therefore, and I will reply to yours.

Blush. I believe we had better drop the subject.

Lady P. By no means. Am I to suppose you alike indifferent to all women? that your heart is entirely disengaged?

Blush. I beg there may be no such supposition made.

Lady P. Am I then to suppose the contrary?

Blush. Madam!

Lady P. Nay, be sincere, hide nothing from your advocate, in your own cause.

Blush. I have no cause; I will not speak a falsity, and I cannot declare the truth.——Farewell!

[*Going.*

Lady P. Where's the man running?—Come back: must I take up that glove, pray, or you? [*Drops her glove, which he takes up*]—Stoop, proud spirit, stoop!

Blush. I humbly ask your pardon.

[*Tenders her the glove.* -

Lady P. A man of gallantry would have kept it.—— Oh! if thou hadst half an eye, the brains but of a wren, the smallest grain of intuition in thee or about thee, thou must ere this have seen and known——

Blush. What? tell me what.

Lady P. What! all ye Powers forbid that I should

C

tell thee what!——Go, get thee gone, thou art good for nothing but to put me out of spirits.

Blush. Turn me not away till you are reconciled: instruct me, I beseech you, how I am to act with Mrs. Phœbe; for I am distress'd beyond measure.

Lady P. Well, then, if you are disposed for a practice, I'll fight this quarter for my aunt, and you shall defend that for yourself.——Speak, are you ready?

Blush. No, no, no; that will never do.

Lady P. Defend yourself, for I am coming on.—— We are now alone, my dear Harry; and as I know you to be the man I may confide in, I shall not scruple to avow you are the man of all the world I must approve and love: a thousand opportunities have occurred for you to discover this, but the delicacy of your principle has determined you to meet my affection with indifference; I am now resolved to prove if that indifference be real or assumed; the measure may seem out of character with strict propriety, but love on my part, and backwardness on yours, compel me to declare myself; and thus I offer you a fond, a faithful, a devoted heart——   .

Blush. Stop, stop, for pity's sake! you put me out of every thing I had to say: I tell you this will never do.

Lady P. You'll tell me of your obligations to my family; I answer, they are offices that leave us your debtors:—you'll say, you are unknown, dependant, destitute; therein you humble me, and aggrandize yourself; for, with all the nobler superiorities of nature on your side, you leave me nothing but a poor advantage on the score of fortune:—as to your scruples that respect my father———   -

Blush. Father! you forget you are speaking for Mrs. Phœbe; you should say brother.

Lady P. Should I?——O, Harry!——Let it pass however; and now for your answer.

Blush. I cannot make any answer.

Lady P. I beg your pardon, you have answered me, completely answer'd; I never saw rebuff more peremptorily given.

Blush. What do you mean? you puzzle me.

Lady P. Then practise it again, till you are perfect; and since I have got so little way on Mrs. Phœbe's side, take it yourself, and I'll reply for Mr. Blushenly.

Blush. Excuse me: I feel myself unfit to take up any other character than of the humblest of your servants, and with all respect entreat you to release me.

Lady P. By all means, for, to own the truth, I am not yet prepared to act your part with the insensibility which it demands.——Farewell! [*Exit hastily.*

Blush. O cruel, cruel honour! [*Exit.*

Enter DAVID, *introducing Major* O'FLAHERTY, *followed by two Servants in Sir* JEFFERY'*s livery.*

David. Pray, sir, walk in; good sir, use no ceremony: I am but a servant, under favour, yet I am bold to say every friend of Mr. Blushenly's is wel-

come in this house.—Thomas!—William! run about
good lads, till you can find Mr. Blushenly—tell him—
but I ask your honour's pardon; you will be pleased
to send your own message.

O'Fla. Make no more words, but tell the young
gentleman a stranger wishes to speak with him.

David. Sha'n't they carry your name, sir?

O'Fla. I can carry that myself; they will be the
nimbler for having nothing to burthen them with.

David. Do as you are bid then, and make haste——
[*Exeunt Servants severally.*]——What can his business
be with Mr. Blushenly? [*Aside.*] I humbly conceive
you have had a long journey, sir; won't you be pleas'd
to repose yourself?

O'Fla. With your leave, I'll stretch my legs awhile,
I have been so long in the saddle, that, except two
or three tumbles and a roll by the way, I have scarce
felt my feet these three days.

David. Bless me! three days in the saddle!——
Where can he be come from? I wish I could get it
out of him. [*Aside.*]——I presume, sir, you are from
foreign parts—no offence, I hope?   .

O'Fla. None in life.

David. It will not out of my head but some good
luck is to happen this day—He looks like a foreigner.
[*Aside.*]——Are you last from Flanders, may I ask?

O'Fla. Indeed you may, sir.

David. He won't plead; what shall I do? [*Aside.*]
—— From the city of Lisle, perhaps?

O'Fla. Are you going thither, that you are so curious?

David. I have been there, sir; I served a lady who is settled there, Mrs. Frances Latimer.

O'Fla. Sir!

David. Perhaps you know the lady, sir; I believe she lives there at this day.

O'Fla. I believe not.——And now I hope you are satisfied with the information I have given you.

David. I ask pardon for my boldness, sir; but I have known Mr. Blushenly from an infant; the first hands that received him at the door of this very house, were mine : I was in hopes you had brought news of good fortune to him; I should have sincerely rejoiced at it, for I love him at my heart; every body loves him—but I won't be troublesome.———Here comes the young gentleman himself.

Enter BLUSHENLY.

Blush. I am told, sir, you would speak with me.

O'Fla. I shall be glad of that honour.——I believe our business does not want a witness; this person may retire.

Blush. David, leave the room.

David. Sir, sir!——I hope no mischief; I shall be within call.   - [*Aside to* Blush.

Blush Go, go! shut the door. [*Exit* David.]—And now permit me to request your name, sir?

O'Fla. O'Flaherty, at your command; you may add Major to it, if you are so pleased.—I have travelled a pretty many miles, by sea and land, out of pure love

C iij

and service to you, young gentleman, if it is you that are called Mr. Blushenly.

Blush. My name is Blushenly.

O'Fla. There's your mistake, my dear;—upon my faith it is not: cann't you take my word at once for what I tell you?

Blush. I have been so called from my birth, I believe; and though neither honour nor inheritance appertains to it, I have to hope you will not take one name from me till you provide me with another.

O'Fla. You speak as prettily, and as much like a gentleman, as heart can wish.——In one word, the true name upon you is Latimer.

Blush. Latimer!

O'Fla. To be sure: didn't I tell you so at first? for if it is Latimer, look you, how can it possibly be Blushenly? · Believe me at a word, and save a long preamble of a story : what grace would there be in my going through the whole catechism with you, when we cann't agree upon the first question?

Blush. Tell your story then in your own way, sir, only be pleased to tell it.

O'Fla. Nothing so easy ; say which story you would have, and I'll tell it as you like.—You had but one mother, depend upon it, and her name was Latimer, Frances Latimer, of Lisle, a lady I had the greatest respect for in life; a dear generous soul she was; a saint upon earth, though she made a small slip in her youth, and bore you over the left shoulder, as the saying is; a frolic, nothing more ; but it laid upon

her mind, which is wonderful to say.——Oh! she
took on piteously about you in her last moments.

Blush. Good Heaven!

O'Fla. Yes, 'twas mighty good of Heaven; you'll
have great cause to sing *Te Deum*, when you see what
a fortune she has left you.

Blush, What is this you tell me? I cannot doubt
but you are serious.

O'Fla. I am not given to be a trifler, and if I were,
'twould be a sorry joke to take so long a journey for:
I have the credentials sign'd and seal'd; you'll have
'em all before you, together with her last dying speech,
and what she said afterwards in her will.——' Take
these papers,' says she to me in her last moments,
' take 'em, Major O'Flaherty, and deliver 'em into
nobody's hands but my son's.'

Blush. And where are the papers?

O'Fla. Where are they! safe enough, trust me for
that;——there's a little ragged boy at the hedge-ta-
vern hard by, where I baited my garran, has got hold
of my saddle-bags, and is bringing them here on his
back.

Blush. Mercy upon me! had you the imprudence
to trust papers of such consequence to a vagabond boy
out of your sight?

O'Fla. Don't believe it, he is not out of my sight,
for I asked him his name before I trusted him with
the bags.

Blush. His name! what signifies his name?

O'Fla. Nay, if his name don't signify, 'tis all the

better, for I have forgot it by the way, 'tis no longer upon my memory: but you'll know it all, when the 'little whipster comes.

Blush. You alarm me beyond measure : let us go in search of him.   [*Going.*

[David *meets them as they are going out.*

David. There is a fellow without, who has brought some baggage belonging to this gentleman.

O'Fla. There, there! now you will be easy; now what becomes of your alarm ?

Blush. Shew me to the fellow.

David. I don't know what to make of all this.

    [*Aside, and exeunt.*

Enter JACK HUSTINGS.

Jack. Sir Jeffery has fled the pit, Harry Blushenly is a flincher of old, the ladies are off, the whole house is a solitude, and nothing is left for me but drowning or marrying, and they both go by destiny ; therefore, if Mrs. Phœbe comes across me, I'll say a short prayer, and wait my fate——Apropos! here she is !————

Enter Mrs. PHOEBE LATIMER.

Mrs. Phœbe, your most humble servant ; I think myself fortunate in this meeting.

Phœbe. Really! then I conclude, Mr. Hustings, you are no friend to contemplation, and do not like your own company: now I am, as the Ancients express it, never less alone than when alone.——Could you not pass an hour with a book? the library is open.

Jack. With a book! yes, madam, I can take up a book, when I've nothing else to do.

Phœbe. And what books do you chiefly read, pray? —poetry, history, philosophy?

Jack. All's one for that; the Racing Calendar, Cock-fighter's Guide, Complete Angler, and the rest of the classics; nothing comes amiss.———Are you fond of fishing, Mrs. Phœbe?

Phœbe. In theory extremely so; I can fish with San- nazarius all the day long.

Jack. He's a happy man, truly; but I cannot say I know the gentleman; does he troll, pray now, or fish with a fly?

Phœbe. I rather believe with a quill; Sannazarius was a poet of the fifteenth century.

Jack. And that's a wonderful old age for a poet; but fishing's a long-liv'd amusement.

Phœbe. 'Tis a solitary one.

Jack. You've hit it, Mrs. Phœbe, 'tis a solitary one; and, to say the truth, I begin to find I must seek out a companion to cheer my solitude, a companion for life, Mrs. Phœbe.

Phœbe. Oh dear heart! if you are in quest of a wife, pass on; don't let me stop you; you have no time to lose. .

Jack. Perhaps I shall go no further.—I have a lady in my thoughts; not one of your flanting young ma- dams, but a staid, sensible, discreet person, of a suit -

able age.——I don't choose by the eye, Mrs. Phœbe; I ask for no more than I bring : youth and beauty are not indispensables in my choice.

Phœbe. If you are contented without them, you are the sooner pleased.——And who may the happy lady be, whom you have so flatteringly described ?

Jack. One you know very well, Mrs. Phœbe; she's not far off.

Phœbe. One of our neighbours ?

Jack. One of your family, the sister of my friend, Sir Jeffery ; if you know the lady's mind, I shall be glad you will inform me of it.

Phœbe. Her mind I know sure enough, but her person I should not have guess'd at by your description of it.——I believe I may answer for that lady, that such addresses, which convey an affront, or any addresses from you, Mr. Hustings, will meet nothing but repulse.

Jack. That's very extraordinary; for Sir Jeffery told me you was determined of marrying out of hand.

Phœbe. Did he so ?

Jack. Yes he did; ' Marry she will,' says he; ' and to be sure I had rather pay her fortune to you than to a stranger:' these were his very words.

Phœbe. Defile not my ears with the vulgar retail of his impertinent discourse. Sir Jeffery shall repent of this insult.

Jack. Now, if I could but fetch her up with the speech ; but, as I am a true man, she has frightened it out of my head.——Come, come, sweet Mrs. Phœbe, don't be angry with me; you and I have long been friends.——Fair bud of beauty! look upon your enamoured lover; suffer him to enfold you in his arms, to clasp you to his panting heart!

Phœbe. Keep off! I avoid the chamber!——

Jack. One kiss, one kind, consenting, reconciling kiss!——   *[Offers to kiss her.*

Phœbe. Off, monster!——Are we amongst woods and wilds, with satyrs, or in a civilized society, with men?——Here is no scene for Lapithean banquets, thou descendant of the Centaurs!——The ancient Scythians were not more barbarous in their cups than thou art; Rome's monarchy was lost by violence not more shocking than this.

Enter Lady PARAGON.

Lady P. Bless me, aunt Phœbe, what's the matter?

Phœbe. Matter enough; this savage would have forced a kiss upon me.

Jack. Why then, as I hope to be saved, I did it for the best.

Lady P. Do you call that your best?—O fye!—— Men are strange animals, and when we women throw out our charms, and look alluring, which you, dear aunt, particularly do this moment, such little fracas will happen.——Come, let me intercede; 'twas but a kiss at most, and I never think a kiss worth fighting for.

Phœbe. Nor I, perhaps, in any other case; but he had the ill-manners to introduce a proposal of marriage, by telling me he did not look.for youth or beauty in a wife.

Lady P. That's the consequence of having too many good qualities.——Had you nothing but youth and beauty to recommend you, you had been sure to have heard of them : foolish women always get the finest things said to them.——Go your way ; take no leave of her, but begone.   [*Aside to* Jack.

Jack. Thou art a dear soul : there's more fuss with these old maids than they are worth.   [*Exit.*

Lady P. Well, my dear aunt, how do you find yourself now ?

Phœbe. Something better; but still in a terrible flutter: my heart beats vehemently.

Lady P. Oh yes, these men do set our hearts a beating; but you see he is gone, the ravisher is gone; I hope you will recover by degrees. I'll stay by you till you are safe : if he should come back I can scream out whilst you are defending yourself; for, let the worst come to the worst, he can stop the mouth but of one of us at a time.

Phœbe. In my days, lovers were on their knees to their ladies for the favour of a salute ; and the concession of the cheek was not then to be obtained without long solicitation, tears, and entreaties.

Lady P. Those were fine days indeed ; then a lady set her favours at some price : now so many give away their goods for nothing, that they have fairly spoil'd the market.——If Mr. Blushenly now————

Phæbe. You do him wrong; in all our intercourse he never once solicited————

Lady P. Oh fie! take care of what you say: remember, remember!

Phæbe. What should I remember?

Lady P. The tapestry bed-chamber, when you was shewing him king Solomon and his concubines in chain-stitch.——Defend me from these modest men! your beef-fed country squires are nothing to them; they have the will, indeed, but not the wit to be mischievous.

Phæbe. Well, well, I sha'n't easily be persuaded out of my good opinion of Mr. Blushenly.

Lady P. Keep to that, and you are safe: good opinion is one thing, and love is another.

Phæbe. True; yet in some cases they go together.

Lady P. And then they drive at a furious rate, truly: when Love holds the whip, Reason drops the reins. [*Exeunt.*

ACT III. SCENE I.

A Hunting-Hall. Sir JEFFERY LATIMER, BLUSH-ENLY, *and* O'FLAHERTY. *A Table with Papers.*

Sir Jeffery.

Joy to you, my dear Harry, all joy attend you!——The will's a good will; you have a brave property;

your title's firm, pen and parchment cann't make a
better. I am beside myself with joy ; I'll have a jubilee
for this month to come; there sha'n't be a sober man
in the county. I could laugh and cry, and be merry
and be sad, or any thing but in my senses.——Come
into my arms, my dear, dear Mr. ——— What's your
name ?

O'Fla. Dennis O'Flaherty is my name. I hope you
like it ; it has been a pretty while in the family, and
I should be loth to change it.

Sir Jeff. I shall love your name and your nation as
long as I have breath. Why, a man of your parts
might have married this cousin of mine, and snapped
her whole fortune,-if you had not been the noblest
fellow upon earth.

O'Fla. Where's the nobleness of not being a rascal ?
I prize the friendship of the fair sex too well to raise
money upon them. It was my fortune in life to inherit nothing at all ; and I have not lessened it : my
good name and my good sword are still my own, and
there is no incumbrance upon either; I have not
mortgaged them to dishonour, and, with the grace of
Heaven, I never intend it.

Blush. Mr. O'Flaherty, I would fain thank you ;
but my heart is too full ; time and my future conduct
must declare my gratitude : whatever may be my
good fortune, you, under Providence, are the father
of it.

O'Fla. It has been my lot, young gentleman, to
meet a great deal of good fortune in the world—be-

longing to other people, I mean—and 'tis a mighty
pleasant thing to carry up and down, though I have
never kept any to my own share.

Sir Jeff. Ah, my good friend, 'tis well my cousin
Frances fell into honest hands; she was a tempting
trust in a distant country.

O'Fla. What difference does the distance make in
my honesty, or her trust? Not but I must own some
of your countrymen, who have had their tempting
trusts at a distance, have remembered to leave the
trust behind 'em, and bring home nothing but the
temptation.

Sir Jeff. That's true, that's true. Oh! that you
had heard what a speech I had like to have made one
day in parliament on this very subject.—'Mr. Speaker,'
says I, starting on my legs, 'shall I tamely sit down?
'shall I sit down tamely, Mr. Speaker?' Would
you think it?—passion choked me, and I did sit
down.

O'Fla. What a pity's that, when a man has got a
full bottle, and cann't pluck out the cork!—I'll tell
you what, Sir Jeffery, you need not be surprised at
finding a poor catholic, like myself, an honest man;
you take a ready way to keep us so, by shutting us out
of your service.

Sir Jeff. And now, Harry, that you are of the
house of the Latimers, if it drops in your hands I
am clear of the blame.

O'Fla. O' my conscience, that's well thought of;
if there's a gap in your pedigree, old gentleman, you

had better trust to him for filling it up than yourself; aye, and let me tell you, you are not a little beholden to the poor dear soul that's dead, for putting a streak in your ladder, when you was on the last step of it: marry! but she made a good job of it, though she had only her left hand to work with.

Blush. Touch not upon that subject! I am to mourn a mother, who, till the last hour of her life, never acknowledged me; I, must remember her, therefore, as a benefactress rather than a parent.— You, sir, have ever been a father to me.

Sir Jeff. Take my daughter into council then, and be a son to me. You see the conditions of your mother's bequest; unless you marry Lady Paragon you have only a life-holding in your estate: Frances, with all her failings, had a family-feeling for the house of Latimer.

Blush. 'Tis that condition, with other reasons of equal delicacy, makes me entreat you both to keep this matter a secret, till I have sounded the affections of your adorable daughter. I would owe my happiness to nothing but her free choice and bounty—I beseech you, therefore, to conceal this event, for a few hours at least, from Lady Paragon, from Mrs. Phœbe, and in short, from all your family, but honest David; his friendly anxiety must be relieved. You will promise me this, Sir Jeffery?

Sir Jeff. Twenty long years and upwards have I brooded upon this nest-egg, and now the chicken's hatcht I mayn't cackle;—'tis a little hard, but I'll do as you bid me.

Blush. Major O'Flaherty, I may expeĉt the same from you ?-

O'Fla. To be sure you may, my dear :—amuse yourself in your own way, ride your own round-about, so you do but come to the right point at last.

Sir Jeff. Come, Harry, this business being dispatched, let us now go and tap the best bottle in my cellar to the health of this worthy gentleman, to whose good offices we are both so highly indebted.

O'Fla. For the bottle, Sir Jeffery, I am your man ; for the good offices you speak of, speak no more about 'em ; honesty is due to every man, and how should you be indebted to me for what I owe you ?

Sir Jeff. Come, sir, let me shew you the way.——
[*Going:*

O'Fla. Mr. Latimer, with your leave, I shall be following you.

Blush. By no means—I am at home ;—but not Latimer, if you please, call me Blushenly.

O'Fla. Aye, aye, that's true—Blushenly—now you go by your wrong name : that's right !—Well, well ! let me see, I call'd you by your right name, but that's wrong—By my soul, between both but it's a very puzzling affair.

Enter JACK HUSTINGS.

Sir Jeff. Hold, hold, hold ! as I live, a very admirable recruit to our party.—Mr. Hustings, this is Major O'Flaherty ; Major O'Flaherty, this is my friend, Mr. Hustings.—I pray you be known to each other, gentlemen both ! honest men don't meet every day.

Blush. This is my moment to escape. [*Exit hastily.*

O'Fla. I am proud to know you, sir; you bear your credentials about you; there's a passport in your countenance that will carry you through every kingdom in Europe.—Sir Jeffery Latimer, your friend here looks as if he could say *Boh !* to a bottle as well as most men.

Sir Jeff. I'll be his sponsor, though it were in the dark.—And now, friend Jack, shall we drink to the health of fair Phœbe, your future bride ?

Jack. Hush, hush ! if you love me ; no more of that, knight : let the wind whistle as it may, if every month in the twelve was November, I'll tuck myself up with a halter, before I'll couple with a wife.

Sir Jeff. Are you so soon disheartened ?—never fear, man ; you and fair Phœbe will make it up before night.

Jack. Then I'll give my skin to the tanner before morning, for you'll find it on the beam—why, she flouted me in a stile as proud as Nebuchadnezzar.

Sir Jeff. And she will be as humble as a trout before this day passes over her head, or I'll never venture at prediction again : retain this gentleman in your cause, and I'll ensure a verdict in your favour.

O'Fla. Is there any quarrel a-foot? What is the matter, may I ask ?

Sir Jeff. A lady's matter; a small suit at matrimony

2

between this worthy gentleman and a maiden sister of mine, Mrs. Phœbe Latimer : the good lady, it must be owned, is rather on the down-hill passage towards the vale of years, and has cast the eyes of her affection on the young gentleman we just now parted with.

O' Fla. When one is going down the hill and t'other up, nothing so natural as that both should meet; but, my life upon it, Mr. Latimer will give her the go-by.

Sir Jeff. Mr. Blushenly, you would say.

O' Fla. Well remembered ; you put that leaf into my book in good time.

Enter DAVID.

Sir Jeff. Now, David, what's the news with you ?

David. Strange news, sir. Mr. Ruefull is coming to visit you.

Sir Jeff. Ruefull to visit me ! I want faith to believe you.

David. His servant is in the house ; and if you like to see a curiosity, gentlemen, you will order him in.

Jack. Oh, bring him in by all means, David ; I should like to see the running-footman to a tortoise. Who is dead in your house, knight, that old Ruefull is come to sit up by the corpse ?　　　[*Exit* David]

O' Fla. Ruefull ! Ruefull ! sure I've heard that name before.

Jack. When a miser or a man-hater is mentioned, Ruefull's name is in every body's mouth.

Sir Jeff. 'Tis a rough shell, but there's virtue at the heart of him.—But I see the fellow coming.—Get yourselves ready, gentlemen, for Death is at the door.

DUMPS *is brought in by* DAVID.

O' Fla. [*Seeing* Dumps *as he enters.*] Oh 'the Beelzebub ! what's here ?—Which of the seven deadly sins begot you ? what gibbet have you defrauded of its furniture ?

Dumps. I am serving-man to Squire Ruefull; I hastened in advance, to signify the coming on of my master.——*Salve, Domine !—Et tu quoque !—Pax in domo !*

O' Fla. What the plague ! which of your evil tongues is that ?

Dumps. 'Tis Latin ; I learnt it when I shewed the tombs in Westminster Abbey.

O' Fla. Oho ! if you come out of the tombs, 'tis no wonder you speak the dead languages.

Dumps. Recté.

Sir Jeff. When will your master be here, fellow ?

Dumps. Anon.

Sir Jeff. Hark ye, David, take this mummy into the cellar, and wet his dust with a cup of October.— You'll find better company in my vaults, friend, than the Abbey's.

Dumps. Oh dear, sir, I was reasonable merry, till I came into my master's service ; he is a monument of a man : we should have had a terrible journey of it, if we had not luckily fallen in with a black job by the way, and kept company with the corpse to Exeter Cathedral.

Jack. I must be acquainted with this fellow.— What is your name ?

Dumps. My name is Dumps, an' please you.

Jack. How long have you been in Mr. Ruefull's service ?

Dumps. Five years by the calendar, five centuries by calculation.—I had indeed the choice of being keeper of a pest-house, but I was fool enough to withstand the offer; and, all other trades failing, took into my present service.

O'Fla. What other trades have you followed ? let us know your history.

Dumps. 'Tis soon told, gentlemen :—I am the son of a sexton, and worked at my father's business in my youth ; I then went into the service of a dissecting surgeon, and with my father's help furnished my master's academy with subjects.

O'Fla. Oh, Lord have mercy upon us !

Dumps. When that trade failed, I hired myself out to the Humane Society.

O'Fla. That was the devil of a jump backwards.

Dumps. Many an honest gentleman now walks about with breath of my blowing ;—but it was too much labour for one pair of lungs ; and, by giving life to a drowned alderman upon a swan-hopping party, I contracted a consumption, and turned murder-monger to a morning paper.

O'Fla. Murder-monger ! there you are in your old quarters once more.—And what's murder-monger, I would fain ask ?

Dumps. Casualty-compiler, an' please you, inventer of murders to amuse our customers; but they said I wanted variety in my violent deaths, I made too much use of the brewer's dray; so they took a tragic poet in my place, and I was turned into Westminster Abbey, as valet-de-chambre to the ragged regiment, to brush the dust off the faces of the wax-work; from thence I came into Squire Ruefull's service; and if I take another step downwards, it must be to the old one, for I can go no lower in this world.

Sir Jeff. Try the depth of my cellar first, and then we'll talk further with you : get you gone.—[*Exit* Dumps.]—But I see the ladies coming—let us step aside, my good friend, and concert our evidence, and then we shall agree in the same story.

O'Fla. Faith, and that's well thought of; for if the truth is not to be spoken, 'tis mighty proper to agree what we shall put in the place of it.   [*Exeunt.*

Enter PHOEBE, *Lady* PARAGON, *and* BLUSHENLY.

Phœbe. Mr. Blushenly, who is that stranger with my brother ?

Blush. His name is O'Flaherty, an officer in the Austrian service.

Phœbe. But what is his business here?

Blush. He comes to announce the death of your relation, Mrs. Frances Latimer.

Phœbe. What do you tell me? Is she dead ? this is news indeed:—do you hear this, Lady Paragon ?

The death of Mrs. Latimer is an event very interesting to us all.

Lady P. As I had scarce the honour of knowing the lady, I cannot say I am particularly affected by the event: if any good person is made happy by her fortune, so far I shall be rejoiced at it.

Phœbe. Why, your father is her heir at law: I wonder you can be so insensible.

Lady P. I hope my father has enough without it; there are people in the world I should rather wish her fortune to.—I recollect, Harry, she was once very good to you, what shall I give you for your legacy?

Blush. I will not sell it, because I have never yet had any good luck to dispose of;—but, promise that you will share it with me, and, believe me, in that case I shall find the old proverb true, and half will be much more than the whole.

Lady P. 'Tis done! I agree to it, so the partition be reciprocal.

Enter Sir JEFFERY LATIMER, *and* O'FLAHERTY.

Sir Jeff. Where are the ladies? I've a budget of news for them.——Sister Phœbe, this is Major O'Flaherty, a friend of our cousin, Mrs. Frances Latimer; I believe his name is not unknown to you.—— Major, this is my daughter, Lady Paragon.

　　　　　　[O'Flaherty *bows to the ladies severally.*

O'Fla. A Paragon indeed!—I am sorry I must put you in mourning, ladies, and strike these fine colours,

that become you so well ; I bring you
dea▊ of a relation.

Phœbe. I understand my cousin Franc

O'Fla. She is all that, madam, the m

Phœbe. Pity indeed! I fear sĥe was
die ; I hope she had time to repent.

O'Fla. Plenty of time—and to make h

Phœbe. In that I suppose you have an

O'Fla. Oh ! a very great one ; I have
to see every shilling bequeathed to her e

Phœbe. Her son ! her own son ! Oh n

O'Fla. Where's the monstrous par
would have been a monster if she had no

Lady P. Do you hear that, Blushenl
gain is drawn.

Blush. I beg your pardon, I shall hold

Phœbe. I never heard she had a son :
what is he ?—She was a single woman, h
have a son ?

O'Fla. I believe there was a very natu
it ; she was not a single woman in that
take it.

Sir Jeff. Puzzle yourself with no mo
—the world says, this son of my cousi
good fortune ; you will see him in this
near at hand, and only waits to know
agreeable he should present himself.—I
I hope you have no objection to a visit f

Lady P. How can I, sir ? an agreeab
always be an accession to our family circ

Sir Jeff. You will be very fond of him when you know him.

Lady P. No doubt I shall, and before I know him, by your character of him.

Sir Jeff. Have a care of yourself, Louisa; for if you should fall desperately in love, and throw yourself away upon the best young man in England, you will go near to break my heart—with joy.

Lady P. The Heavens forbid! I would not be guilty of such a thing for the world.

Sir Jeff. 'Tis no matter, in spite of all my warning you will do it.

Lady P. Impossible!

Sir Jeff. I tell you, you will do it;—sister Phœbe, remember I predict it.

Phœbe. Stay till the event happens, brother Jeffery, and then you may safely risque a prediction.

Sir Jeff. What do you say in the case, Major O'Flaherty, are you with me in opinion?

O'Fla. Oh! most clearly; and the more her ladyship protests against it, give me leave to say, the more I am persuaded of it.

Lady P. That's severe indeed, if ladies are to be taken by contraries.

O'Fla. Ladies like you, madam, must be taken as we can get them; such prizes don't fall to every man's lot: if Sir Jeffery has a mind for a wager, I shall be very glad to go sharer with him.

Lady P. Agreed! what shall the wager be?

O'Fla. Any thing but money.

Lady P. I'll put my life upon the stake.

O'Fla. Any thing but murder : for your money, I don't value it ; and for your life, it is in my opinion above all value.

Lady P. Name your own terms, then ; the bet is lost before 'tis laid.

O'Fla. Let it be a wedding-favour, then : a cockade to mount in our hats, and a courtesy to wear upon our lips.—Will you strike hands to this ?

Lady P. Hands and heart—Blushenly shall hold stakes.

Blush. Give them to me, then, and let me seal the treasure thus, and thus—[*Kisses her hand.*]—When I forfeit this deposit, it must be death that takes it from me.

Sir Jeff. All this does not stagger me : I tell you, daughter, you have laid a losing wager, and so good b'ye to you.—Come, gentlemen. [*Exit.*

O'Fla. I am your ladyship's most obedient—I shall call upon you for payment ; 'tis true I have only half a share, but any half of your ladyship's favours is more by half than any man deserves. [*Exeunt.*

Enter DAVID *and* DUMPS.

David. Well, Master Dumps, how do you find yourself now ?

Dumps. Gayly.

David. How sits his honour's old October on your stomach ?

Dumps. Bravely.

David. Now you are free of Merryfield-Hall: every body that comes here goes through a wetting.

Dumps. Bene.

David. 'Tis the custom of the house.

Dumps. Floreat!

Enter Servant, and speaks to DUMPS.

Serv. Are not you servant to the gentleman just arrived?

Dumps. Who, old Ruefull?

Serv. I don't know his name; but if your's be Dumps, he is calling out lustily for you in the hall. —Run, and see what he wants; for he won't be pacified without you.

Dumps. I run! no, if I could have done that, I would have run out of his service long enough ago. —Hang him, earthworm, let him crawl to me; I'll not budge.

David. Hush, hush! keep a good tongue in your head, Dumps; here your master comes.

[*Exeunt* David *and Servant.*

Dumps *retires to the back Scene. Enter* RUEFULL.

Rue. Are they fools born, or fools bewitcht, in this house?——'Twere better I took lodgings in a belfry, and slept to the ringing of bob-majors, than harbour in this academy of confusion.——Here have I been calling for my rascal, and every rascal runs but the right one; half a score tongues to answer, not a hand to help: the building of Babel was a Quaker's meeting to it.——Where is this fellow of mine? 'tis plain he ● not broken his neck, else I should have stumbled upon his corpse.——Dumps! why Dumps, I say!

Dumps. Here am I.

Rue. Here am I! hedge-hog:——well, and here I am. Why don't you move at my call? Are you in the stocks? Are you in the conjurer's circle?

Dumps. Very likely, for my head runs round.

Rue. Why, you are tipsy; you have been drinking, sirrah: your eyes are set in your head.

Dumps. I hope so.

Rue. Sot, did not I warn you against this?——How often have I preached to you on the virtue of sobriety?

Dumps. Yes, but you made a virtue of necessity; you never gave me a chance to get tipsy in your service.

Rue. And I'll take care you never shall again, sirrah. I'll muzzle you for this: I'll shut you up in the Eddystone upon rotten biscuit and rain-water, for a twelvemonth.

Dumps. Do; then I shall go out of the world in a blaze.——*Vale.*　　　　　　　　　　[*Exit.*

Enter *Sir* JEFFERY.

Sir Jeff. What, old acquaintance! are you come amongst us? Welcome to Merryfield Hall; stay with me an hour, stay with me a month, once for all you are heartily welcome!

Rue. I am obliged to you : it becomes the master of the mansion to welcome his guests : but when his servants do the office for him, they are apt to overact their parts. Your fellows have intoxicated my fool with their western hospitality; and I am as much to seek without him, as a blind beggar without his dog. ——I pray you get some body to lead me about the house.

Sir Jeff. I will be your servant; every body will be your servant.

Rue. Let it be some civil gentleman, then, and none of those powdered coxcombs I met in your lobby. Servants now-a-days dress so like gentlemen, and gentlemen so like servants, that the less ceremony is with the better sort: if Harry Blushenly is with you, turn me over to him.

Sir Jeff. He'll be happy to attend upon you; I expect him every moment.

Rue. I have a foolish liking to the lad—but no matter.——Hark ye, friend Jéffery; if you foist me into one of your state-beds, with a villanous Dutch device of fair Bathsheba, or the queen of Sheba, to keep me company, I had rather you should shut me into your old tower, with a screech-owl at my casement, and a death-watch at my tester.——If you make a stranger of me that way, you'll be sure to keep me so.

Sir Jeff. 'Fore George, you have hit it: the chamber in the old Tower will suit you to a truth——But hold, hold! that won't do, neither—if you ring your bell there, not a soul will come to it, was it to save your life or their own.

Rue. What's the matter with it?

Sir Jeff. 'Tis haunted : Tom Dismal walks there.

Rue. I knew him when I was a boy ; he was your father's butler : a melancholy man he was ; he taught me the history of the great plague, and the fire of London.

Sir Jeff. He tuck'd himself up on the beam, in the great frost, thirty-nine.

Rue. He could not do it in a cooler moment.—But look! here comes your young man; go to your company, and leave us together.

Sir Jeff. You shall have your humour; so good bye to you.   [*Exit.*

Enter Blushenly.

Blush. I am happy to see you, sir; I hope you are in good health.

Rue. No, no, child, no such thing : I am never in good health : throw away no time in such silly compliments. Shut the door, for your owls in this house are broad awake in noon-day.——So, so! that's well.——I have taken an idle whim in my head, youngster, since you was at the Hermitage, that I am rather ashamed of, and therefore, do you see, I choose to make all fast, before I come to confession.

Blush. I believe, sir, nobody can overhear us, if you have any commands in private for me.

Rue. Was not it three days you passed at my cottage?

Blush. I think it was, sir.

Rue. I dare say you thought them thirteen; but you played the hypocrite well.

Blush. Oh for shame, sir! you must believe to the contrary, or think me the most ungrateful of all men.

Rue. No, no, no, no! I tell you I don't think it.—I have an odd humour of my own, I know I have, but I like you, I have a regard for you, young man; and that's more than I have said to any body these thirty years; I suppose if I was better acquainted with you, I should be cured of my weakness.

Blush. Perhaps you would, sir, for I'll not boast of my own deservings.

Rue. I like you the better for it, I like you the better for it. I hate professions; I am sick when I meet a fellow bolstered up with bladders, puff'd full of his own empty praises. I hope you don't think I am fool enough to come here upon a visit to old Jeffery.—— Not I, nor to Dame Partlet, his cackling sister, either.—He has got his daughter home, has he not?

Blush. Yes, sir, Lady Paragon is part of the family.

Rue. A blockhead that he was, to marry her to a gamester.—He deserves to be hung up by the heels, with a warning pasted on the gibbet to all fathers, mothers, and guardians. Why didn't he give her to you?

Blush. Alas! sir, I had neither father, mother, nor fortune.

Rue. What then? you had a better pedigree without parents, than she has with them; and for fortune, what's that? if you was of my way of thinking, you would not take it was it offered to you; why, I have got a fortune, youngster, a great fortune, if that be all, and a great house; but *Magna domus magnum malum* is my motto; a hut by the sea-side is the castle of my comfort.——I have something to say to you on the subject of this young woman; but first let me have a sight of her.

Blush. She is now taking her walk in the garden; shall we join her?

Rue. With all my heart—shew me the way.

[*Exeunt.*

ACT IV.   SCENE I.

Mrs. PHOEBE LATIMER, *alone.*

Mrs. *Phœbe.*

IF this silly brother of mine was not the strangest compound of contraries in nature, I should think there was some plot in his proceeding; for it seems as if he encouraged Blushenly, whilst he was recommending Latimer; yet he protests to me his heart is set upon the match: but you may as well teach method to a monkey, as expect consistency in him.——

Well met, sir! I must beg your patient answer to a few questions.

Enter BLUSHENLY.

Blush. Propose them.

Phœbe. What are you doing in this family, Mr. Blushenly? Are you, or are you not apprised of my brother's wishes for the disposal of his daughter to the heir of my cousin Latimer?

Blush. I am, madam.

Phœbe. Are you disposed to promote, or to obstruct that alliance?

Blush. Warmly to promote it.

Phœbe. Then you take a very extraordinary method of doing it, let me tell you:——I can hardly believe Lady Paragon will be the more disposed to give her hand to Mr. Latimer, for the ardor with which Mr. Blushenly kisses it.

Blush. She has hampered me; but I cannot disclose myself to her yet.   [*Aside.*

Phœbe. I perceive you are embarassed.——Female hearts, young gentleman, cannot resist such gallantries; there is nothing else wanting in your character to render you irresistible.——You must not kiss her hand again, indeed you must not.

Blush. If it was done to recommend Mr Blushenly, and not Mr. Latimer, set me down in your opinion for the meanest of mankind.

Phœbe. Whom but yourself can it recommend?——

Nature is your advocate, Mr. Blushenly; she wants
no help : she has bestowed upon you attractions more
than enough; no one is secure within the sphere of
their activity; I speak upon conviction:—Oh! had
you dealt so by me! but you are altered, you are
estranged from me; you treat me disdainfully, Mr.
Blushenly.

Blush. For which of my sins am I to be thus tor-
mented?—[*Aside.*]—How so, I beseech you? When
have I been thus guilty?

Phœbe. When I——Have you forgot then how, in
spite of all I could devise to stop you, you run to the
coquettish lure of Lady Paragon, like a quail to the
call, whilst the net was spreading to entrap you?

Blush. Well, madam, perhaps I cannot defend every
little inattention to prudence; you must take me on
the tenor of my life; and I trust it will never happen
to me to be found wanting in esteem for you : as to
Lady Paragon, be assured, I will never oppose the
presumptuous addresses of a Foundling, to the just
pretensions of a man of fortune.

Phœbe. You judge wisely, Mr. Blushenly; I commend your resolution; she is not fit to be a wife.

Blush. She is not fit to be a wife to a Blushenly, I
confess to you : when that name comes into union
with a Latimer, it will not be with Lady Paragon, depend upon it.

Phœbe. Now, now indeed I understand you;—that
was kindly said; that was like yourself : you have re-

lieved an anxious throbbing heart.—Oh, Mr. Blushenly,.you must not kiss her hand again——Indeed I
cannot bear it.

Blush. Be content I every thing shall be cleared up.
before this day is at an end—At present, I must take
my leave; but an hour sha'n't pass before I will see
you again.

. *Phœbe.* Indeed I shall we meet so soon again ?

Blush. Without fail——Then I will hold back nothing from you.

Phœbe. Nor I from you ; till then, farewell I—[*Exit
Blush.*] 'Tis.done I 'tis settled I that important matter is at last adjusted. As for their jeers and jibes, I
value them not. I'll draw my fortune into my own
hands.——Let me see!——Twenty thousand, at five
per cent.—a neat income in a cheap country; a re-
tired little box, with a spare room for a nursery; a
post-chaise for myself, and a nag for my husband.—
Why, 'tis affluence; 'tis luxury; 'tis the paradise of
human life I——Pshaw I this fellow again I

Enter JACK HUSTINGS.

Jack. Don't be frightened, Mrs. Phœbe I you have
nothing to fear : I have seen my error, and thoroughly
repent of it.

Phœbe. 'Tis well you have, sir.

Jack. Very true ; 'tis a happy reformation——but
who can command himself at all times, Mrs. Phœbe ?
——Where's the man that can do it ? I was surprised,
taken unawares, passion ran away with me like an un-

broke horse: but I have got him under now; I can govern him with a twine of thread.

Phœbe. 'Tis well you can, sir.

Jack. Very true, Mrs. Phœbe, 'tis a joyful change. ——I see I am not the man; a lady of your talents cann't take up with a country 'squire; 'tis not to be thought of—Blushenly carries all before him.

Phœbe. Where did your sagacity collect that, Mr. Hustings?

Jack. 'Tis not I only that see it; all the neighbours talk of nothing else. I thought indeed disparity of years might have stood in his way; but I see you do not start at trifles, your generosity has surmounted that objection: as for fortune, I know you have a spirit above that.

Phœbe. Whether you know it or not, I have that spirit, sir.

Jack. Yes, Mrs. Phœbe, I am ready to bear witness to your spirit; and, though a discarded lover, have some hopes, by the blessing of a good constitution, to survive it, and dance at your wedding still.——Happy be the man! he has the merit of admiring you for your youth and beauty——I had the misfortune to address you for your virtue and discretion.

Enter Sir JEFFERY LATIMER, RUEFULL, *and Lady* PARAGON.

Sir Jeff. Sister Phœbe, here is an old friend, and servant of yours, Mr. Ruefull: he is not quite so

jovial as Jack Hustings, nor so young as Harry Blushenly; but, if you like a melancholy lover, I'll pit my
friend against all England.

Rue. Ah, Mrs. Phœbe! a pretty many years have
gone over our heads since I handed you to your ber-
lin from the opera of Griselda. I was then a young
man just come home from my travels, and you a fine
gay girl in your bloom, just setting out in your career
of conquests.——By the same token, I remember I
broke a glass hoop-ring, which it was then a fashion
to wear, into your finger by squeezing your hand; I
shall never forget the pretty flutter it threw you into,
when the blood started through your glove: I penn'd
a sonnet on the occasion, in elegiac metre, that had
some points in it; but it did not move; you was ever
inexorable.

Phœbe. Such a thing may have passed, but I was
too young to carry the impression in remembrance.

Rue. Very likely, for I dare say your wound healed
quicker than mine.——I retired from the gay world
soon after, where I had no desire to pass for a sple-
netic companion amongst men of pleasure; since when
I have made some friendships with the dead, merely
that we may not be absolute strangers to each other'
when we meet; however, I have this advantage in it,
that I am going to my connections, and you are parting from yours. Not that I would be understood to
insinuate that you have any symptoms of immediate
decay about you, Mrs. Phœbe; on the contrary, I
think your air and apparel more gay and juvenile than

F

I should have looked for in a person of your years; and I rejoice to see you carry them off so much above my expectation.—Truly you are a fine woman of your age, a very fine woman of your age still.

[*Mrs.* Phœbe *walks aside in a passion.*

Jack. Wormwood, knight, wormwood! She is broiling with vexation.

Sir Jeff. Hark ye, daughter Paragon, cut her lace, and save her stays from bursting.

Lady P. Worse and worse! Here's Blushenly coming; I cannot bear to see her suffer.—Mr. Rue-full, I shall grow jealous if you make all these fine speeches to my aunt, and not let me have my turn.—— Go to my aunt, Harry, go; I can assure you she has her full share of admiration in this company, and you are throwing weight into the heavier scale.——Why don't you do as I bid you?   [*Apart to* Blushenly.

[Blushenly *having entered during this speech of Lady* Paragon's, *she makes signs to him to go to Mrs.* Phœbe; *which he at first misunderstands, but afterwards goes and converses apart with her.*

Rue. There is something very sincere in your challenge, young lady, I like the manner of it well; and, to tell you the truth, I came hither purposely to see you; for though I am an old fellow with one foot in my coffin, I hope there's no harm if I take a parting peep at youth and beauty before death shuts down the lid. I was curious, you must know, to see you with my own eyes, and hear with my own ears; for had I taken what that idle young fellow reported upon trust, I should have the strangest opinion of you in nature.

Lady P. How so, I pray, how so? I should expect he, of all men, would report of me as a friend.

Rue. I should doubt that, for he made you out to be a miracle of human goodness—Now that's a shot point-blank against all my experience and belief.

Phœbe. Oh! that I had that man's tongue in my pocket!—Will nobody silence him!

Lady P. You are justified in your incredulity; for I shall not scruple to confess that I am more proud of his partiality than I could be of the truth itself.

Rue. That's a fair confession at least; and if it does not serve to convey a very favourable impression of your judgment, it enables me to guess at your affections towards the young man at your elbow: and I am persuaded I shall have my old friend Mrs. Phœbe on my side, if I wish you both happy in each other.

Phœbe. Are you so, sir? are you so? Why do you take upon yourself to answer for me in the case?

Rue. Because I think you have lived long enough in the world to see the misery of unequal matches:—where affections meet, where characters tally, where tempers agree, who regards fortune?

Jack. Not Mrs. Phœbe, I assure you;—she has a spirit above that—you know you told me so yourself just now.

Phœbe. Who desired you to interfere?

F ij

Rue. Then their ages, madam—there, I'm sure, you'll own they're match'd. Now I hold it in abhorrence, and equally a sin against nature in either sex, were an old fellow, like myself, to couple his infirmities to the youth and beauty of Lady Paragon, or a woman of your gravity to befool herself with a ridiculous passion for him there.

Jack. Lack-a-day, sir! Mrs. Phœbe can get over that too.

Phœbe. Who told you what I can get over, or what I cannot get over? I desire I may neither be quoted for an example, nor referred to as a witness in these matters.—And you must give me leave to tell you, Mr. Ruefull, that it is unusual for strangers, like you, to interfere in family matters, and take up the concerns of other people's alliances, as if they were their own.

Rue. Whether I am officious or not, madam, time must shew; but I trust there is no offence in saying, that if this young lady was my daughter, I would bestow her on Mr. Blushenly; or was he my son, I would recommend him to Lady Paragon: this is my opinion, Mrs. Phœbe, and I am ready to back it with my purse, if it is wanted. I believe I have as good an estate as my old friend here, perhaps I might say a better, for I have nursed it pretty carefully, and lived upon the gnawing of a crust;—'twas my humour, and I had nobody's leave to ask for mortifying myself. I am going out of the world, this young man is coming into it.—If Sir Jeffery will step aside with me, perhaps I shall convince him at least that I did not come here officiously, and for nothing.

[*Exit.*

Jack. Who calls this man a miser ?

Lady P. I am in love with him ; he has won my heart for ever.

Blush. 'Tis a rough humour, but a most benevolent nature.

Sir Jeff. Sister Phœbe, what do you think of all this ?

Phœbe. I think it a mere mouthful of moonshine ; true lunatic's diet ; the cookery of a crack'd brain ; froth to feed fools with ; you will find a better legacy in Don Diego's will : the man is in his dotage.

Sir Jeff. A word in your ear.—You are still for Mr. Latimer ? [*Aside.*

Phœbe. I am. [*Aside.*

Sir Jeff. Positively ? [*Aside.*

Phœbe. Peremptorily. [*Aside.*

Sir Jeff. Here's my hand, then : my daughter marries Frances Latimer's son, or I'll make the house too hot to hold her. [*Aside. Exit.*

Phœbe. So far all is safe—but I don't like these whisperings—I must interrupt their conference. [*Aside.*
Mr. Blushenly !—Niece Paragon !—You will forgive me, but——

Blush. Stay, madam, let me speak a word in private with your aunt. [*To Lady* Paragon.]——Mrs. Phœbe, you betray yourself by this impatience ; leave me, if you please, with Lady Paragon.

F iij

Phœbe. Why must I leave you ?

Blush. Because—because you must.

Phœbe. Sure!—You're grown very peremptory.

Blush. I make it my condition—my request—will that suffice ?

Phœbe. Well!—but you'll keep faith with me——you'll remember!—I'm gone.——[*Aside.*] How provokingly handsome she looks! I cann't bear the sight of her. [*Exit.*

Blush. At last we are alone ; and I now press the moment that decides upon my hope.—This Latimer, whom she so anxiously expects, whom your father recommends, and who is prepared to throw himself at your feet, is now in this very house.

Lady P. Well, if he is, what then ? Nor he nor they have supernatural power ; and human means shall never force me to a second sacrifice.

Blush. Are you so resolute ?

Lady P. My heart is pledged : you know the holder of it.

Blush. Then I have undertaken a hard task indeed ; for I am to move you for that very Latimer.

Lady P. Come, come, I've found you out : this is a return for my raillery about my aunt's strong box ; but, unless you can find pleasure in putting me to pain, I beg you to be serious.

Blush. I never was more serious in my life.

Lady P. Sir!—Mr. Blushenly!—I did not think you could be cruel to me.——We never meet again.
[*Going.*

Blush. Stop, I conjure you, stop!

Lady P. Why should I ?—Oh, Harry! if you are still so blind as not to see the openest heart in nature, legible by every eye but yours, I'll sooner do a violence to my sex's delicacy, by an avowal of my love, than leave it in your power to make a plea of ignorance.

Blush. You shall not do your dignity that wrong; I see and know your heart.

Lady P. You see it by false lights, you know it by unfair reports; else would you treat it as you do ?—No, you mistake a playful spirit for a levity of principle ; you think me a coquette, who likes and dislikes by caprice, and whose favours, like false coin received in payment, you are impatient to pass off to any other dupe that will take them.

Blush. I were a brute without reason could I so judge of you. The playfulness of your spirit shews the purity of your nature ; a heart like yours would make an angel's face superfluous ; I think with too much reverence of your virtue to recollect that you are beautiful.

Lady P. For which then of these two perfections do you reject me ? Is it my virtue, or my beauty you revolt from ?—Inconsistent flattery! Who throws away what he admires ? who draws back from proffered happiness ? either too proud to receive a blessing, or too suspicious to believe it is intended.

Blush. I neither have the pride nor the suspicion you describe ; and I only regret there is any thing

between us, which you have not the pleasure of be-
stowing. '

Lady P. Why then do you assume a disinterested-
ness which cuts me to the heart ? and with a cold air
of prudence, as fruitless as it is cruel, attempt to turn
inflexible affections from yourself to Latimer ?

Blush. Because I am that Latimer.

Lady P. What do I hear !

Blush. Oh, let me clasp you to my heart ! words
are too weak to tell you how I love.

Lady P. Oh ! what a head for stratagem is thine !
—a notable experiment, to prove that it is day by the
light of the sun !—Oh, Harry, Harry ! if I could
play the hypocrite, I would revoke all I have said,
and turn your own game upon you :—but I have
ways enough to be revenged ; and, as you have been
so very backward in discerning a lady's advances, I'll
take care you shall be as slow in making your own ;
you have seized a strong post by surprise, but I have
other defences in reserve ; and, with my aunt Phœbe
in front, I can still protract a surrender.

Blush. Whilst you look upon me with those eyes
of love, I may defy your menaces, because I have
your mercy to depend upon.

Lady P. Well, I protest you are insufferably vain.

Blush. And I swear you are insupportably handsome.

Lady P. Oh ! then you are come down from your
high-flown sentiment to a little plain sense at last :
you have drawn off the angel, and the woman ap-

'ery glad to find that I am not quite too
ttered.

soul dotes on you : I adore you.

1eel, then, and worship at a distance.

' privilege.—There lies your retreat ;

: my own.

I you break parole with me ? No, you
:red, and I'll carry off my prisoner, or
1e with me, loveliest of women, come !·

lon't know that I dare; I shall grow
: I thought to stroke a lamb, and I
:d a lion.   [*Exeunt.*

Mrs. PHOEBE *and* O'FLAHERTY.

ere, there, there! did you see that, sir ?

yes; mighty close truly, mighty close.

Mr. Latimer's friend, methinks, you
/ well pleased with this discovery.

indeed, and I am surprised to see you
iently ; but you are of a sweet gentle
:eive : and, as a reward for your pa-
safely promise you shall hear no more
after this night.

w so, how so ? make me understand
:n to do.

er ask about it : never vex your lovely
: a way of our own in Ireland.

)lain yourself, I conjure you.

y, you know there is such a thing in the
)st-chaise—Well !—and here you live

upon the coast, hard by the sea, do you mind me?—
Very well!—Mighty convenient, you'll allow, for
shipping off contraband commodities, alias live-stock,
for the continent.—Now if we can catch this young
ram by the horns, and smuggle him into Dunkirk,
we shall stop his breed at home, and nobody the
wiser.

Phœbe. Horrible! would you take the young man
out of the kingdom? would you murder him?

O'Fla. Why that shall be just as you like; it
would make his voyage the shorter.

Phœbe. Barbarian! I'll not suffer it: my blood
chills with the idea.

O'Fla. Oh then take another recipe to warm it:—
Elope with him yourself.

Phœbe. Myself.

O'Fla. 'Tis done every day; the most effectual
mode in nature to pique the jealousy of the young
lady at home; she'll marry Latimer, out of revenge,
in a week: the only thing is, to put a small force upon
your modesty; if you have friendship enough for
your niece to do this, all difficulties are over.

Phœbe. Do you propose this in ridicule, or in insult
to me?

O'Fla. Nay, if it shocks the delicacy of your nature, away with it at once; and, to say the truth, I
was afraid your modesty could not put up with it.—
What will become of her reputation? says I to Mr.
Latimer. Would you put a fair innocent creature
side by side with a tempting young rogue in a close

carriage ? I'm ashamed of you, says I.—Oh ! I rattled him off roundly, for dreaming of it; for I was of your way of thinking, that it would be best to knock him on the head at once, and save mischief.   .

Phœbe. Murder to save mischief !——Murder my reputation rather! inclose me in the odious post-chaise! let my innocence be your sacrifice, sooner than meditate an act so horrible: if no means else can be devised to separate him from Lady Paragon, behold me ready to devote myself a voluntary victim to preserve the honour and the interests of my family!

O'Fla. Why then, as I am a sinner, there is not a martyr in the calendar can go beyond you.——Oh, sweet Phœbe, if you were of the right persuasion, you would be the first saint of your name!—Make up your mind, dear creature, for the journey: pack up a few trifles for your occasions by the way; put a good book in your pocket to keep the foul fiend at a distance;—for, mind what I tell you, there's no trusting to these close carriages: as for holding him in talk about the weather, and the prospects, and all that, don't depend upon it, for the night will be as dark as a hedge; then there's such a cracking and a rattling with your iron work, screaming goes for nothing in an English post-chaise.   -

Phœbe. Talk no more of such idle prospects; I have other resources than you know of; and shall take care to prevent mischief, both to him, to her, or myself.   [*Exit*

O'Fla. Mercy on me! what a fermentation does a
little learning raise in a female scull! No wonder that
our fortune hunters poach among these petticoated
pe-ants; they fall into the snare like a pheasant from
its perch.   [*Exit.*

ACT V. SCENE I.

Enter RUEFULL *and* DUMPS.

Ruefull.

GET you gone, sirrah! I dismiss you from my service.

Dumps. Thank you heartily; 'tis the only kindness
you ever did me.

Rue. Leave the room.

Dumps. To leave is to obey—to obey is to serve.—
You are no longer my master, therefore I do not
leave the room.

Rue. Incomparable impudence! This is as it should
be, it feeds my spleen, and serves to put me out of
humour with the world.

Enter JACK HUSTINGS.

Jack. Who finds fault with the world?—I say 'tis a
good world.

Rue. I never said it was not good enough for those
who live in it.

Jack. Philosophers do but mar it.

Rue. Fox-hunters don't mend it.

Jack. You have a fellow here in your service of admirable humour.

Rue. He is an admirable fellow, if impudence be a recommendation.—I have done with him : he is upon his promotion ; if you have a mind for a purchase, you have nothing to do but to outbid the gallows, and the lot is your own.

Dumps. Take me whilst you can have me, good sir! if you put it by till to-morrow, you will have to seek for me at the bottom of the moat ;—I shall lay this old scare-crow of a livery on the bank for a mark : 'twill be in its seventh generation when I take leave of it, and every one of my predecessors left a family behind to be provided for ;——give the devil his due, as the saying is, my master has some credit in this old coat ; for 'tis made for all mankind, 'tis the only thing in our house that does not go by measure.

Jack. And can you find in your heart to part from this fellow ?

Rue. Parting from Dumps is like the practice of repentance : it costs some struggle to wean one's self from one's vices.——Fare thee well, Dumps! I wish I were certain thou wouldst never come back to me ; for if thou dost, I shall surely take thee in, and 'twould be hard if the plague could be had above once in one's life. [*Exit.*

Jack. Well, Dumps, what are you pondering upon?

G

Dumps. A reprieve at the gallows is a very serious thing.

Jack. After all your changes in life, you have had one change for the better; 1 have no melancholy faces in my family.——You must have led the life of a dog in this old fellow's service.

Dumps. Bad enough! but if I had little food, I had less work; if I had no merriment, I had no care. A man may live in a prison till he likes it: when I was with my master, I pined for liberty; now I am loose, I long to go back again. In short, I don't know how it is; I had made up my mind, and, with your leave, I'll return to my execution.——You don't know that old gentleman's character, sir.

Jack. I know what he passes for in the world's opinion—a miser and a man hater.

Dumps. Miser enough I own he is, and has gone near to starve me; but then he starves himself, so I cann't complain of him for that: a man-hater he is, I don't deny it; but then he does good to people out of spite.——He can be charitable enough, whilst other folks take the praise of it; find him out, and you are sure to lose his good-will.——He was a rake in his young days.

Jack. Was he so? pr'ythee, if thou canst, tell me something of his history.

Dumps. There's a lady of family (I don't know who she is) that he behaved very ill to: it lies on his conscience, and has turned his temper to vinegar:—she had a child by him—when he went abroad and left her;—he buried himself many years amongst the mountains, where the Swiss live, as' I believe.

Jack. Is the child alive ?

Dumps. I know nothing of that : so much I know, that he has been making enquiries since I've been with him, but all to no purpose, as far as I can find. He has a brave estate, and a fine house upon it, but he lives in a poor little cottage-like place, with an old woman and myself, and sees nobody. Folks think him a white-witch or wizard, and are afraid to come near him.

Jack. He seems to have taken strongly to our young man here.

Dumps. Mr. Blushenly, you mean ?

Jack. The same ;—he is very earnest to promote a match between him and Lady Paragon.

Dumps. Is he so? why then you must excuse me, sir, I cannot think of leaving him : if he is Mr. Blushenly's friend, I'll follow him whilst there is land or water to carry me; and so I will tell him;——here he comes.——*Peccavi, Domine!*——Master, forgive me !

Enter RUEFULL, *and Sir* JEFFERY.

Rue. Get thee gone, blockhead, get thee gone!—I have no time to forgive thee.

Dumps. Rather say, you have no leisure to hold out.

Rue. I have better business to mind.

Dumps. 'Tis done with a word : pray, sir, be quick about it, for repentance comes but seldom, and 'tis not good manners to keep a stranger waiting.

Rue. Well, well, well ! I will keep thee on, if it be only to torment thee; thy pardon shall be thy punishment.—Away with thee. [*Exit* Dumps.

Sir Jeff. Friend Jack, we are upon business.

Jack. A moment's patience !——Mr. Ruefull, give me your hand ; nay, good sir, give it me !——I honour you from my soul :——I beg pardon for the false opinion I have had of you ;—I am a country-bred fellow, 'tis true, but I have an honest heart, and a warm one—so Heaven bless you! that's enough,
[*Exit.*

Rue. Ahem !——What's the matter with my eyes ?——A plague upon the fellow, say I, for putting me in humour with mankind.——Go on with your story——

Sir Jeff. I educated him in all points as my own son.

Rue. And at your own expence ?

Sir Jeff. No, I was privately supplied by his mother for that purpose.

Rue. Thank you, sir ! thank you heartily for that ; I should else have been compelled to confess it was a benevolent action.—And who is his mother?—Stop, though ! if it is one of your secrets, keep it to yourself.

Sir Jeff. It has been a secret, an inviolable secret, from the day of his birth to this hour ;—it is now no longer so; for the death of his mother, who was a kinswoman of mine——   ·

Rue. How's that? what do you say? a kinswoman of yours!

Sir Jeff. A near one; my cousin, Frances Latimer——

Rue. Sir!

Sir Jeff. What alarms you?

Rue. Is Blushenly the son of Mrs. Fanny Latimer? are you sure of this? have you no trick in it?

Sir Jeff. Trick! you may see her will.

Rue. Shew it to me.—Had she no other son, no other child but this? answer me this.

Sir Jeff. No other child.—After putting him into my hands, she left England, shut herself into a convent at Lisle in Flanders, and led an exemplary life in retirement from the world, though she would never be induced to acknowledge her son, or discover his father.

Rue. Let me see the will, let me see the will.

Sir Jeff. Come into my closet with me, and you shall see it.

Rue. Shew me the way.—Hey-day! what ails me? how my head swims!—Give me your arm.—So, so! 'tis better.

Sir Jeff. Bear up, my good friend; I see you are agitated by this discovery.

Rue. Do you think so? Cann't an old man be sick suddenly, but you must spy a mystery in it?—— Pshaw! [*Exeunt.*

Enter Lady PARAGON *and* BLUSHENLY.

Lady P. A situation of more hazard than mine could not well be; for I was courted by my admirers, and neglected by my husband.· Oh! let no woman wed a gamester! human misery cannot exceed it.—And now, my dear Harry, that I have given you a portrait of myself, the best I can say for it is, that it is a faithful likeness; some faulty tints there may be, which the pencil of vanity has thrown in, but they will fly off in time; and I flatter myself it is no where dashed with the dark shades of guilt or deformity: as for the colours which love has given it, they will never fade in your keeping, for they are burnt in with fire, and can only perish with the piece itself.   [*They embrace.*

Enter Mrs. PHŒBE LATIMER, *as they are embracing.*

Phœbe. I can support this no longer.—Mr. Blushenly, you are a traitor! Lady Paragon, you are—I won't say what—I renounce you!

Blush. Recollect yourself, madam! speak without passion, and I will answer you without reproach.

Phœbe. No, sir, I will not speak without passion, nor will I enter upon any explanation with you.——There is a couching lion in your path, ready to spring upon you, and devour you both: an awful secret is in my keeping, nature extorts it from me; and before you rush into the crime of incest, know, young man—and tremble whilst I tell it—you are her fa-

ther's son.—How now! have you no feeling to your
situation, that you receive it thus calmly? if you can
doubt it, I'll produce my brother, and he shall con-
firm it to your faces.

Lady P. Stay, madam, if you please; there is no
occasion to spread our family disgrace any further.

Phœbe. How you both stand!—Lady Paragon, I'm
astonished at your insensibility: you don't even
change colour.

Lady P. That's much indeed; for I'm very apt to
blush for those who assert a falsehood to my face.

Phœbe. A falsehood! what do you insinuate?

Blush. Patience, I beseech you, and let us save
you whilst we can.—Your zeal for Mr. Latimer hurries you too far, when it puts you to invention and
the abuse of truth.—In some degree I take the fault
upon myself; for I could sooner have told you that
his interest in this lady's affections stands on the security of honour, and does not want the aid of fic-
tion—I am that happy man! I am that Latimer!

Phœbe. You! you!

Blush. O'Flaherty brought the proofs; Sir Jeffery
will impart them to you.

Phœbe. Then I am ruined and undone!—I have
exposed myself to shame and derision:—I am sink-
ing with confusion!

Lady P. No, my dear aunt, you shall not sink; we
are your friends, and we will hold you up.

Phœbe. Impossible! I never can recall what I've
said.

Blush. Nor shall you; for if time shall ever extinguish in your breast its partial affection for Blushenly, gratitude shall continue to record it in the heart of Latimer: therefore I pray you be at peace with yourself. What now is done, is done in secret; and whoever, in my hearing, dares to vent a sneer at the aunt of my Louisa, makes an enemy of me.

Phœbe. I thank you; you both are truly generous; —but I am much agitated, and wish to retire to my chamber.

Lady P. No, no, persist, if it be possible!—My father will soon be here; meet him with congratulations; meet the whole family!—Look! here comes O'Flaherty.

Phœbe. The man of all the world I cannot meet; he knows my weakest thoughts: save me from this meeting, if you have pity for me.

Enter O'FLAHERTY, *and is met by* BLUSHENLY.

Blush. Stop, my good friend!—and, before a word can pass your lips, let me exact from you, as a soldier and a man of honour, to look at these ladies, and if there be here present one, to whose thoughts in some weak moment (for we all have such moments) you have been privy, bury them in generous silence for ever, and approve yourself deserving of the favours of the sex, by your gallantry in concealing their foibles!

O'Fla. I understand you, sir, perfectly; and when I pledge my honour, I pledge that which neither to man nor woman has been ever forfeited—so there's an end of the matter.——Now be so good as to say which name you are pleased to be called by, and whether I am to give you joy as Mr. Latimer; or how much longer I am to keep it secret.

Blush. You are fairly released.

O'Fla. And, does your ladyship bear in mind our wager?

Lady P. I acknowledge it lost, and will pay it the first moment I am able.

O'Fla. O dear heart alive! what a joy it is to hear you say so!—but there is a part at least, and the best part too, which you can always pay on demand.

Lady P. Well then, if you wish it, 'tis before you; serve yourself.

O'Fla. May the blessing of blessings light upon your generous heart! [*Salutes her respectfully.*] May the cheek which I have touched be unstained with a tear! And may your lips, which I had not the bold-ness to approach, be the sacred treasure of your husband! Mrs. Phœbe Latimer, I hope I shall not offend if I offer at the same presumption.—Be con-fident, dear madam, that you have not in the world a more faithful humble servant than myself!

[*Aside to her.*

Phœbe. I have entire reliance on your honour. I begin to feel the return of tranquillity.

Enter Sir JEFFERY LATIMER.

Lady P. Bless me, sir, what ails you? You alarm me.

Sir Jeff. Tears of joy, tears of joy—don't be alarm'd!—I am a father myself; the feelings of nature are very strong.

Blush. What are you speaking of?

Sir Jeff. The surprise was sudden, and overpowered him; but we have fetched him to himself: Jack Hustings opened a vein—he can turn his hand to any thing.—Here comes the good man!—Now let nobody be in a bustle; recollect yourself, Harry! Let nobody be in a bustle—Be as quiet and composed as I am.

RUEFULL *is led in between* JACK HUSTINGS *and* DUMPS, DAVID *attending behind with a Chair.*

Rue. Put the chair in its place again! methinks you are very troublesome.—[Dumps *puts a bottle of salts to his nose.*] What does the blockhead thrust his salts up my nostrils for? Keep 'em till my funeral, they'll serve to draw tears in your eyes.

Jack How do you find yourself now, sir?

Rue. Exceedingly annoyed by your officiousness.—Who made you a surgeon, I would fain know? Why am I to be blooded like a calf at the whim of a butcher?

Jack. You might have died, if we had not opened a vein.

Rue. Might have died!—well, and what might I do better? I have always reckoned upon one happy hour in life—the hour at the end of it.——Hark ye, Sir Jeffery, ask your daughter if she resolves upon marrying that young man by her side.

Sir Jeff. Her heart is centered in that hope—I an-swer you in her own words.

Rue. Pray, madam, let me ask you why you make this choice?

Lady P. Because I know him, love him, and ad-mire him; his honour, gentleness, modesty, and be-nevolence, endear him to me. _

Rue. And is this a world for such a man to live in? With all these qualities, what sort of figure will he make in high life?

Lady P. I should be sorry if a man of your good sense gave into hackneyed invectives against high life; I suspect it is the vices of the vulgar which are precipitating this country to its grave!

Rue. It may be so; I stand corrected. But it is fitting you should know there is one objection to your future husband: he is the son of a humoursome, capricious old fellow, whom all the world sets down for a snarler and a miser.—I am his father.

Blush. Then nature is a faithful prophetess: I felt her at my heart.—Give me your blessing, sir!—My benefactor, friend, and father.

[*Throws himself on his knee.*

Rue. There, there! [*Blesses him.*]—I do these of-fices scurvily; a fellow of no feeling would make you a fine speech on the occasion.—I desire there may be no more said of the matter; it won't tell to my re-putation—Old Jeffery knows all about it.—The world was a bad world, even in my young days, and I con-tributed to make it worse: I used your mother like a

rascal, the more shame for me! She never forgave
it, and I never ceased repenting of it : if she would
have told me where to find you, you should not have
been so long without a father.

O'Fla. O *Jubilate!* what a hurricane of good luck
is fallen upon us.—Hark ye, Mr. Jack Hustings, you
and I will make the corks crack for this.

Blush. Louisa, may I not present you to my father?
[*Presents her.*

Rue. Happy be your lot, young lady! May the
son repair the injuries of the'father! and, by the honour of his conduct to your family, atone for the
shame which mine has brought upon it!

Lady P. I am not the less confident of his conduct,
when I find he is honourable and virtuous by inheritance.

Rue. I am only afraid he is too rich to be virtuous ;
if I was to consult his true interest I should disinherit
him.

Blush. Fear me not, sir, whilst there is an honest
man in this company in want of that which we abound
in.—Captain O'Flaherty, I hold myself accountable
for Lady Paragon's debts; they are gaming debts
indeed, but no less debts of honour : she has lost a
wager to you of a wedding-favour—It is not very ele-
gantly made up, but it is cordially bestowed—I hope
you'll wear it for her sake. [*Gives a paper folded up.*

Rue. Well said, boy! you are my own son ;—you
have put my money out to use already.

O'Fla. Out upon it! 'tis a subsidy for a German

prince! I'll not touch a stiver of it. Zooks! man, I never wanted money, for I've always lived without it.

Lady P. Take it, however, if it be only to do honour to the friend that gives it.

Phœbe. Let me join interest with my niece in the request: and now let's see if you dare to hold out against the petition of the ladies.

Sir Jeff. Sister Phœbe! sister Phœbe! give me your hand—by the bones of the Latimers you are an honour to my family. Henceforward we strike up harmony and good fellowship for our lives.

Phœbe. Let us all be friends, and all be happy!—Call in your neighbours, brother Jeffery, and let Merryfield-Hall blaze on this joyful occasion!——Mr. Hustings, as you are looking out amongst the old and ugly for a partner, let the fiddles strike up, and you and I will join in the dance.

Jack. 'Tis a bargain!. now you are fair Phœbe again.—Away with all bickerings for ever! let those take them up that like 'em.—I should wish to know what punishment you could find in your heart to inflict, if I dared to repeat my offence in the face of this good company.

Lady P. I'll answer you that question—Transportation for life.

Sir Jeff. To the land of matrimony.

Jack. I am resigned to my fate—Let the law take its course!

Sir Jeff. Get the warrants ready: here is double duty for the Ordinary.

H

O'Fla. Ladies and gentlemen, a word with you before you are turned off—I hope I am not to be your
executor, for I have enough already on my hands
with these papers.—Will you be my banker, old gentleman ? and lay out for a purchase of just such another little cot as your own; where, with a rood of
potatoes in my front, and an acre of bog at my back,
I can sit chirping like an old cricket in my chimney-
corner, and ruminate on the occurrences of this
happy day.

[*Exeunt omnes.*

EPILOGUE.

Written for Miss FARREN;

BY EDWARD TOPHAM, ESQ.

IN this gay age, when all the heart is waste,
And frighted Nature flies the realms of taste,
's there a well-bred dame, whose cheek discloses
The bloom —of rouge, cold cream, and milk of roses,
Who deigns these splendid side-boxes to grace,
In Figaro feathers and Lunardi lace,
And, gently lolling on her favourite page,
Laughs—and talks somewhat louder than the Stage ?
If some sweet girl—another Werter's pride—
In pure simplicity should grace her side,
And feeling what she hears, devoid of art——
Drop a soft tear—expressive of the heart ;
Would not the fashion'd dame our child reprove,
And cry—' Indeed—you're vastly wrong—my love !
' What, weep ? O fie !—I blush :—this strange disorder
' Will make folks think you enter'd with an Order!'
While in high life our hearts the fashions steel,
Too gay to listen, and too fine to feel——
Honest John Bull—before a sturdy elf——
Now claims no right of judging for himself;
To PUFFS *from Theatres gives up his vote,*
And kindly thinks all true—*because 'tis wrote ;*
For when no plaudits strike our duller ear,
The papers hear a voice we cannot hear——
And when for seats no beauties disagree,
They see a crowd, alas ! we cannot see ;

——And while you clamber o'er the empty rows,
In SWEET ADVERTISEMENT—*the House o'erflows!*
Puff is the word : where fame is NOT *a breath,*
——How many an Actress Puff has sav'd from death!
And Actors, for whom Mutes were full enough,
Have risen Alexanders—from a Puff!
While generous paragraphs all-lavish give
Sums total, which our Treasurers ne'er receive.

   With added force—the other House comes after——
Here, dead with grief, you there revive with laughter—
Beaumarchais's Muse—a favourite of the nation——
Now rises like some Bishop—by translation.
Jest, repartee, and stage effect still tease you,
With wit made English, and with French made easy.
Say, then—as humble copyists—shall WE *borrow*
A sketch of what some pens may say to-morrow?
' The Comedy, where laughter knows no pause——
' Went off with most astonishing applause!
' The dresses, scenery—and situation,
' Exceeded all the bounds of commendation!
' The great demand for side-boxes, from Monday
' Will know no intermission—but on Sunday!
' The eighth, tenth, twentieth nights—each place is chosen——
' About the fiftieth you may pop your nose in.
' The Actors all—were wonderfully clever ;
' The like was never seen, nor heard—no never.
' Miss Farren's widow—above all—d'ye see,
*' Was—*YOU *must fill that vacancy for* ME.'

THE END.

De Wilde pinx.ᵗ   Audin.

Mʳ BENSLEY as OAKLY,
Lord this is the strangest Misapprehension!
I am quite astonished.

London, Printed for J. Bell British Library Strand, Octʳ 27, 1792

.THE

JEALOUS WIFE.

A

COMEDY,

By GEORGE COLMAN.

ADAPTED FOR

THEATRICAL REPRESENTATION,

AS PERFORMED AT THE

THEATRES-ROYAL,

DRURY-LANE AND COVENT-GARDEN.

REGULATED FROM THE PROMPT-BOOKS,

By Permission of the Managers.

"The Lines distinguished by inverted Commas, are omitted in the Representation."

LONDON:

Printed for the Proprietors, under the Direction of
JOHN BELL, British Library, STRAND,
Bookseller to His Royal Highness the Prince of Wales.

MDCCXCII.

ADVERTISEMENT.

THE use that has been made in this comedy of Fielding's *admirable novel of* Tom Jones, *must be obvious to the most ordinary reader. Some hints have also been taken from the account of Mr. and Mrs.* Freeman, *in No.* 212, *and No.* 216, *of the* Spectator; *and the short scene of* Charles's *intoxication, at the end of the third act, is partly an imitation of the behaviour of* Syrus, *much in the same circumstances, in the* Adelphi *of* Terence. *There are also some traces of the character of the Jealous Wife, in one of the latter papers of the* Connoisseur.

It would be unjust, indeed, to omit mentioning my obligations to Mr. Garrick. *To his inspection the comedy was submitted in its first rude state; and to my care and attention to follow his advice in many particulars, relating both to the fable and characters, I know that I am much indebted for the reception which this piece has met with from the public.*

PROLOGUE.

WRITTEN BY MR. LLOYD.

Spoken by Mr. GARRICK.

THE Jealous Wife! a comedy! poor man!
A charming subject! but a wretched plan.
His skittish wit, o'erleaping the due bound,
Commits flat trespass upon tragic ground.
Quarrels, upbraidings, jealousies, and spleen,
Grow too familiar in the comic scene.
Tinge but the language with heroic chime,
'Tis passion, pathos, character, sublime!
What round big words had swell'd the pompous scene,
A king the husband, and the wife a queen!
Then might distraction rend her graceful hair,
See sightless forms, and scream, and gape, and stare.
Drawcansir Death *had rag'd without controul,*
Here the drawn dagger, there the poison'd bowl.
What eyes had stream'd at all the whining wo!
What hands had thunder'd at each Hah! *and* Oh!

But peace! the gentle prologue custom sends,
Like drum and serjeant, to beat up for friends.
At vice and folly, each a lawful game,
Our author flies, but with no partial aim.

He read the manners, open as they lie
In Nature's volume to the general eye.
Books too he read, nor blush'd to use their store——
He does but what his betters did before.
Shakespere *has done it, and the* Grecian *stage*
Caught truth of character from Homer's page.

"If in his scenes an honest skill is shewn,
And borrowing little, much appears his own;
If what a master's happy pencil drew
He brings more forward in dramatic view;
To your decision he submits his cause,
Secure of candour, anxious for applause.

But if, all rude, his artless scenes deface
The simple beauties which he meant to grace,
If, an invader upon others land,
He spoil and plunder with a robber's hand,
Do justice on him!——As on fools before,
And give to Blockheads *past* one Blockhead *more.*

Dramatis Personae.

DRURY-LANE.

Men.

OAKLY	- Mr. Bensley.
Major OAKLY	- Mr. Baddeley.
CHARLES	- Mr. Barrymore.
RUSSET	- Mr. Aickin.
Sir HARRY BEAGLE	- Mr. R. Palmer.
Lord TRINKET	- Mr. Dodd.
Captain O'CUTTER	- Mr. Moody.
PARIS	- Mr. Maddocks.
WILLIAM	- Mr. Phillimore.
JOHN	- Mr. Webb.
TOM	- Mr. Alfred.
Servant *to Lady* Freelove	- Mr. Lyons.

Women.

Mrs. OAKLY	- Miss Farren.
Lady FREELOVE	- Mrs. Hopkins.
HARRIOT	- Mrs. Kemble.
TOILET	- Miss Tidswell.
Chambermaid	- Mrs. Heard.

COVENT-GARDEN.

Men.

OAKLY	- Mr. Farren.
Major OAKLY	- Mr. Ryder.
CHARLES	- Mr. Macready.
RUSSET	- Mr. Fearon.
Sir HARRY BEAGLE	- Mr. Edwin.
Lord TRINKET	- Mr. Lewis.
Captain O'CUTTER	- Mr. Aickin.
PARIS	- Mr. Wewitzer.
WILLIAM	- Mr. Ledger.
JOHN	- Mr. Evatt.
TOM	- Mr. Rock.
Servant *to Lady* Freelove	- Mr. Lee.

Women.

Mrs. OAKLY	- Mrs. Pope.
Lady FREELOVE	- Mrs. Bernard.
HARRIOT	- Mrs. Merry.
TOILET	- Miss Stuart.
Chambermaid	- Miss Brangin.

THE

JEALOUS WIFE.

ACT I. SCENE I.

A Room in OAKLY'*s House.* *Noise heard within.*

Mrs. Oakly, within.

DON'T tell me—I know it is so—It's monstrous, and I will not bear it.

Oak. [*Within.*] But, my dear!——

Mrs. Oak. Nay, nay, &c.   [*Squabbling within.*

Enter Mrs. OAKLY, *with a Letter,* OAKLY *following.*

Mrs. Oak. Say what you will, Mr. Oakly, you shall never persuade me, but this is some filthy intrigue of yours.

Oak. I can assure you, my love!——

Mrs. Oak. Your love!—Don't I know your—Tell me, I say, this instant, every circumstance relating to this letter.

Oak. How can I tell you, when you will not so much as let me see it?

B ij

Mrs. Oak. Look you, Mr. Oakly, this usage is not to be borne. You take a pleasure in abusing my tenderness and soft disposition.—To be perpetually running over the whole town, nay, the whole kingdom too, in pursuit of your amours!—Did not I discover that you was great with mademoiselle, my own woman?—Did not you contract a shameful familiarity with Mrs. Freeman?—Did not I detect your intrigue with Lady Wealthy?—Was not you——

Oak. Oons! madam, the Grand Turk himself has not half so many mistresses—You throw me out of all patience—Do I know any body but our common friends?—Am I visited by any body, that does not visit you?—Do I ever go out, unless you go with me?—And am I not as constantly by your side, as if I was tied to your apron-strings?

Mrs. Oak. Go, go, you are a false man——Have not I found you out a thousand times? And have not I this moment a letter in my hand, which convinces me of your baseness?——Let me know the whole affair, or I will——

Oak. Let you know? Let me know what you would have of me——You stop my letter before it comes to my hands, and then expect that I shou'd know the contents of it.

Mrs. Oak. Heaven be praised! I stopt it.—I suspected some of these doings for some time past—But the letter informs me who she is, and I'll be revenged on her sufficiently. Oh, you base man, you!

Oak. I beg, my dear, that you would moderate your passion!—Shew me the letter, and I'll convince you of my innocence.

Mrs. Oak. Innocence!—Abominable!—Innocence! —But I am not to be made such a fool—I am convinced of your perfidy, and very sure that——

Oak. 'Sdeath and fire! your passion hurries you out of your senses——Will you hear me?

Mrs. Oak. No, you are a base man; and I will not hear you.

Oak. Why then, my dear, since you will neither talk reasonably yourself, nor listen to reason from me, I shall take my leave till you are in a better humour. So, your servant! [*Going.*

Mrs. Oak. Ay, go, you cruel man!——Go to your mistresses, and leave your poor wife to her miseries. ——How unfortunate a woman am I!—I could die with vexation—— [*Throwing herself into a chair.*

Oak. There it is—Now dare not I stir a step further—If I offer to go, she is in one of her fits in an instant—Never sure was woman at once of so violent and so delicate a constitution! What shall I say to sooth her? Nay, never make thyself so uneasy, my dear—Come, come, you know I love you. Nay, nay, you shall be convinced.

Mrs. Oak. I know you hate me; and that your unkindness and barbarity will be the death of me.
[*Whining.*

Oak. Do not vex yourself at this rate—I love you
B iij

most passionately—Indeed I do—This must be some mistake.

Mrs. Oak. O, I am an unhappy woman! [*Weeping.*

Oak. Dry up thy tears, my love, and be comforted! You will find that I am not to blame in this matter — Come, let me see this letter——Nay, you shall not deny me.   [*Taking the letter.*

Mrs. Oak. There! take it, you know the hand, I am sure.

Oak. To Charles Oakly, Esq. [*Reading.*]—Hand! 'Tis a clerk-like hand, indeed! a good round text! and was certainly never penned by a fair lady.

Mrs. Oak. Ay, laugh at me, do!

Oak. Forgive me, my love, I did not mean to laugh at thee——But what says the letter ?——[*Reading.*] *Daughter eloped—you must be privy to it—scandalous— dishonourable—satisfaction—revenge—*um, um, um—— *injured father.*

HENRY RUSSET.

Mrs. Oak. [*Rising.*] Well, sir—you see I have detected you——Tell me this instant where she is concealed.

Oak. So—so—so——This hurts me—I'm shock'd—
            [*To himself.*

Mrs. Oak. What, are you confounded with your guilt? Have I caught you at last?

Oak. O that wicked Charles! To decoy a young lady from her parents in the country! The profli-

gacy of the young fellows of this age is abominable.   [*To himself.*

  Mrs. Oak. [*Half aside and musing.*] Charles!—Let
me see!——Charles!—No! Impossible. This is
all a trick.

   Oak. He has certainly ruined this poor lady.
                          [*To himself.*

  Mrs. Oak. Art! art! all art! There's a sudden
turn now! You have ready wit for an intrigue, I
find.

  Oak. Such an abandoned action! I wish I had
never had the care of him.   [*To himself.*

  Mrs. Oak. Mighty fine, Mr. Oakly! Go on, sir,
go on! I see what you mean.——Your assurance
provokes me beyond your very falsehood itself. So
you imagine, sir, that this affected concern, this flimsy
pretence about Charles, is to bring you off. Match-
less confidence! But I am armed against every thing
——I am prepared for all your dark schemes : I am
aware of all your low stratagems.

  Oak. See there now! Was ever any thing so provoking? To persevere in your ridiculous——For
Heaven's sake, my dear, don't distract me. When
you see my mind thus agitated and uneasy, that a
young fellow, whom his dying father, my own brother, committed to my care, should be guilty of such
enormous wickedness; I say, when you are witness of
my distress on this occasion, how can you be weak
enough and cruel enough to——

  Mrs. Oak. Prodigiously well, sir! You do it very

well. Nay, keep it up, carry it on, there's nothing like going through with it. O you artful creature! But, sir, I am not to be so easily satisfied. I do not believe a syllable of all this——Give me the letter—[*Snatching the letter.*]——You shall sorely repent this vile business, for I am resolved that I will know the bottom of it. [*Exit.*

Oak. This is beyond all patience. Provoking woman! Her absurd suspicions interpret every thing the wrong way. She delights to make me wretched, because she sees I am attached to her, and converts my tenderness and affection into the instruments of my own torture. But this ungracious boy! In how many troubles will he involve his own and his lady's family——I never imagined that he was of such abandon'd principles. O, here he comes!

Enter Major OAKLY, *and* CHARLES.

Char. Good-morrow, sir!

Maj. Good-morrow, brother, good-morrow!—— What! you have been at the old work, I find. I heard you—ding! dong! i'faith!—She has rung a noble peal in your ears. But how now? Why sure you've had a remarkable warm bout on't.———You seem more ruffled than usual.

Oak. I am, indeed, brother! Thanks to that young gentleman there. Have a care, Charles! you may be called to a severe account for this. The honour of a family, sir, is no such light matter.

Char. Sir!

1

Maj. Hey-day! What, has a curtain-lecture produced a lecture of morality? What is all this?

Oak. To a profligate mind, perhaps, these things may appear agreeable in the beginning. But don't you tremble at the consequences?

Char. I see, sir, that you'are displeased with me, but I am quite at a loss to guess at the occasion.

Oak. Tell me, sir!—where is Miss Harriot Russet?

Char. Miss Harriot Russet!—Sir—Explain.

Oak. Have not you decoy'd her from her father?

Char. I!—Decoy'd her—Decoy'd my Harriot!——I would sooner die than do her the least injury.—— What can this mean?

Maj. I believe the young dog has been at her, after all.

Oak. I was in hopes, Charles, you had better principles. But there's a letter just come from her father——

Char. A letter!—What letter? Dear sir, give it me. Some intelligence of my Harriot, Major!—— The letter, sir, the letter this moment, for Heaven's sake!

Oak. If this warmth, Charles, tends to prove your innocence——

Char. Dear sir, excuse me——I'll prove any thing —Let me but see this letter, and I'll——

Oak. Let you see it?——I could hardly get a sight of it myself. Mrs. Oakly has it.

Char. Has she got it? Major, I'll be with you again directly.   [*Exit hastily.*

Maj. Hey-day! The devil's in the boy! What a fiery set of people! By my troth, I think the whole family is made of nothing but combustibles.

Oak. I like this emotion. It looks well. It may serve too to convince my wife of the folly of her suspicions. Wou'd to Heaven I could quiet them for ever!

Maj. Why, pray now, my dear naughty brother, what heinous offence have you committed this morning? What new cause of suspicion? You have been asking one of the maids to mend your ruffle, I suppose, or have been hanging your head out of window, when a pretty young woman has past by, or——

Oak. How can you trifle with my distresses, Major? Did not I tell you it was about a letter?

Maj. A letter!—hum—A suspicious circumstance, to be sure! What, and the seal a true-lover's knot now, hey! or an heart transfixt with darts; or possibly the wax bore the industrious impression of a thimble; or perhaps the folds were lovingly connected by a wafer, pricked with a pin, and the direction written in a vile scrawl, and not a word spelt as it should be; ha, ha, ha!

Oak. Pooh! brother——Whatever it was, the letter, you find, was for Charles, not for me——this outrageous jealousy is the devil.

Maj. Mere matrimonial blessings and domestic comfort, brother! jealousy is a certain sign of love.

Oak. Love! it is this very love that hath made us both so miserable. Her love for me has confined

me to my house, like a state prisoner, without the
liberty of seeing my friends, or the use of pen, ink,
and paper; while my love for her has made such a
fool of me, that I have never had the spirit to contradict her.

Maj. Ay, ay, there you've hit it; Mrs. Oakly
would make an excellent wife, if you did but know
how to manage her.

Oak. You are a rare fellow, indeed, to talk of ma
naging a wife——A debauch'd bachelor——a rat-
tle-brain'd, rioting fellow——who have pick'd up
your common-place notions of women in bagnios, ta-
verns, and the camp; whose most refined commerce
with the sex has been in order to delude country girls
at your quarters, or to besiege the virtue of abigails,
milliners, or mantua-maker's 'prentices.

Maj. So much the better!—so much the better!
women are all alike in the main, brother, high or
low, married or single, quality or no quality. I have
found them so, from a duchess down to a milk-maid.

Oak. Your savage notions are ridiculous. What
do you know of a husband's feelings ?——You, who
comprise all your qualities in your *honour*, as you call
it!—Dead to all sentiments of delicacy, and incapable
of any but the grossest attachments to women. This
is your boasted refinement, your thorough knowledge
of the world! While with regard to women, one poor
train of thinking, one narrow set of ideas, like the
uniform of the regiment, serves the whole corps.

Maj. Very fine, brother!—there's common-place

for you with a vengeance. Henceforth, expect no quarter from me. I tell you again and again, I know the sex better than you do. They all love to give themselves airs, and to have power: every woman is a tyrant at the bottom. But they could never make a fool of me.——No, no! no woman should ever domineer over me, let her be mistress or wife.

Oak. Single men can be no judges in these cases. They must happen in all families. But when things are driven to extremities—to see a woman in uneasiness—a woman one loves too—one's wife—who can withstand it? You neither speak nor think like a man that has lov'd, and been married, major!

Maj. I wish I could hear a married man speak my language——I'm a bachelor, it's true; but I am no bad judge of your case for all that. I know yours and Mrs. Oakly's disposition to a hair. She is all impetuosity and fire—A very magazine of touchwood and gunpowder. You are hot enough too upon occasion, but then it's over in an instant. In comes love and conjugal affection, as you call it;—that is, mere folly and weakness—and you draw off your forces, just when you shou'd pursue the attack, and follow your advantage. Have at her with spirit, and the day's your own, brother!

Oak. I tell you, brother, you mistake the matter. Sulkiness, fits, tears!——These, and such as these, are the things which make a feeling man uneasy. Her passion and violence have not half such an effect on me.
2

Maj. Why, then, you may be sure, she'll play that upon you, which she finds does most execution. But you must be proof against every thing. If she's furious, set passion against passion; if you find her at her tricks, play off art against art, and foil her at her own weapons. That's your game, brother!

Oak. Why, what would you have me do?

Maj. Do as you please, for one month, whether she likes it or not; and, I'll answer for it, she will consent you shall do as you please all her life after.

Oak. This is fine talking. You do not consider the difficulty that———.

Maj. You must overcome all difficulties. Assert your right boldly, man! give your own orders to servants, and see they observe them; read your own letters, and never let her have a sight of them; make your own appointments, and never be persuaded to break them; see what company you like; go out when you please; return when you please, and don't suffer yourself to be called to account where you have been. In short, do but shew yourself a man of spirit, leave off whining about love and tenderness, and nonsense, and the business is done, brother!

Oak. I believe you are in the right, major! I see you're in the right. I'll do it, I'll certainly do it.— But then it hurts me to the soul, to think what uneasiness I shall give her. The first opening of my design will throw her into fits, and the pursuit of it perhaps may be fatal.

Maj. Fits! ha, ha, ha!—Fits!—I'll engage to cure

C

her of her fits. Nobody understands hysterical cases better than I do: besides, my sister's symptoms are not very dangerous. Did you ever hear of her falling into a fit when you was not by?——Was she ever found in convulsions in her closet?——No, no, these fits, the more care you take of them, the more you will increase the distemper—let them alone, and they will wear themselves out, I warrant you.

Oak. True—very true—you're certainly in the right—I'll follow your advice. Where do you dine to-day? I'll order the coach, and go with you.

Maj. O brave! keep up this spirit, and you're made for ever.

Oak. You shall see now, major! Who's there?

Enter Servant.

Order the coach directly. I shall dine out to-day.

Serv. The coach, sir!——Now? Sir!

Oak. Ay, now, immediately.

Serv. Now? Sir!——the—the—coach! Sir!——that is——my mistress——

Oak. Sirrah! do as you're bid. Bid them put to this instant.

Serv. Ye——yes, sir——yes, sir.   [*Exit.*

Oak. Well, where shall we dine?

Maj. At the St. Alban's, or where you will. This is excellent, if you do but hold it.

Oak. I will have my own way, I am determined.

Maj. That's right.

Oak. I am steel.

Maj. Bravo!

Oak. Adamant.

Maj. Bravissimo!

Oak. Just what you'd have me.

Maj. Why that's well said. But *will* you do it?

Oak. I will.

Maj. You won't.

Oak. I will. I'll be a fool to her no longer. But hark ye, major! my hat and sword lie in my study. I'll go and steal them out, while she is busy talking with Charles.

Maj. Steal them! for shame! Pr'ythee take them boldly, call for them, make them bring them to you here, and go out with spirit, in the face of your whole family.

Oak. No, ho—you are wrong—let her rave after I am gone, and when I return, you know, I shall exert myself with more propriety, after this open affront to her authority.

Maj. Well, take your own way.

Oak. Ay, ay——let me manage it, let me manage it.   [*Exit.*

Maj. Manage it! ay, to be sure, you're a rare manager! It is dangerous, they say, to meddle between man and wife. I am no great favourite of Mrs. Oakly's already; and in a week's time I expect to have the door shut in my teeth.

Enter CHARLES.

How now, Charles, what news?

Char. Ruin'd and undone! she's gone, uncle! my Harriot's lost for ever.

Maj. Gone off with a man?—I thought so: they are all alike.

Char. O no! Fled to avoid that hateful match with Sir Harry Beagle.

Maj. Faith, a girl of spirit!—Joy! Charles, I give you joy; she is your own, my boy!—A fool and a great estate! Devilish strong temptations!

Char. A wretch! I was sure she would never think of him.

Maj. No! to be sure! commend me to your modesty! Refuse five thousand a year, and a baronet, for pretty Mr. Charles Oakly! It is true, indeed, that the looby has not a single idea in his head besides a hound, a hunter, a five-barred gate, and a horse-race; but then he's rich, and that will qualify his absurdities. Money is a wonderful improver of the understanding.——But whence comes all this intelligence?

Char. In an angry letter from her father.——How miserable I am! If I had not offended my Harriot, much offended her by that foolish riot and drinking at your house in the country, she would certainly, at such a time, have taken refuge in my arms.

Maj. A very agreeable refuge for a young lady to be sure; and extremely decent!

Char. I am all uneasiness. Did not she tell me, that she trembled at the thoughts of having trusted her affections with a man of such a wild disposition? What a heap of extravagancies was I guilty of!

Maj. Extravagancies with a witness! Ah, you silly young dog, you would ruin yourself with her father, in spite of all I could do. There you sat, as drunk as a lord, telling the old gentleman the whole affair, and swearing you would drive Sir Harry Beagle out of the country, though I kept winking and nodding, pulling you by the sleeve, and kicking your shins under the table, in hopes of stopping you, but all to no purpose.

Char. What distress may she be in at this instant! Alone and defenceless!——Where? Where can she be?

Maj. What relations or friends has she in town?

Char. Relations! let me see.—Faith! I have it.—If she is in town, ten to one but she is at her aunt's, Lady Freelove's. I'll go thither immediately.

Maj. Lady Freelove's! Hold, hold, Charles!—— do you know her ladyship?

Char. Not much; but I'll break through all forms to get to my Harriot.

Maj. I do know her ladyship.

Char. Well, and what do you know of her?

Maj. O nothing!——Her ladyship is a woman of the world, that's all——she'll introduce Harriot to the best company.

Char. What do you mean?

Maj. Yes, yes, I would trust a wife, or a daughter, or a mistress with Lady Freelove, to be sure!——

I'll tell you what, Charles! you're a good boy, but you don't know the world. Women are fifty times oftener ruined by their acquaintance with each other, than by their attachment to men. One thorough-paced lady will train up a thousand novices. That Lady Freelove is an arrant——By the bye, did not she, last summer, make formal proposals to Harriot's father from Lord Trinket?

Char. Yes! but they were received with the utmost contempt. The old gentleman, it seems, hates a lord, and he told her so in plain terms.

Maj. Such an aversion to the nobility may not run in the blood. The girl, I warrant you, has no objection. However, if she's there, watch her narrowly, Charles! Lady Freelove is as mischievous as a monkey, and as cunning too.—Have a care of her. I say, have a care of her.

Char. If she's there, I'll have her out of the house within this half hour, or set fire to it.

Maj. Nay, now you're too violent.——Stay a moment, and we'll consider what's best to be done.

Re-enter OAKLY.

Oak. Come, is the coach ready? Let us be gone. Does Charles go with us?

Char. I go with you!——What can I do? I am so vext and distracted, and so many thoughts crowd in upon me, I don't know which way to turn myself.

Mrs. Oak. [*Within.*] The coach!—dines out!—— where is your master?

Oak. Zounds! brother, here she is!

Enter Mrs. OAKLY.

Mrs. Oak. Pray, Mr. Oakly, what is the matter you
cannot dine at home to-day?

Oak. Don't be uneasy, my dear!——I have a little business to settle with my brother; so I am only
just going to dinner with him and Charles to the
tavern.

Mrs. Oak. Why cannot you settle your business
here as well as at a tavern? But it is some of your
ladies business, I suppose, and so you must get rid of
my company.——This is chiefly your fault, Major
Oakly!

Maj. Lord! sister, what signifies it, whether a
man dines at home or abroad? [*Coolly.*

Mrs. Oak. It signifies a great deal, sir! and I don't
choose——

Maj. Phoo! let him go, my dear sister, let him go!
he will be ten times better company when he comes
back. I tell you what, sister—you sit at home till
you are quite tired of one another, and then 'you
grow cross, and fall out. If you would but part a
little now and then, you might meet again in good
humour.

Mrs. Oak. I beg, Major Oakly, that you would
trouble yourself about your own affairs; and let me
tell you, sir, that I——

Oak. Nay, do not put thyself into a passion with the

Major, my dear!—It is not his fault; and I shall come back to thee very soon.

Mrs. Oak. Come back!——why need you go out ?—I know well enough when you mean to deceive me : for then there is always a pretence of dining with Sir John, or my Lord, or somebody ; but when you tell me, that you are going to a tavern, it's such a bare-faced affront——

Oak. This is so strange now !——Why, my dear, I shall only just——

Mrs. Oak. Only just go after the lady in the letter, I suppose.

Oak. Well, well, I won't go then.—Will that convince you ?—I'll stay with you, my dear!——will that satisfy you ?

Maj. For shame! hold out, if you are a man.

[*Apart.*

Oak. She has been so much vext this morning already, I must humour her a little now.   [*Apart.*

Maj. Fie, fie! go out, or you're undone.   [*Apart.*

Oak. You see it's impossible——   [*Apart.*

[*To Mrs.* Oakly.] I'll dine at home with thee, my love.

Mrs. Oak. Ay, ay, pray do, sir.——Dine at a tavern indeed!   [*Going.*

Oak. [*Returning.*] You may depend on me another time, Major.

Maj. Steel and adamant!——Ah!

Mrs. Oak. [*Returning.*] Mr. Oakley!

Oak. O, my dear!   [*Exeunt Mr. and Mrs. Oakly.*

Maj. Ha, ha, ha! there's a picture of resolution! there goes a philosopher for you! ha! Charles!

Char. O, uncle! I have no spirits to laugh now.

Maj. So! I have a fine time on't between you and my brother. Will you meet me to dinner at the St. Alban's by four? We'll drink her health, and think of this affair.

Char. Don't depend on me. I shall be running all over the town in pursuit of my Harriot. I have been considering what you have said, but at all events I'll go directly to Lady Freelove's. If I find her not there, which way I shall direct myself, Heaven knows.

Maj. Hark'e, Charles! If you meet with her, you may be at a loss. Bring her to my house. I have a snug room, and——

Char. Phoo! pr'ythee, uncle, don't trifle with me now.

Maj. Well, seriously then, my house is at your service.

Char. I thank you: but I must be gone.

Maj. Ay, ay, bring her to my house, and we'll settle the whole affair for you. You shall clap her into a post-chaise, take the chaplain of our regiment along with you, wheel her down to Scotland, and when you come back, send to settle her fortune with her father: that's the modern art of making love, Charles!   [*Exeunt.*

ACT II. SCENE I.

A Room in the Bull and Gate Inn. Enter *Sir* HARRY BEAGLE *and* TOM.

Sir Harry.

TEN guineas a mare, and a crown the man? hey, Tom!

Tom. Yes, your honour.

Sir H. And are you sure, Tom, that there is no flaw in his blood?

Tom. He's a good thing, sir, and as little beholden to the ground, as any horse that ever went over the turf upon four legs. Why, here's his whole pedigree, your honour!

Sir H. Is it attested?

Tom. Very well attested: it is signed by Jack Spur, and my Lord Startall.   [*Giving the Pedigree.*

Sir H Let me see—[*Reading.*]—Tom-come-tickle-me was out of the famous Tantwivy mare, by Sir Aaron Driver's chesnut horse White Stockings. White Stockings his dam was got by Lord Hedge's South Barb, full sister to the Proserpine Filley, and his sire Tom Jones; his grandam was the Irish Duchess, and his grandsire 'Squire Sportly's Trajan; his great grandam, and great, great grandam, were Newmarket Peggy and Black Moll, and his great grandsire, and great, great grandsire, were Sir

Ralph Whip's Regulus, and the famous Prince Anamaboo.

his

JOHN X SPUR,

mark.

STARTAL.

Tom. All fine horses, and won every thing! a foal out of your honour's Bald-faced Venus, by this horse, would beat the world.

Sir. H. Well then, we'll think on't.——But, pox on't, Tom, I have certainly knock'd up my little roan gelding, in this dam'd wild-goose chase of threescore miles an end.

Tom. He's deadly blown to be sure, your honour; and I am afraid we are upon a wrong scent after all. Madam Harriot certainly took across the country, instead of coming on to London.

Sir H. No, no, we traced her all the way up.—But d'ye hear, Tom, look out among the stables and repositories here in town, for a smart road nag, and a strong horse to carry a portmanteau.

Tom. Sir Roger Turf's horses are to be sold—I'll see if there's ever a tight thing there——but I suppose, sir, you would have one somewhat stronger than Snip——I don't think he's quite enough of a horse for your honour.

Sir H. Not enough of a horse! Snip's a powerful gelding; master of two stone more than my weight. If Snip stands sound, I would not take a hundred guineas for him. Poor Snip! go into the stable, Tom, see they give him a warm mash, and look at his heels and his eyes.—But where's Mr. Russet all this while ?

Tom. I left the 'squire at breakfast on a cold pigeon-pye, and enquiring after madam Harriot in the kitchen. I'll let him know your honour would be glad to see him here.

Sir H. Ay, do: but hark'e, Tom, be sure you take care of Snip.

Tom. I'll warrant your honour.

Sir H. I'll be down in the stables myself by and by. [*Exit* Tom.] Let me see——out of the famous Tantwivy by White Stockings ; White Stockings his dam, full sister to the Proserpine Filley, and his sire —pox on't, how unlucky it is, that this damn'd accident should happen in the Newmarket week !——ten to one I lose my match with Lord Choakjade, by not riding myself, and I shall have no opportunity to hedge my betts neither——what a damn'd piece of work have I made on't !—I have knock'd up poor Snip, shall lose my match, and as to Harriot, why, the odds are, that I lose my match there too——a skittish young tit ! If I once get her tight in hand, I'll make her wince for it.——Her estate join'd to my own, I would have the finest stud, and the noblest kennel in the whole country.——But here comes her father, puffing and blowing, like a broken-winded horse up hill.

Enter RUSSET.

Rus. Well, Sir Harry, have you heard any thing of her ? ,

2

Sir H. Yes, I have been asking Tom about her, and he says, you may have her for five hundred guineas.

Rus. Five hundred guineas! how d'ye mean? where is she? which way did she take?

Sir H. Why, first she went to Epsom, then to Lincoln, then to Nottingham, and now she is at York.

Rus. Impossible! she could not go over half the ground in the time. What the devil are you talking of?

Sir H. Of the mare you was just now saying you wanted to buy.

Rus. The devil take the mare!——who would think of her, when I am mad about an affair of so much more consequence?

Sir H. You seemed mad about her a little while ago. She's a fine mare, and a thing of shape and blood.

Rus. Damn her blood!——Harriot! my dear provoking Harriot! Where can she be? Have you got any intelligence of her?

Sir H. No, faith, not I: we seem to be quite thrown out here—but however I have ordered Tom to try if he can hear any thing of her among the ostlers.

Rus. Why don't you enquire after her yourself? why don't you run up and down the whole town after her?——t'other young rascal knows where she is, I warrant you.——What a plague it is to have a daughter! When one loves her to distraction, and has toil'd and labour'd to make her happy, the un-

D

grateful slut will sooner go to hell her own way—but she shall have him—I will make her happy, if I break her heart for it.—A provoking gipsy!—to run away, and torment her poor father, that dotes on her! I'll never see her face again.—Sir Harry, how can we get any intelligence of her? Why don't you speak! why don't you tell me?——Zounds! you seem as indifferent as if you did nor care a farthing about her.

Sir H. Indifferent! you may well call me indifferent!——this damn'd chace after her will cost me a thousand——if it had not been for her, I would not have been off the course this week, to have sav'd the lives of my whole family——I'll hold you six to two that——

Rus. Zounds! hold your tongue, or talk more to the purpose——I swear, she is too good for you—you don't deserve such a wife—a fine, dear, sweet, lovely, charming girl!—She'll break my heart.—How shall I find her out?——Do, pr'ythee, Sir Harry, my dear honest friend, consider how we may discover where she is fled to.

Sir H. Suppose you put an advertisement into the news-papers, describing her marks, her age, her height, and where she strayed from. I recover'd a bay mare once by that method.

Rus. Advertise her!—What! describe my daughter and expose her in the publick papers, with a reward for bringing her home, like horses stolen or stray'd!——recovered a bay mare!——the devil's in the fellow!——he thinks of nothing but racers, and bay mares, and stallions.——'Sdeath I wish your——

Sir H. I wish Harriot was fairly pounded; it would save us both a deal of trouble.

Rus. Which way shall I turn myself?——I am half distracted.——If I go to that young dog's house, he has certainly conveyed her somewhere out of my reach——if she does not send to me to-day, I'll give her up for ever——perhaps though, she may have met with some accident, and has nobody to assist her. —No, she is certainly with that young rascal.—I wish she was dead, and I was dead——I'll blow young Oakly's brains out.

Enter TOM.

Sir H. Well, Tom, how is poor Snip?

Tom. A little better, sir, after his warm mash : but Lady, the pointing bitch that followed you all the way, is deadly foot-sore.

Rus. Damn Snip and Lady!—have you heard any thing of Harriot?

Tom. Why I came on purpose to let my master and your honour know, that John Ostler says as how, just such a lady as I told him madam Harriot was, came here in a four-wheel chaise, and was fetch'd away soon after by a fine lady in a chariot.

Rus. Did she come alone?

Tom. Quite alone, only a servant-maid, please your honour.

Rus. And what part of the town did they go to?

Tom. John Ostler says as how, they bid the coachman drive to Grosvenor-square.

Sir H. Soho! puss——Yoics!

Rus. She is certainly gone to that young rogue——
he has got his aunt to fetch her from hence——or else
she is with her own aunt Lady Freelove——they both
live in that part of the town. I'll go to his house,
and in the mean while, Sir Harry, you shall step to
Lady Freelove's. We'll find her, I warrant you.
I'll teach my young mistress to be gadding. She
shall marry you to-night. Come along, Sir Harry,
come along; we won't lose a minute. Come along.

Sir H. Soho! hark forward! wind 'em and cross
'em! hark forward! Yoics! Yoics!   [*Exeunt.*

SCENE II.

Changes to OAKLY'S. *Enter Mrs.* OAKLY.

Mrs. Oak. After all, that letter was certainly intended for my husband. I see plain enough they are
all in a plot against me. My husband intriguing,
the major working him up to affront me, Charles
owning his letters, and so playing into each other's
hands.——They think me a fool, I find——but I'll
be too much for them yet.——I have desired to speak
with Mr. Oakley, and expect him here immediately.
His temper is naturally open, and if he thinks my
anger abated, and my suspicions laid asleep, he will
certainly betray himself by his behaviour. I'll assume

an air of good-humour, pretend to believe the fine
story they have trumped up, throw him off his guard,
and so draw the secret out of him.—Here he comes.
—How hard it is for to dissemble one's anger! O, I
could rate him soundly! but I'll keep down my in-
dignation at present, though it chokes me.

Enter OAKLY.

O my dear! I am very glad to see you. Pray sit
down. [*They sit.*] I longed to see you. It seemed an
age till I had an opportunity of talking over the silly
affair that happened this morning.   [*Mildly.*

Oak. Why really, my dear———

Mrs. Oak. Nay don't look so grave now. Come—
it's all over. Charles and you have cleared up matters. I am satisfied.

Oak. Indeed! I rejoice to hear it! You make me
happy beyond my expectation. This disposition will
insure our felicity. Do but lay aside your cruel unjust suspicion, and we should never have the least
difference.

Mrs. Oak. Indeed I begin to think so. I'll endeavour to get the better of it. And really sometimes
it is very ridiculous. My uneasiness this morning,
for instance! ha, ha, ha! To be so much alarmed
about that idle letter, which turned out quite another
thing at last—was not I very angry with you? ha, ha,
ha!   [*Affecting a laugh.*

Oak. Don't mention it. Let us both forget it.

Your present cheerfulness makes amends for every thing.

Mrs. Oak. I am apt to be too violent : I love you too well to be quite easy about you. [*Fondly.*]—Well —no matter—what is become of Charles?

Oak. Poor fellow! he is on the wing, rambling all over the town in pursuit of this young lady.

Mrs. Oak. Where is he gone, pray?

Oak. First of all, I believe, to some of her relations.

Mrs. Oak. Relations! Who are they? Where do they live?

Oak. There is an aunt of her's lives just in the neighbourhood; Lady Freelove.

Mrs. Oak. Lady Freelove! Oho! gone to Lady Freelove's, is he?—and do you think he will hear any thing of her?

Oak. I don't know; but I hope so with all my soul.

Mrs. Oak. Hope! with all your soul; do you hope so. [*Alarmed.*

Oak. Hope so! ye—yes—why don't you hope so? [*Surprised.*

Mrs. Oak. Well—yes—[*Recovering.*]—O ay, to be sure. I hope it of all things. You know, my dear, it must give me great satisfaction, as well as yourself, to see Charles well settled.

Oak. I should think so; and really I don't know where he can be settled so well. She is a most deserving young woman, I assure you.

Mrs. Oak. You are well acquainted with her then?

Oak. To be sure, my dear! after seeing her so often

last summer at the Major's house in the country, and at her father's.

Mrs. Oak. So often!

Oak. O ay, very often—Charles took care of that —almost every day.

Mrs. Oak. Indeed! But pray—a—a—a—I say— a—a—   [*Confused.*

Oak. What do you say? my dear!

Mrs. Oak. I say—a—a—[*Stammering.*] Is she hand-some?

Oak. Prodigiously handsome indeed.

Mrs. Oak. Prodigiously handsome! and is she reckoned a sensible girl?

Oak. A very sensible, modest, agreeable young lady as ever I knew. You would be extremely fond of her, I am sure. You cann't imagine how happy I was in her company. Poor Charles! she soon made a conquest of him, and no wonder, she has so many elegant accomplishments! such an infinite fund of cheerfulness and good humour! Why, she's the dar-ling of the whole country.

Mrs. Oak. Lord! you seem quite in raptures about her.

Oak. Raptures!—not at all. I was only telling you the young lady's character. I thought you would be glad to find that Charles had made so sensible a choice, and was so likely to be happy.

Mrs. Oak. O, Charles! True, as you say, Charles will be mighty happy.

Oak. Don't you think so?

Mrs. Oak. I am convinced of it. Poor Charles! I am much concern'd for him. He must be very uneasy about her. I was thinking whether we could be of any service to him in this affair.

Oak. Was you, my love? that is very good of you. Why, to be sure, we must endeavour to assist him. Let me see? How can we manage it? Gad! I have hit it. The luckiest thought! and it will be of great service to Charles.

Mrs. Oak. Well, what is it? [*Eagerly.*]—You know I would do any thing to serve Charles, and oblige you. [*Mildly.*

Oak. That is so kind! Lord, my dear, if you would but always consider things in this proper light, and continue this amiable temper, we should be the happiest people——

Mrs. Oak. I believe so: but what's your proposal?

Oak. I am sure you'll like it.—Charles, you know, may perhaps be so lucky as to meet with this lady.——

Mrs. Oak. True.

Oak. Now I was thinking, that he might, with your leave, my dear——

Mrs. Oak. Well!

Oak. Bring her home here——

Mrs. Oak. How!

Oak. Yes, bring her home here, my dear!—it will make poor Charles's mind quite easy: and you may take her under your protection till her father comes to town.

Mrs. Oak. Amazing! this is even beyond my expectation.

Oak. Why!——what!——

Mrs. Oak. Was there ever such assurance? Take her under my protection! What! would you keep her under my nose?

Oak. Nay, I never conceiv'd—I thought you would have approv'd——

Mrs. Oak. What! make me your convenient woman!——No place but my own house to serve your purposes?

Oak. Lord, this is the strangest misapprehenion! I am quite astonished.

Mrs. Oak. Astonished! yes——confused, detected, betrayed by your vain confidence of imposing on me. Why, sure you imagine me an ideot, a driveller. Charles, indeed! yes, Charles is a fine excuse for you. The letter this morning, the letter, Mr. Oakly!

Oak. The letter! why sure that——

Mrs. Oak. Is sufficiently explained. You have made it very clear to me. Now I am convinced. I have no doubt of your perfidy. But I thank you for some hints you have given me, and you may be sure I shall make use of them: nor will I rest, till I have full conviction, and overwhelm you with the strongest proof of your baseness towards me.

Oak. Nay, but——

Mrs. Oak. Go, go! I have no doubt of your falsehood: away!   [*Exit Mrs. Oakly.*

Oak. Was there ever any thing like this? Such

unaccountable behaviour! angry I don't know why!
jealous of I know not what! pretending to be satisfied merely to draw me in, and then creating ima-
ginary proofs out of an innocent conversation!——
Hints!——hints I have given her!—What can she
mean?———

TOILET *crossing the Stage.*

Toilet! where are you going?

Toilet. To order the porter to let in no company to
my lady to-day. She won't see a single soul, sir.

[*Exit.*

Oak. What an unhappy woman! Now will she
sit all day feeding on her suspicions, till she has convinced herself of the truth of them.

JOHN *crossing the Stage.*

Well, sir, what's your business?

John. Going to order the chariot, sir!—my lady's
going out immediately.   [*Exit.*

Oak Going out! what is all this?—But every way
she makes me miserable. Wild and ungovernable
as the sea or the wind! made up of storms and tem-
pests! I cann't bear it: and one way or other I will
put an end to it.   [*Exit.*

SCENE III.

Lady FREELOVE'S *House*——*Enter Lady* FREELOVE
with a card—Servant following.

L. Free. [*Reading as she enters.*]—' And will take

the liberty of waiting on her ladyship *en cavalier*, as he comes from the menége.' Does any body wait that brought this card ?

Serv. Lord Trinket's servant is in the hall, madam.

L. Free. My compliments, and I shall be glad to see his lordship.—Where is Miss Russet ?

Serv. In her own chamber, madam.

L. Free. What is she doing ?

Serv. Writing, I believe, madam.

L. Free. Oh! ridiculous!—scribbling to that Oakly, I suppose. [*Apart.*]—Let her know I should be glad of her company here.   [*Exit* Servant.

L. Free. It is a mighty troublesome thing to manage a simple girl, that knows nothing of the world. Harriot, like all other girls, is foolishly fond of this young fellow of her own choosing, her first love, that is to say, the first man that is particularly civil, and the first air of consequence which a young lady gives herself. Poor silly soul!—But Oakly must not have her positively. A match with Lord Trinket will add to the dignity of the family. I must bring her into it. I will throw her into his way as often as possible, and leave him to make his party good as fast as he can. But here she comes.

Enter HARRIOT.

Well! Harriot, still in the pouts! nay, pr'ythee, my dear little run-away girl, be more cheerful! your everlasting melancholy puts me into the vapours.

Har. Dear madam, excuse me. How can I be

cheerful in my present situation? I know my father's temper so well, that I am sure this step of mine
must almost distract him. I sometimes wish that I
had remained in the country, let what would have
been the consequence.

L. Free. Why, it is a naughty child, that's certain;
but it need not be so uneasy about papa, as you know
that I wrote by last night's post to acquaint him that
his little lost sheep was safe, and that you are ready to
obey his commands in every particular, except marrying that oaf, Sir Harry Beagle.——Lord! Lord!
what a difference there is between a country and town
education! Why, a London lass would have jumped
out of a window into a gallant's arms, and without
thinking of her father, unless it were to have drawn
a few bills on him, been an hundred miles off in nine
or ten hours, or perhaps out of the kingdom in twen-
ty-four.

Har. I fear I have already been too precipitate. I
tremble for the consequences.

L. Free. I swear, child, you are a downright prude.
Your way of talking gives me the spleen; so full of
affection, and duty, and virtue, 'tis just like a funeral
sermon. And yet, pretty soul! it can love.—Well,
I wonder at your taste; a sneaking simple gentleman! without a title! and when to my knowledge
you might have a man of quality to-morrow.

Har. Perhaps so. Your ladyship must excuse me,
but many a man of quality would make me miserable.

L. Free. Indeed, my dear, these antideluvian no-

tions will never do now a-days; and at the same
time too, those little wicked eyes of yours speak a
very different language. Indeed you have fine eyes,
child! And they have made fine work with Lord
Trinket.

Har. Lord Trinket!   *[Contemptuously.*

L. Free. Yes, Lord Trinket: you know it as well
as I do, and yet, you ill-natured thing, you will not
vouchsafe him a single smile. But you must give
the poor soul a little encouragement, pr'ythee do.

Har. Indeed I cann't, madam, for of all mankind
Lord Trinket is my aversion.

L. Free. Why so? child! He is counted a well-
bred, sensible young fellow, and the women all
think him handsome.

Har. Yes, he is just polite enough to be able to be
very unmannerly with a great deal of good breeding;
is just handsome enough to make him most exces-
sively vain of his person; and has just reflection
enough to finish him for a coxcomb; qualifications,
which are all very common among those whom your
ladyship calls men of quality.

L. Free. A satirist too! Indeed, my dear, this affectation sits very aukwardly upon you. There will
be a superiority in the behaviour of persons of
fashion.

Har. A superiority, indeed! For his lordship always behaves with so much insolent familiarity, that
I should almost imagine he was soliciting me for

E

other favours, rather than to pass my whole life with him.

L. Free. Innocent freedoms, child, which every fine woman expects to be taken with her, as an acknowledgment of her beauty.

Har. They are freedoms, which, I think, no innocent woman can allow.

L. Free. Romantic to the last degree !—Why, you are in the country still, Harriot !

Enter Servant.

Serv. My Lord Trinket, madam ! [*Exit Servant.*
L. Free. I swear now I have a good mind to tell him all you have said.

Enter Lord TRINKET *in boots, &c. as from the Riding-House.*

Your lordship's most obedient humble servant.

L. Trink. Your ladyship does me too much honour. Here I am *en bottine* as you see,—just come from the menége. Miss Russet, I am your slave. I declare it makes me quite happy to find you together. 'Pon honour, ma'am, [*To* Harriot.] I begin to conceive great hopes of you : and as for you, Lady Freelove, I cannot sufficiently commend your assiduity with your fair pupil. She was before possessed of every grace that nature could bestow on her, and nobody is so well qualified as your ladyship to give her the *Bon Ton.*

Har. Compliment and contempt all in a breath!
My lord, I am obliged to you. But waving my acknowledgments, give me leave to ask your lordship,
whether nature and the *Bon Ton* (as you call it) are so
different, that we must give up one in order to obtain
the other?

L. Trink. Totally opposite, madam. The chief
aim of the *Bon Ton* is to render persons of family different from the vulgar, for whom indeed nature
serves very well. For this reason it has, at various
times, been ungenteel to see, to hear, to walk, to be
in good health, and to have twenty other horrible
perfections of nature. Nature indeed may do very
well sometimes. It made you, for instance, and it
then made something very lovely; and if you would
suffer us of quality to give you the *Ton*, you would be
absolutely divine: but now—me—madam—me——
nature never made such a thing as me.

Har. Why, indeed, I think your lordship has very
few obligations to her.

L. Trink. Then you really think it's all my own?
I declare now that is a mighty genteel compliment.
Nay, if you begin to flatter already, you improve
apace. 'Pon honour, Lady Freelove, I believe we
shall make something of her at last.

L. Free. No doubt on't. It is in your lordship's
power to make her a complete woman of fashion at
once.

L. Trink. Hum! Why, ay——

Har. Your lordship must excuse me. I am of a

very tasteless disposition. I shall never bear to be
carried out of nature.

L. Free. You are out of nature now, Harriot! I
am sure no woman but yourself ever objected to being
carried among persons of quality. Would you believe it? my lord! here has she been a whole week
in town, and would never suffer me to introduce her
to a rout, an assembly, a concert, or even to court,
or to the opera; nay, would hardly so much as mix
with a living soul that has visited me.

L. Trink. No wonder, madam, you do not adopt
the manners of persons of fashion, when you will not
even honour them with your company. Were you
to make one in our little coteries, we should soon
make you sick of the boors and bumpkins of the horrid country. By the bye, I met a monster at the
riding-house this morning, who gave me some intelligence, that will surprise you, concerning your family.

Har. What intelligence?

L. Free. Who was this monster, as your lordship
calls him? A curiosity, I dare say. .

L. Trink. This monster, madam, was formerly my
head groom, and had the care of all my running
horses, but growing most abominably surly and extravagant, as you know all these fellows do, I turned
him off; and ever since my brother Slouch Trinket
has had the care of my stud, rides all my principal
matches himself, and——

Har. Dear my lord, don't talk of your groom and

your brother, but tell me the news. Do you know any thing of my father?

L. Trink. Your father, madam, is now in town. This fellow, you must know, is now groom to Sir Harry Beagle, your sweet rural swain, and informed me, that his master and your father were running all over the town in quest of you; and that he himself had orders to enquire after you; for which reason, I suppose, he came to the riding-house stables, to look after a horse, thinking it, to be sure, a very likely place to meet you. Your father, perhaps, is gone to seek you at the Tower, or Westminster-Abbey, which is all the idea he has of London; and your faithful lover is probably cheapening a hunter, and drinking strong beer at the Horse and Jockey in Smithfield.

L. Free. The whole set admirably disposed of!

Har. Did not your lordship inform him where was?

L. Trink. Not I, 'pon honour, madam: that I left to their own ingenuity to discover.

L. Free. And pray, my lord, where in this town have this polite company bestowed themselves?

L. Trink. They lodge, madam, of all places in the world, at the Bull and Gate Inn, in Holborn.

L. Free. Ha, ha, ha! The Bull and Gate! Incomparable! What, have they brought any hay or cattle to town?

L. Trink. Very well, Lady Freelove, very well, indeed!—There they are, like so many graziers;

and there, it seems, they have learned that this lady is certainly in London.

Har. Do, dear madam, send a card directly to my father, informing him where I am, and that your ladyship would be glad to see him here. For my part, I dare not venture into his presence till you have, in some measure, pacified him; but, for Heaven's sake, desire him not to bring that wretched fellow along with him.

L. Trink. Wretched fellow! Oho! *Courage,* Milor Trinket!   [*Aside,*

L. Free. I'll send immediately. Who's there?

. *Enter Servant.*

Serv. [*Apart to L.* Freelove.] Sir Harry Beagle is below, madam.

L. Free. [*Apart to Serv.*] I am not at home.—— Have they let him in?

Serv. Yes, madam.

L. Free. How abominably unlucky this is! Well, then shew him into my dressing-room. I will come to him there.   [*Exit Serv.*

L. Trink. Lady Freelove! No engagement, I hope. We won't part with you, 'pon honour.

L. Free. The worst engagement in the world. A pair of musty old prudes! Lady Formal and Miss Prate.

L. Trink. O the beldams! As nauseous as ipecacuanha, 'pon honour.

L. Free. Lud! lud! what shall I do with them?

Why do these foolish women come troubling me now?
I must wait on them in the dressing-room, and you
must excuse the card, Harriot, till they are gone. I'll
dispatch them as soon as I can, but Heaven knows
when I shall get rid of them, for they are both everlasting gossips; though the words came from her ladyship one by one, like drops from a still, while the
other tiresome woman overwhelms us with a flood of
impertinence. Harriot, you'll entertain his lordship
till I return.   [*Exit.*

L. Trink. Gone!—'Egad, my affairs here begin to
grow very critical,—the father in town!—lover in
town!—Surrounded by enemies!——What shall I
do?—[*To* Harriot.] I have nothing for it but a *coup
de main.* 'Pon honour, I am not sorry for the coming
in of these old tabbies, and am much obliged to her
ladyship for leaving us such an agreeable tête-a-tête.

Har. Your lordship will find me extremely bad
company.

L. Trink. Not in the least, my dear! We'll entertain ourselves one way or other, I'll warrant you.—
'Egad, I think it a mighty good opportunity to esta-
blish a better acquaintance with you.

Har. I don't understand you.

L. Trink. No?——Why then I'll speak plainer.—
[*Pausing and looking her full in the face.*] You are an
amazing fine creature, 'pon honour.

Har. If this be your lordship's polite conversation,
I shall leave you to amuse yourself in soliloquy.
                                    [*Going.*

L. Trink. . . No, no, no, madam, that must not be. [*Stopping her.*] This place, my passion, the opportunity, all conspire——

Har. How, sir! you don't intend to do me any violence.

L. Trink. 'Pon honour, ma'am, it will be doing great violence to myself if I do not. You must excuse me.   [*Struggling with her.*

Har. Help! help! murder! help!

L. Trink. Your yelping will signify nothing; nobody will come.   [*Struggling.*

Har. For Heaven's sake!——Sir! My lord!——
                                   [*Noise within.*

L. Trink. Pox on't, what noise?——Then I must be quick.   [*Still struggling.*

Har. Help! murder! help! help!

Enter CHARLES *hastily.*

Char. What do I hear? My Harriot's voice calling for help? Ha! [*Seeing them.*] Is it possible? Turn ruffian!—I'll find you employment.   [*Drawing.*

L. Trink. You are a most impertinent scoundrel, and I'll whip you through the lungs, 'pon honour.

          [*They fight,* Harriot *runs out screaming help,* &c.

Enter Lady FREELOVE, *Sir* HARRY BEAGLE, *and Servants.*

L. Free. How's this?—Swords drawn in my house!—Part them——[*They are parted.*] This is the most impudent thing.

L. Trink. Well, rascal, I shall find a time, I know you, sir!

Char. The sooner the better, I know your lordship too.

Sir H. I'faith, madam, [*To L.* Free.] we had like to have been in at the death.

L. Free. What is all this? Pray, sir, what is the meaning of your coming hither to raise this disturbance? Do you take my house for a brothel?

.[*To* Charles.

Char. Not I, indeed, madam! but I believe his lordship does.

L. Trink. Impudent scoundrel!

L. Free. Your conversation, sir, is as insolent as your behaviour. Who are you? What brought you here?

Char. I am one, madam, always ready to draw my sword in defence of innocence in distress, and more especially in the cause of that lady I delivered from his lordship's fury; in search of whom I troubled your ladyship's house.

L. Free. Her lover, I suppose, or what?

Char. At your ladyship's service; though not quite so violent in my passion as his lordship there.

L. Trink. Impertinent rascal!

L. Free. You shall be made to repent of this insolence.

L. Trink. Your ladyship may leave that to me.

Char. Ha! ha!

Sir H. But pray what is become of the lady all this

while? Why, Lady Freelove, you told me she was not here, and, i'faith, I was just drawing off another way, if I had not heard the view-halloo.

L. Free. You shall see her immediately, sir! Who's there?

Enter a Servant.

Where is Miss Russet?

Serv. Gone out, madam.

L. Free. Gone out! where?

Serv. I don't know, madam: but she ran down the back stairs crying for help, crossed the servants hall in tears, and took a chair at the door.

L. Free. Blockheads! To let her go out in a chair alone!——Go, and enquire after her immediately.

[*Exit* Servant.

Sir H. Gone! What a pox had I just run her down, and is the little puss stole away at last?

L. Free. Sir, if you will walk in [*To Sir* Har.] with his lordship and me, perhaps you may hear some tidings of her; though it is most probable she may be gone to her father. I don't know any other friend she has in town.

Char. I am heartily glad she is gone. She is safer any where than in this house.

L. Free. Mighty well, sir!——My lord! Sir Harry! ——I attend you.

L. Trink. You shall hear from me, sir!

[*To* Charles.

Char. Very well, my lord.

Sir H. Stole away !——Pox on't——stole away.

[*Exeunt Sir* H. *and Lord* Frink.

L. Free. Before I follow the company, give me leave to tell you, sir, that your behaviour here has been so extraordinary—— ·

Char. My treatment here, madam, has indeed been very extraordinary.

L. Free. Indeed !—Well—no matter—permit me to acquaint you, sir, that there lies your way out, and that the greatest favour you can do me, is to leave the house immediately.

Char. That your ladyship may depend on. Since you have put Miss Russet to flight, you may be sure of not being troubled with my company. I'll after her immediately—I can't rest till I know what is become of her

L. Free. If she has any regard for her reputation, she'll never put herself into such hands as yours.

Char. O, madam, there can be no doubt of her regard for that, by her leaving your ladyship.

L. Free. Leave my house.

Char. Directly.——A charming house! and a charming lady of the house too ! Ha, ha, ha !

L. Free. Vulgar fellow !

Char. Fine lady !   [*Exeunt severally.*

ACT III. SCENE I.

Lady FREELOVE's *House. Enter Lady* FREELOVE, *and Lord* TRINKET.

Lord Trinket.

Doucement, *Doucement,* my dear Lady Freelove!——Excuse me! I meant no harm, 'pon honour.

L. Free. Indeed, indeed, my Lord Trinket, this is absolutely intolerable. What, to offer rudeness to a young lady in my house! What will the world say of it?

L. Trink. Just what the world pleases.——It does not signify a doit what they say.——However, I ask pardon; but, 'egad, I thought it was the best way.

L. Free. For shame, for shame, my lord! I am quite hurt at your want of discretion. Leave the whole conduct of this affair to me, or I'll have done with it at once. How strangely you have acted! There I went out of the way on purpose to serve you, by keeping off that looby Sir Harry Beagle, and preventing him or her father from seeing the girl, till we had some chance of managing her ourselves.——And then you chose to make a disturbance, and spoiled all.

L. Trink. Devil take Sir Harry and t'other scoundrel too!——That they should come driving hither just at so critical an instant!——And that the wild little thing should take wing, and fly away the lord know whither!

L. Free. Ay,——And there again you was indiscreet past redemption. To let her know, that hei
father was in town, and where he was to be found
too! For there I am confident she must be gone, as
she is not acquainted with one creature in London.

L. Trink. Why a father is in these cases the *pis-
aller* I must confess. 'Pon honour, Lady Freelove,
I can scarce believe this obstinate girl a relation of
yours. Such narrow notions! I'll swear, there is
less trouble in getting ten women of the *prémiere volée,*
than in conquering the scruples of a silly girl in that
stile of life.

L. Free. Come, come, my lord, a truce with your
reflections on my niece! Let us consider what is best
to be done.

L. Trink. E'en just what your ladyship thinks proper.——For my part, I am entirely *dérangée.*

L. Free. Will you submit to be governed by me
then?

L. Trink. I'll be all obedience——your ladyship's
slave, 'pon honour.

L. Free. Why then, as this is rather an ugly affair
in regard to me, as well as your lordship, and may
make some noise, I think it absolutely necessary,
merely to save appearances, that you should wait on
her father, palliate matters as well as you can, and
make a formal repetition of your proposal of marriage.

L. Trink. Your ladyship is perfectly in the right.
——You are quite *au fait* of the affair. It shall be

done immediately, and then your reputation will be
safe, and my conduct justified to all the world.——
But should the old rustic continue as stubborn as his
daughter, your ladyship, I hope, has no objections to
my being a little *rusée*, for I must have her, 'pon
honour.

 L. Free. Not in the least.

 L. Trink. Or if a good opportunity should offer,
and the girl should be still untractable——

 L. Free. Do what you will, I wash my hands of it.
She's out of my care now, you know.——But you
must beware your rivals. One, you know, is in the
house with her, and the other will lose no opportunities of getting to her.

 L. Trink. As to the fighting gentleman, I shall cut
out work for him in his own way. I'll send him a
petit billet to-morrow morning, and then there can be
no great difficulty in outwitting her bumkin father,
and the baronet.

Enter a Servant.

 Serv. Captain O'Cutter to wait on your ladyship.

 L. Free. O the hideous fellow! The Irish sailor-
man, for whom I prevailed on your lordship to get
the post of regulating captain. I suppose he is come
to load me with his odious thanks. I won't be troubled
with him now.

 L. Trink. Let him in, by all means. He is the best
creature to laugh at in nature. He is a perfect sea-
monster, and always looks and talks as if he was upon

deck. Besides, a thought strikes me.——He may be of use.

L. Free. Well——send the creature up then.

[*Exit* Servant.

But what fine thought is this ?

L. Trink. A *coup de maitre*, 'pon honour ! I intend ——but hush ! Here the porpus comes.

Enter Captain O'CUTTER.

L. Free. Captain, your humble servant ! I am very glad to see you.

O'Cut. I am much oblaged to you, my lady ! Upon my conscience, the wind favours me at all points. I had no sooner got under way to tank your ladyship, but I have born down upon my noble friend his lordship too. I hope your lordship's well ?

L. Trink. Very well, I thank you, captain !—But you seem to be hurt in the service : what is the meaning of that patch over your right eye ?

O'Cut. Some advanced wages from my new post, my lord ! This pressing is hot work, tho' it entitles us to smart-money.

L. Free. And pray in what perilous adventure did you get that scar, captain ?

* *O'Cut.* Quite out of my element, indeed my lady ! I got in an engagement by land. A day or two ago I spied three stout fellows, belonging to a merchant-man. They made down Wapping. I immediately gave my lads the signal to chace, and we bore down right upon them. They tacked, and lay to. We

Fij

gave them a thundering broadside, which they re-saved like men ; and one of them made use of small arms, which carried off the weathermost corner of Ned Gage's hat ; so I immediately stood in with him, and raked him, but resaved a wound on my starboard eye, from the stock of the pistol.   However, we took them all, and they now lie under the hatches, with fifty more, a-board a tender off the Tower.

L. Trink. Well done, noble captain :—— But how-ever you will soon have better employment, for I think the next step to your present post, is commonly a ship.

O'Cut. The sooner the better, my lord!   Honest Terence O'Cutter shall never flinch, I warrant you ; and has had as much sea-sarvice as any man in the navy.

L. Trink. You may depend on my good offices, cap-tain!—But in the mean time it is in your power to do me a favour.

O'Cut. A favour! my lord! your lordship does me honour.   I would go round the world, from one end to the other, by day or by night, to sarve your lord-ship, or my good lady here.

L. Trink. Dear madam, the luckiest thought in na-ture! [*Apart to L.* Free.]—The favour I have to ask of you, captain, need not carry you so far out of your way.   The whole affair is, that there are a couple of impudent fellows at an inn in Holborn, who have af-fronted me, and you would oblige me infinitely, by pressing them into his Majesty's service.

L. Free. Now I understand you.———Admirable!

　　　　　　　　　　　　[*Apart to L.* Trink.

O'Cut. With all my heart, my lord, and tank you too, fait. But, by the bye, I hope they are not house-keepers, or freemen of the city. There's the devil to pay in meddling with them. They boder one so about liberty and property, and stuff. It was but t'other day that Jack Trowser was carried before my Lord Mayor, and lost above a twelvemonth's pay, for nothing at-all—at-all.

L. Trink. I'll take care you shall be brought into no trouble. These fellows were formerly my grooms. If you'll call on me in the morning, I'll go with you to the place.

O'Cut. I'll be with your lordship, and bring with me four or five as pretty boys as you'll wish to clap your two lucking eyes upon of a summer's day.

L. Trink. I am much obliged to you. But, captain, I have another little favour to beg of you.

O'Cut. Upon my shoul, and I'll do it.

L. Trink. What, before you know it?

O'Cut. Fore and aft, my lord!

L. Trink. A gentleman has offended me in a point of honour———

O'Cut. Cut his troat.

L. Trink. Will you carry him a letter from me?

O'Cut. Indeed and I will: and I'll take you in tow too, and you shall engage him yard-arm and yard-arm.

L. Trink. Why then, captain, you'll come a little earlier to-morrow morning than you proposed, that you may attend him with my billet, before you proceed on the other affair.

O'Cut. Never fear it, my lord!——Your sarvant!—— My ladyship, your humble sarvant!

L. Free. Captain, yours! Pray give my service to my friend Mrs O'Cutter. How does she do?

O'Cut. I tank your ladyship's axing——The dear creature is purely tight and we l.

L. Trink. How many children have you, captain?

O'Cut. Four, and please your lordship, and another upon the stocks.

L. Trink. When it is launched, I hope to be at the christening. I'll stand godfather, captain!

O'Cut. Your lordship's very good.

L. Trink. Well, you'll come to-morrow.

O'Cut. O, I'll not fail, my lord! Little Terence O'Cutter never fails, fait, when a troat is to be cut.

[*Exit.*

L. Free. Ha, ha, ha! But sure you don't intend to ship off both her father and her country lover for the Indies?

L. Trink. O no! Only let them contemplate the inside of a ship for a day or two.

L. Free. Well, but after all, my lord, this is a very bold undertaking. I don't think you'll be able to put it in practice.

L. Trink. Nothing so easy, 'pon honour. To press a gentleman——a man of quality——one of us—— would not be so easy, I grant you. But these fellows, you know, have not half so decent an appearance as

one of my footmen: and from their behaviour, conversation, and dress, it is very possible to mistake
them for grooms and ostlers.

L. Free. There may be something in that indeed.
But what use do you propose to make of this stratagem?

L. Trink. Every use in nature. This artifice must
at least take them out of the way for some time, and
in the mean while measures may be concerted to carry
off the girl.

Enter. à Servant.

Serv. Mrs. Oakly, madam, is at the door, in her
chariot, and desires to have the honour of speaking to
your ladyship, on particular business.

L. Trink. Mrs. Oakly! what can that jealous-pated
woman want with you?

L. Free. No matter what.—I hate her mortally.—
Let her in.   [*Exit* Servant.

L. Trink. What wind blows her hither?

L. Free. A wind that must blow us some good.

L. Trink. How?——I was amazed you chose to see
her.

L. Free. How can you be so slow of apprehension?
——She comes you may be sure on some occasion relating to this girl: in order to assist young Oakly
perhaps, to sooth me, and gain intelligence, and so
forward the match; but I'll forbid the banns, I warrant you.——Whatever she wants, I'll draw some
sweet mischief out of it.——But away! away!——I
think I hear her—slip down the back stairs——or,

stay, now I think on't, go out this way—meet her—
and be sure to make her a very respectful bow, as
you go out.

L. Trink. Hush! here she is.

Enter Mrs. OAKLY.

[*L* Trinket *bows, and exit.*]

Mrs. Oak. I beg pardon for giving your ladyship
this trouble.

L. Free. I am always glad of the honour of seeing
Mrs. Oakly.

Mrs. Oak. There is a letter, madam, just come from
the country, which has occasioned some alarm in our
family. It comes from Mr. Russet——

L. Free. Mr. Russet!

Mrs. Oak. Yes, from Mr. Russet, madam! and is
chiefly concerning his daughter. As she has the honour of being related to your ladyship, I took the liberty of waiting on you.

L. Free. She is indeed, as you say, madam, a relation of mine! but after what has happened, I scarce
know how to acknowledge her.

Mrs. Oak. Has she been so much to blame then?

L. Free. So much, madam?——Only judge for
yourself.——Though she had been so indiscreet, not
to say indecent in her conduct, as to elope from her
father, I was in hopes to have hush'd up that matter,
for the honour of our family.——But she has run
away from me too, madam!—went off in the most ab-
rupt manner, not an hour ago.

Mrs. Oak. You surprise me. Indeed her father, by his letter, seems apprehensive of the worst consequences.—But does your ladyship imagine any harm has happened ?

L. Free. I can't tell——I hope not——But indeed she is a strange girl. You know, madam, young women cann't be too cautious in their conduct. She is, I am sorry to declare it, a very dangerous person to take into a family.

Mrs. Oak. Indeed!   [*Alarmed.*

1. Free. If I was to say all I know !

Mrs. Oak. Why sure your ladyship knows of nothing that has been carried on clandestinely between her and Mr. Oakly.   [*In disorder.*

L. Free. Mr. Oakly !

Mrs. Oak. Mr. Oakly—no, not Mr. Oakly—that is, not my husband—I don't mean him—not him—but his nephew—young Mr. Oakly.

L. Free. Jealous of her husband! So, so! Now I know my game.   [*aside.*

Mrs. Oak. But pray, madam, give me leave to ask, was there any thing very particular in her conduct, while she was in your ladyship's house ?

L. Free. Why really, considering she was here scarce a week, her behaviour was rather mysterious ; —letters and messages, to and fro, between her and I don't know who——I suppose you know that Mr. Oakly's nephew has been here, madam.

Mrs. Oak. I was not sure of it. Has he been to wait on your ladyship already on this occasion ?

L. Free. To wait on me!——The expression is much too polite for the nature of his visit.—My lord Trinket, the nobleman whom you met as you came in, had, you must know, madam, some thoughts of my niece, and as it would have been an advantageous match, I was glad of it; but I believe, after what he has been witness to this morning, he will drop all thoughts of it.

Mrs. Oak. I am sorry that any relation of mine should so far forget himself——

L. Free. It's no matter—his behaviour indeed, as well as the young lady's, was pretty extraordinary ——and yet after all, I don't believe he is the object of her affections.

Mrs. Oak. Ha!   [*Much alarmed.*

L. Free. She has certainly an attachment somewhere, a strong one; but his lordship, who was present all the time, was convinced, as well as myself, that Mr. Oakly's nephew was rather a convenient friend, a kind of go-between, than the lover.——Bless me, madam, you change colour! you seem uneasy! what's the matter?

Mrs. Oak. Nothing,——madam,——nothing;——a little shock'd that my husband should behave so.

L. Free. Your husband, madam!

Mrs. Oak. His nephew, I mean.——His unpardonable rudeness——but I am not well——I am sorry I have given your ladyship so much trouble——I'll take my leave.

L. Free. I declare, madam, you frighten me. Your

being so visibly affected, makes me quite uneasy. I
hope I have not said any thing——I really don't be-,
lieve your husband is in fault. Men, to be sure,
allow themselves strange liberties. But I think, nay
I am sure, it cannot be so. It is impossible. Don't
let what I have said have any effect on you.

Mrs. Oak. No, it has not——I have no idea of such
a thing.——Your ladyship's most obedient—[*Going*,
returns]——But sure, madam, you have not heard or
don't know any thing.

L. Free. Come, come, Mrs. Oakly, I see how it is,
and it would not be kind to say all I know. I dare
not tell you what I have heard. Only be on your
guard—there can be no harm in that. Do you be
against giving the girl any countenance, and see what
effect it has.

Mrs. Oak. I will——I am much obliged——But
does it appear to your ladyship then that Mr.
Oakly——

L. Free. No, not at all—nothing in't, I dare say—
I would not create uneasiness in a family—but I am
a woman myself, have been married, and cann't help
feeling for you.—But don't be uneasy, there's nothing
in't, I dare say.

Mrs. Oak. I think so.——Your ladyship's humble
servant.

L. Free. Your servant, madam.——Pray don't be
alarmed, I must insist on your not making yourself
uneasy.

Mrs Oak. Not at all alarmed—not in the least un-easy.—Your most obedient.   [*Exit.*

L. Free. Ha, ha, ha! There she goes, brimful of anger and jealousy, to vent it all on her husband. Mercy on the poor man!

Enter Lord TRINKET.

Bless me! my lord, I thought you was gone.

L. Trink. Only into the next room. My curiosity would not let me stir a step further. I heard it all, and was never more diverted in my life, 'pon honour. Ha, ha, ha!

L. Free. How the silly creature took it! Ha, ha, ha!

L. Trink. Ha, ha, ha!—My dear Lady Freelove, you have a deal of ingenuity, a deal of *esprit*, 'pon honour.

L. Free. A little shell thrown into the enemy's works, that's all.

Both. Ha, ha, ha, ha!

L. Free. But I must leave you. I have twenty visits to pay. You'll let me know how you succeed in your secret expedition.

L. Trink. That you may depend on.

L. Free. Remember then that to-morrow morning I expect to see you.——At present your lordship will excuse me.——Who's there? [*Calling to the servants.*] Send Epingle into my dressing-room.   [*Exit.*

L. Trink. So!——If O'Cutter and his myrmidons are alert, I think I cann't fail of success, and then *prenez garde*, Mademoiselle Harriot!——This is one of the drollest circumstances in nature.——Here is my lady Freelove, a woman of sense, a woman that knows the world too, assisting me in this design. I never knew her ladyship so much out.——How, in the name of wonder, can she imagine that a man of quality, or any man else 'egad, would marry a fine girl, after——not I, 'pon honour. No—no—when I have had the *entamure*, let who will take the rest of the loaf. [*Exit.*

SCENE II.

Changes to Mr. OAKLY's *House.* Enter HARRIOT *following a Servant.*

Har. Not at home!——Are you sure that Mrs. Oakly is not at home, sir?

Serv. She is just gone out, madam.

Har. I have something of consequence——If you will give me leave, sir, I will wait till she returns.

Serv. You would not see her, if you did, madam. She has given positive orders not to be interrupted with any company to-day.

Har. Sure, sir, if you was to let her know that I had particular business——

Serv. I should not dare to trouble her, indeed, madam.

Har. How unfortunate this is! What can I do?—Pray, sir, can I see Mr. Oakly then?

G

Serv. Yes, madam : I'll acquaint my master, if you please.

Har. Pray do, sir.

Serv. Will you favour me with your name, madam?

Har. Be pleased, sir, to let him know that a lady desires to speak with him.

Serv. I shall, madam.　　　•　　[*Exit servant.*

Har. I wish I could have seen Mrs. Oakly. What an unhappy situation am I reduced to! What will the world say of me?—And yet what could I do? To remain at Lady Freelove's was impossible. Charles, I must own, has this very day revived much of my tenderness for him; and yet I dread the wildness of his disposition. I must now, however, solicit Mr. Oakly's protection, a circumstance (all things considered) rather disagreeable to a delicate mind, and which nothing, but the absolute necessity of it, could excuse. Good heavens! What a multitude of difficulties and distresses am I thrown into, by my father's obstinate perseverance to force me into a marriage, which my soul abhors!

Enter OAKLY.

Oak. [*At entering.*] Where is this lady?——[*Seeing her.*] Bless me, Miss Russet, is it you?——Was ever any thing so unlucky? [*Aside.*] Is it possible, madam, that I see you here?

Har. It is too true, sir; and the occasion on which I am now to trouble you is so much in need of an apology, that——

Oak. Pray make none, madam.—If my wife should return before I get her out of the house again I——
[*Aside.*

Har. I dare say, sir, you are not quite a stranger to the attachment your nephew has professed to me.

Oak. I am not, madam. I hope Charles has not been guilty of any baseness towards you. If he has, I'll never see his face again.

Har. I have no cause to accuse him. But——

Oak. But what, madam? Pray be quick I——The very person in the world I would not have seen I
[*Aside.*

Har. You seem uneasy, sir I

Oak. No, nothing at all——Pray go on, madam.

Har. I am at present, sir, through a concurrence of strange accidents, in a very unfortunate situation, and do not know what will become of me without your assistance.

Oak. I'll do every thing in my power to serve you, I know of your leaving your father, by a letter we have had from him. Pray let me know the rest of your story.

Har. My story, sir, is very short. When I left my father's I came immediately to London, and took refuge with a relation, where, instead of meeting with the protection I expected, I was alarmed with the most infamous designs upon my honour. It is not an hour ago, since your nephew rescued me from the attempts of a villain. I tremble to think, that I left him actually engaged in a duel.

' G ij

Oak. He is very safe. He has just sent home the chariot from the St. Alban's tavern, where he dines to-day. But what are your commands for me, madam?

Har. I am heartily glad to hear of his safety.—The favour, sir, I would now request of you is, that you would suffer me to remain for a few days in your house.

Oak. Madam!

Har. And that in the mean time you will use your utmost endeavours to reconcile me to my father, without his forcing me into a marriage with Sir Harry Beagle.

Oak. This is the most perplexing situation!—— Why did not Charles take care to bestow you properly?

Har. It is most probable, sir, that I should not have consented to such a measure myself. The world is but too apt to censure, even without a cause : and if you are so kind as to admit me into your house, I must desire not to consider Mr. Oakly in any other light than as your nephew; as in my present circumstances I have particular objections to it.

Oak. What an unlucky circumstance!——Upon my soul, madam, I would do any thing to serve you—— but being in my house, creates a difficulty that——

Har. I hope, sir, you do not doubt the truth of what I have told you.

Oak. I religiously believe every tittle of it, madam, but I have particular family considerations, that——

Har. Sure, sir, you cannot suspect me to be base enough to form any connections in your family contrary to your inclinations, while I am living in your house.

Oak. Such connections, madam, would do me and all my family great honour. I never dreamt of any scruples on that account.—What can I do?—Let me see—let me see—suppose——— [*Pausing.*

Enter Mrs. OAKLY *behind, in a capuchin, tippet, &c.*

Mrs. Oak. I am sure I heard the voice of a woman conversing with my husband———Ha! [*Seeing* Harriot.] It is so, indeed! Let me contain myself—I'll listen.

Har. I see, sir, you are not inclin'd to serve me— good heaven! what am I reserv'd to?———Why, why did I leave my father's house to expose myself to greater distresses? [*Ready to weep.*

Oak. I would do any thing for your sake : indeed I would. So pray be comforted, and I'll think of some proper place to bestow you in.

Mrs. Oak. So! so!

Har. What place can be so proper as your own house?

Oak. My dear madam, I———I———

Mrs. Oak. My dear madam———mighty well!

Oak. Hush!—hark!———what noise———no———nothing. But I'll be plain with you, madam, we may be interrupted.———The family consideration I hinted at, is nothing else than my wife. She is a little un-

G iij

happy in her temper, madam!—and if you was to be admitted into the house, I don't know what would be the consequence.

Mrs. Oak. Very fine——

Har. My behaviour, sir!

Oak. My dear life, it would be impossible for you to behave in such a manner, as not to give her suspicion.

Har. But if your nephew, sir, took every thing upon himself——

Oak. Still that would not do, madam!——Why this very morning, when the letter came from your father, though I positively denied any knowledge of it, and Charles owned it, yet it was almost impossible to pacify her.

Mrs. Oak. The letter!—How I have been bubbled!

Har. What shall I do? What will become of me?

Oak. Why, look'e, my dear madam, since my wife is so strong an objection, it is absolutely impossible for me to take you into the house. Nay if I had not known she was gone out, just before you came, I should be uneasy at your being here even now. So we must manage as well as we can. I'll take a private lodging for you a little way off, unknown to Charles or my wife, or any body; and if Mrs. Oakly should discover it at last, why the whole matter will light upon Charles you know.

Mrs. Oak. Upon Charles!

Har. How unhappy is my situation! [*Weeping*] I am ruined for ever.

Oak. Ruin'd! Not at all. Such a thing as this has happened to many a young lady before you, and all has been well again——Keep up your spirits! I'll contrive, if I possibly can, to visit you every day.

Mrs. Oak. [*Advancing.*] Will you so? O, Mr. Oakly! have I discovered you at last? I'll visit you, indeed. And you, my dear madam, I'll——

Har. Madam, I don't understand——

Mrs. Oak. I understand the whole affair, and have understood it for some time past.—You shall have a private lodging, miss!——It is the fittest place for you, I believe.—How dare you look me in the face?

Oak. For heaven's sake, my love, don't be so violent.—You are quite wrong in this affair—you don't know who you are a talking to. That lady is a person of fashion.

Mrs. Oak. Fine fashion, indeed! to seduce other women's husbands!

Har. Dear madam; how can you imagine——

Oak. I tell you, my dear, this is the young lady that Charles——

Mrs. Oak. Mighty well! but that won't do, sir!—Did not I hear you lay the whole intrigue together? Did not I hear your fine plot of throwing all the blame upon Charles?——

Oak. Nay, be cool a moment.——You must know, my dear, that the letter which came this morning related to this lady——

Mrs. Oak. I know it.

Oak. And since that, it seems, Charles has been so fortunate as to——

Mrs. Oak. O, you deceitful man!——That trick is too stale to pass again with me.——It is plain now what you meant by your proposing to take her into the house this morning.——But the gentlewoman could introduce herself, I see.

Oak. Fie! fie! my dear, she came on purpose to enquire for you.

Mrs. Oak. For me!——better and better!——Did not she watch her opportunity, and come to you just as I went out? But I am obliged to you for your visit, madam. It is sufficiently paid. Pray don't let me detain you.

Oak. For shame! for shame, Mrs. Oakly! How can you be so absurd? Is this proper behaviour to a lady of her character!

Mrs. Oak. I have heard her character. Go, my fine run-away madam! Now you've eloped from your family, and run away from your aunt! Go!——You shan't stay here, I promise you.

Oak. Pr'ythee, be quiet. You don't know what you are doing. She shall stay.

Mrs. Oak. She shan't stay a minute.

Oak. She shall stay a minute, an hour, a day, a week, a month, a year!——'Sdeath, madam, she shall stay for ever if I choose it.

Mrs. Oak. How!

Har. For heaven's sake, sir, let me go. I am frighted to death.

Oak. Don't be afraid, madam!——She shall stay, I insist upon it.

Rus. [*within.*] I tell you, sir, I will go up. I am sure the lady'is here, and nothing shall hinder me.

Har. O my father! my father!   [*Faints away.*

Oak. See! she faints. [*Catching her.*]——Ring the bell! Who's there?

Mrs. Oak. What! take her into your arms too!—— I have no patience.

Enter RUSSET *and Servants.*

Rus. Where is this——ha! fainting! [*Running to her.*] O my dear Harriot! my child! my child!

Oak. Your coming so abruptly shocked her spirits. But she revives. How do you, madam?

Har. [*To* Russet] O, sir!

Rus. O my dear girl! How could you run away from your father, that loves you with such fondness! ——But I was sure I should find you here——

Mrs. Oak. There—there!—sure he should find her here! Did not I tell you so?——Are not you a wicked man, to carry on such base underhand doings, with a gentleman's daughter?

Rus. Let me tell you, sir, whatever you may think, of the matter, I shall not easily put up with this be-haviour.—How durst you encourage my daughter to an elopement, and receive her in your house.

Mrs. Oak. There, mind that!——The thing is as plain as the light.

Oak. I tell you, you misunderstand——

Rus. Look you, Mr. Oakly, I shall expect satis-faction from your family for so gross an affront.——

Zouns, sir, I am not to be used ill by any man in England. .

Har. My dear sir, I can assure you ———

Rus. Hold your tongue, girl! You'll put me in a passion.

Oak. Sir, this is all a mistake.

Rus. A mistake! Did not I find her in your house?

Oak. Upon my soul, she has not been in my house above———

Mrs. Oak. Did not I hear you say you would take her a lodging? a private lodging!

Oak. Yes, but that———

Rus. Has not this affair been carried on a long time in spite of my teeth?

Oak. Sir, I never troubled myself———

Mrs. Oak. Never troubled yourself!—Did not you insist on her staying in the house, whether I would or no?

Oak. No.

Rus. Did not you send to meet her, when she came. to town?

Oak. No.

Mrs. Oak. Did not you deceive me about the letter this morning?

Oak. No—no—no—I tell you, no.

Mrs. Oak. Yes—yes—yes——I tell you, yes.

Rus. Shan't I believe my own eyes?

Mrs. Oak. Shan't I believe my own ears?

Oak. I tell you, you are both deceived.

Rus. Zouns, sir, I'll have satisfaction.

Mrs. Oak. I'll stop these fine doings, I warrant you.

Oak. 'Sdeath, you will not let me speak—and you are both alike I think.——I wish you were married to one another with all my heart. . . ,

Mrs. Oak. Mighty well! mighty well!

Rus. I shall soon find a time to talk with you. ,

Oak. Find a time to talk! you have talked enough now for all your lives. ,

Mrs. Oak. Very fine! Come along, sir! Leave that lady with her father. Now she is in the properest hands.

Oak. I wish I could leave you in his hands. [*Going, returns.*] I shall follow, you, madam! One word with you, sir!——The height of your passion, and Mrs. Oakly's strange misapprehension of this whole affair, makes it impossible to explain matters to you at present. I will do it when you please, and how you please.

. *Rus.* Yes, yes: I'll have satisfaction.——So, madam! I have found you at last.——You have made a fine confusion here.

Har. I have, indeed, been the innocent cause of a great deal of confusion.

Rus. Innocent!—— What business had you to be running hither after——

Har. My dear sir, you misunderstand the whole affair. I have not been in this house half an hour.

Rus. Zounds, girl, don't put me in a passion!—— You know I love you——but a lie puts me in a pas-

sion. But come along—we'll leave this house directly
—[Charles *singing without.*] Heyday ! what now ?

After a noise without, enter CHARLES, *drunk.*

Char. *But my wine neither nurses nor babies can bring,*
And a big-bellied bottle's a mighty good thing.
[Singing.

What's here ? a woman ? Harriot ! impossible ! My
dearest, sweetest Harriot ! I have been looking all
over the town for you, and at last——when I was
tired—— and weary—and disappointed—why then the
honest Major and I sat down together to drink your
health in pint bumpers. [*Running up to her.*

Rus. Stand off——How dare you take any liberty
with my daughter before me ? Zounds, sir, I'll be the
death of you.

Char. Ha ! 'Squire Russet too !——You jolly old
cock, how do you do?—But Harriot ! my dear girl !
[*Taking hold of her.*] My life, my soul, my——

Rus. Let her go, sir—come away Harriot !—Leave
him this instant, or I'll tear you asunder. [*Pulling her.*

Har. There needs no violence to tear me from a
man who could disguise himself in such a gross manner, at a time when he knew I was in the utmost distress. [*Disengages herself, and exit with* Russet.

Charles. Only hear me, sir——madam !——my dear
Harriot——Mr. Russet——gone !——she's gone !—
and 'egad in very ill humour, and in very bad company !——I'll go after her—but hold !—I shall only
make it worse——as I did—now I recollect—once be-

fore.   How the devil came they here,?—Who would
have thought of finding her in my own house?——
My head turns round with conjectures.—I believe I
am drunk—very drunk——so 'egad, I'll e'en go and
sleep myself sober, and then enquire the meaning of
all this.   For,

> *I love Sue, and Sue loves me, &c.*

[Exit singing.

ACT IV.   SCENE I.

OAKLY's *House.* Enter Mrs. OAKLY *and Major* OAKLY.

Major.

WELL——well——but sister!——

Mrs. Oak. I will know the truth of this matter.
Why cann't you tell me the whole story?

Maj. I'll tell you nothing.——There's nothing to
tell——you know the truth already.——Besides, what
have I to do with it? Suppose there was a disturbance
yesterday, what's that to me? was I here? it's no
business of mine.

Mrs. Oak. Then why do you study to make it so?
Am not I well assured that this mischief commenced
at your house in the country? And now you are
carrying it on in town.

Maj. This is always the case in family squabbles.
My brother has put you out of humour, and you
choose to vent your spleen upon me.

H

Mrs. Oak. Because I know that you are the occasion of his ill usage. Mr. Oakly never behaved in such a manner before.

Maj. I? Am I the occasion of it?

Mrs. Oak. Yes, you. I am sure on't.

Maj. I am glad on't with all my heart.

Mrs. Oak. Indeed!

Maj. Ay, indeed: and you are the more obliged to me.—Come, come, sister, it's time you should reflect a little. My brother is become a public jest; and by-and-bye, if this foolish affair gets wind, the whole family will be the subject of town-talk.

Mrs. Oak. And well it may, when you take so much pains to expose us.——The little disquiets and uneasiness of other families are kept secret; but here quarrels are fomented, and afterwards industriously made public.——And you, sir, you have done all this——you are my greatest enemy.

Maj. Your truest friend, sister.

Mrs. Oak. But it's no wonder. You have no feelings of humanity, no sense of domestic happiness, no idea of tenderness or attachment to any woman.

Maj. No idea of plague or disquiet—no, no—and yet I can love a woman for all that——heartily—— as you say, tenderly——But then I always choose a woman should shew a little love for me too.

Mrs. Oak. Cruel insinuation!—But I defy your malice——Mr. Oakly can have no doubt of my affection for him.

Maj. Nor I neither; and yet your affection, such

as it is, has all the evil properties of aversion. You absolutely kill him with kindness. Why, what a life he leads! He serves for nothing but a mere whetstone of your ill-humour.

Mrs. Oak. Pray now, sir!——

Maj. The violence of your temper makes his house uncomfortable to him, poisons his meals, and breaks his rest.

Mrs. Oak. I beg, Major Oakly, that——

Maj. This it is to have a wife that dotes upon one! ——the least trifle kindles your suspicion; you take fire in an instant, and set the whole family in a blaze.

Mrs. Oak. This is beyond all patience.—No, sir, 'tis you are the incendiary—you are the cause of—I cann't bear such—[*ready to weep.*]—from this instant, sir, I forbid you my house. However Mr. Oakly may treat me himself, I'll never be made the sport of all his insolent relations.   [*Exit.*

Maj. Yes, yes, I knew I should be turn'd out of doors. There she goes—— back again to my brother directly. Poor gentleman !——'Slife, if he was but half the man that I am, I'd engage to keep her going to and fro all day, like a shuttlecock.

Enter CHARLES.

What, Charles!

Char. O major! have you heard of what happened after I left you yesterday?

Maj. Heard! Yes, yes, I have heard it plain enough. But poor Charles! Ha, ha, ha! What a scene of confusion! I would give the world to have been there.

Char. And I would give the world to have been any where else. Cursed fortune!

Maj. To come in so opportunely at the tail of an adventure!——Was not your mistress mighty glad to see you? You was very fond of her, I dare say.

Char. I am upon the rack. Who can tell what rudeness I might offer her! I can remember nothing ——I deserve to lose her——to make myself a beast! ——and at such a time too!——O fool, fool, fool!

Maj. Pr'ythee, be quiet, Charles!——Never vex yourself about nothing; this will all be made up the first time you see her.

Char. I should dread to see her——and yet the not knowing where she is, distracts me——her father may force her to marry Sir Harry Beagle immediately.

Maj. Not he, I promise you. She'd run plump into your arms first, in spite of her father's teeth.

Char. But then her father's violence, and the mildness of her disposition——

Maj. Mildness!——Ridiculous!——Trust to the spirit of the sex in her. I warrant you, like all the rest, she'll have perverseness enough not to do as her father would have her.

Char. Well, well—But then my behaviour to her To expose myself in such a condition to her again! The very occasion of our former quarrel!——

Maj. Quarrel! ha, ha, ha! What signifies a quar-

rel with a mistress ? Why, the whole affair of making
love, as they call it, is nothing but quarrelling and
making it up again. They quarrel o'purpose to kiss
and be friends.

Char. Then indeed things seemed to be taking a fortunate turn——To renew our difference at such a
time!——Just when I had some reason to hope for a
reconciliation !——May wine be my poison if ever I
am drunk again !

Maj. Ay, ay, so every man says the next morning.

Char. Where, where can she be ? Her father would
hardly carry her back to lady Freelove's, and he has
no house in town himself, nor Sir Harry——I don't
know what to think——I'll go in search of her,
though I don't know where to direct myself.

Enter a Servant.

Serv. A gentleman, sir, that calls himself Captain
O'Cutter, desires to speak with you.

Char. Don't trouble me——I'll see nobody——I'm
not at home——

Serv. The gentleman says he has very particular
business, and he must see you.

Char. What's his name ? Who did you say ?

Serv. Captain O'Cutter, sir.

Char. Captain O'Cutter ! I never heard of him
before. Do you know any thing of him, major ?

Maj. Not I——But you hear he has particular business. I'll leave the room.

Char. He can have no business that need be a secret

H iij

to you.——Desire the Captain to walk up.——[*Exit
Servant.*]——What would I give if this unknown
Captain was to prove a messenger from my Harriot!

Enter Captain O'CUTTER.

O'Cut. Jóntlemen, your sarvant. Is either of your
names Charles Oakly, esq.

Char. Charles Oakly, sir, is my name, if you have
any business with it.

O'Cut. Avast, avast, my dear!—I have a little business with your name, but as I was to let nobody
know it, I cann't mention it till you clear the decks,
fait.——   [*Pointing to the major.*

Char. This gentleman, sir, is my most intimate
friend, and any thing that concerns me may be mentioned before him.

O'Cut. O, if he's your friend, my dear, we may do
all above-board. It's only about your deciding a de-
'ferance with my Lord Trinket. He wants to shew
you a little warm work; and as I was steering this
way, he desired me to fetch you this letter. [*Giving
a letter.*]

Maj. How, sir, a challenge!

O'Cut. Yes, fait, a challenge. I am to be his lordship's second; and if you are fond of a hot birth,
and will come along with that jontleman, we'll all go
to it together, and make a little line of battle a-head
of our own, my dear.

Char. [*Reading.*] Ha! what's this? This may be
useful.   [*Aside.*

Maj. Sir, I am infinitely obliged to you.—A rare fellow this. [*Aside.*] Yes, yes, I'll meet all the good company. I'll be there in my waistcoat and pumps, and take a morning's breathing with you. Are you very fond of fighting, sir?

O'Cut. Indeed and I am; I love it better than salt beef or biscuit.

Maj. But pray, sir, how are you interested in this difference? Do you know what it is about?

O'Cut. O, the devil burn me, not I. What signifies what it's about, you know? so we do but tilt a little.

Maj. What, fight and not know for what?

O'Cut. When the signal's out for engaging, what signifies talking?

Maj. I fancy, sir, a duel is a common breakfast with you. I'll warrant now, you have been engag'd in many such affairs.

O'Cut. Upon my shoul, and I have: sea or land, its all one to little Terence O'Cutter.—When I was last in Dublin, I fought one jontleman for cheating me out of a tousand pounds: I fought two of the Mermaid's crew about Sally Macguire; tree about politicks; and one about the play-house in Smock-Alley. But upon my fait, since I am in England, I have done noting at-all, at-all.

Char. This is lucky—but my transport will discover me. [*Aside.*] Will you be so kind, sir, [*To* O'Cutter.] as to make my compliments to his Lord-

ship, and assure him that I shall do myself the honour
of waiting on him.

O'Cut. Indeed and I will.—Arrah, my dear, won't
you come too?　　　　　　　　' [*To Major* Oakly.

Maj. Depend upon't. We'll go through the whole
exercise : carte, tierce, and segoon, captain.

Char. Now to get my intelligence. [*Aside.*] I think
the time, sir, his lordship appoints in his letter, is—
a———

O'Cut. You say right——Six o'clock.

Char. And the place—a—a—is——I think, behind
Montague-House.

O'Cut. No, my dear!——Avast, by the Ring in
Hyde-Park, fait——I settled it there myself, for
fare of interruption.

Char. True, as you say, the Ring in Hyde-Park—
I had forgot—Very well, I'll not fail you, sir.

O'Cut. Devil burn me, not I. Upon my shoul,
little Terence O'Cutter will see fair play, or he'll
know the reason—And so, my dear, your sarvant.

Maj. Ha, ha, ha! What a fellow!——He loves
fighting like a game cock.

Char. O uncle! the luckiest thing in the world!

Maj. What, to have the chance of being run
through the body! I desire no such good fortune.

Char. Wish me joy, wish me joy! I have found
her, my dear girl, my Harriot!——She is at an inn in
Holborn, major!

Maj. Ay! how do you know?

Char. Why, this dear, delightful, charming, blundering captain, has delivered me a wrong letter.

Maj. A wrong letter!

Char. Yes, a letter from Lord Trinket to Lady Freelove.

Maj. The devil! What are the contents?

Char. The news I told you just now, that she's at an inn in Holborn :—and besides, an excuse from my lord, for not waiting on her ladyship this morning, according to his promise, as he shall be entirely taken up with his design upon Harriot.

Maj. So!—so!—A plot between the lord and the lady.

Char. What his plot is I don't know, but I shall beg leave to be made a party in it : so perhaps his lordship and I may meet, and *decide* our *deferance*, as the captain calls it, before to-morrow morning.——There! read, read, man! 　　　[*Giving the letter.*

Maj. [*Reading*] Um—um—um——Very fine! And what do you propose doing?

Char. To go thither immediately.

Maj. Then you shall take me with you. Who knows what his lordship's designs may be? I begin to suspect foul play.

Char. No, no; pray mind your own business. If I find there is any need of your assistance, I'll send for you.

Maj. You'll manage this affair like a boy now—Go on rashly with noise and bustle, and fury, and get yourself into another scrape.

Char. No—no—Let me alone; I'll go *incog.*—Leave my chariot at some distance—Proceed prudently, and take care of myself, I warrant you. I did not imagine that I should ever rejoice at receiving a challenge, but this is the most fortunate accident that could possibly have happened. B'ye, b'ye, uncle!　　　　　　　　　　　　　　*[Exit hastily.*

Maj. I don't half approve of this—and yet I can hardly suspect his lordship of any very deep designs neither.—Charles may easily outwit him. Hark ye, William!　　　　*[At seeing a servant at some distance.*

Enter Servant.

Serv. Sir!

Maj. Where's my brother?

Serv. In his study——alone, sir.

Maj. And how is he, William?

Serv. Pretty well, I believe, sir.

Maj. Ay, ay, but is he in good humour, or——

Serv. I never meddle in family affairs, not I, sir.

　　　　　　　　　　　　　　　　　[Exit.

Maj. Well said, William!——No bad hint for me, perhaps!—What a strange world we live in!—No two people in it love one another better than my brother and sister, and yet the bitterest enemies could not torment each other more heartily.——Ah, if he had but half my spirit!——And yet he don't want it neither—But I know his temper—He pieces out the matter with maxims, and scraps of philosophy, and odds and ends of sentences—I must live in peace——

Patience is the best remedy—Any thing for a quiet
life! and so on——However, yesterday, to give him
his due, he behaved like a man.   Keep it up, brother! keep it up! or it's all over with you.   Since
mischief is on foot, I'll even set it forwards on all
sides.   I'll in to him directly, read him one of my
morning lectures, and persuade him, if I possibly
can, to go out with me immediately; or work him up
to some open act of rebellion against the sovereign
authority of his lady-wife.   Zounds, brother! rant,
and roar, and rave, and turn the house out of the
window.   If I was a husband!——'Sdeath, what a
pity it is, that nobody knows how to manage a wife
but a batchelor.   [*Exit.*

SCENE II.

Changes to the Bull and Gate Inn.   Enter HARRIOT.

Har. What will become of me? My father is en-
raged, and deaf to all remonstrances, and here I am
to remain by his positive orders, to receive this booby
baronet's odious addresses.——Among all my distresses, I must confess that Charles's behaviour yesterday is not the least.   So wild! So given up to excesses! And yet——I am ashamed to own it even
myself——I love him: and death itself shall not prevail on me to give my hand to Sir Harry.——But
here he comes! What shall I do with him?

Enter Sir HARRY BEAGLE.

Sir H. Your servant, miss!——What? Not speak!——Bashful, mayhap—Why then I will.—Look'e, miss, I am a man of few words.—What signifies hagling? It looks just like a dealer.——What d'ye think of me for a husband?——I am a tight young fellow—sound wind and limb—free from all natural blemishes—Rum all over, d'amme.

Har. Sir, I don't understand you. Speak English, and I'll give you an answer.

Sir H. English! Why so I do—and good plain English too.——What d'ye think of me for a husband?—That's English—e'nt it?——I know none of your French lingo, none of your *parlyvoos*, not I.—What d'ye think of me for a husband? The 'squire says you shall marry me.

Har. What shall I say to him? I had best be civil. [*Aside.*]——I think, sir, you deserve a much better wife, and beg——

Sir H. Better! No, no,—though you're so knowing, I'm not to be taken in so.——You're a fine thing——Your points are all good.

Har. Sir Harry! Sincerity is above all ceremony. Excuse me, if I declare I never will be your wife. And if you have a real regard for me, and my happiness, you will give up all pretension to me. Shall I beseech you, sir, to persuade my father not to urge a marriage, to which I am determined never to consent?

Sir H. Hey! how! what!—be off!——Why, it's a match, miss!——It's done and done on both sides.

Har. For Heaven's sake, sir, withdraw your claim to me.——I never can be prevailed on——indeed I cann't——

Sir H. What, make a match and then draw stakes! That's doing of nothing—Play or pay all the world over.

Har. Let me prevail on you, sir!——I am determined not to marry you at all events.

Sir H. But your father's determined you shall, miss. —So the odds are on my side.——I am not quite sure of my horse, but I have the rider hollow.

Har. Your horse! Sir—d'ye take me for—but I forgive you.—I beseech you come into my propeal. It will be better for us both in the end.

Sir H. I cann't be off.

Har. Let me intreat you.

Sir H. I tell you, it's impossible.

Har. Pray, pray do, sir.

Sir H. I cann't, damme.

Har. I beseech you.

Sir H. [*Whistles.*]

Har. How! laughed at?-

Sir H. *Will you marry me? Dear Ally, Ally Croker!*
            · [*Singing.*

Har. Marry you? I had rather be married to a slave, a wretch——You!   [*Walks about.*

Sir H. A fine going thing.——She has a deal of

I

foot——treads well upon her pasterns——goes above her ground——

Har. Peace, wretch!—Do you talk to me as if I were your horse?

Sir H. Horse! Why not speak of my horse? If your fine ladies had half as many good qualities, they would be much better bargains.

Har. And if their wretches of husbands liked them half so well as they do their horses, they would lead better lives.

Sir H. Mayhap so.——But what signifies talking to you?——The 'Squire shall know your tricks—— He'll doctor you.——I'll go and talk to him.

Har. Go any where, so that you go from me.

Sir H. He'll break you in—If you won't go in a snaffle, you must be put in a curb——He'll break you, damme.   [*Exit.*

Har. A wretch!——But I was to blame to suffer his brutal behaviour to ruffle my temper.——I could expect nothing else from him, and he is below my anger.——How much trouble has this odious fellow caused both to me and my poor father!—I never disobeyed him before, and my denial now makes him quite unhappy. In any thing else I would be all submission; and even now, while I dread his rage, my heart bleeds for his uneasiness——I wish I could resolve to obey him.

Enter RUSSET.

Rus. Are not you a sad girl? a perverse, stubborn, obstinate——

Har. My dear sir——

Rus. Look ye, Harriot, don't speak,——you'll put me in a passion——Will you have him?——Answer me that—Why don't the girl speak?—Will you have him?

Har. Dearest sir, there is nothing in the world else——

Rus. Why there!—there!——Look ye there!—— Zounds, you shall have him——Hussy, you shall have him——You shall marry him to night——Did not you promise to receive him civilly?—How came you to affront him?

Har. Sir, I did receive him very civilly; but his behaviour was so insolent and insupportable ——

Rus. Insolent!—Zounds, I'll blow his brains out. ——Insolent to my dear Harriot!—A rogue! a villain! a scoundrel! I'll—but it's a lie—I know it's a lie—He durst not behave insolent—Will you have him? Answer me that. Will you have him?—— Zounds, you shall have him.

Har. If you have any love for me, sir——

Rus. Love for you!—You know I love you—You know your poor fond father dotes on you to madness. ——I would not force you, if I did not love you—— Don't I want you to be happy?——But I know what you would have. You want young Oakly, a rake-helly, drunken——

Har. Release me from Sir Harry, and if I ever marry against your consent, renounce me for ever.

I ij

Rus. I *will* renounce you, unless you'll have Sir Harry.

Har. Consider, my dear sir, you'll make me miserable. I would die to please you, but cannot prostitute my hand to a man my heart abhors.——Absolve me from this hard command, and in every thing else it will be happiness to obey you.

Rus. You'll break my heart, Harriot, you'll break my heart——Make you miserable!—Don't I want to make you happy? Is not he the richest man in the county?—That will make you happy.——Don't all the pale-faced girls in the country long to get him?——And yet you are so perverse, and wayward, and stubborn——Zounds, you shall have him.

Har. For Heaven's sake, sir——

Rus. Hold your tongue, Harriot!—I'll hear none of your nonsense.——You shall have him, I tell you, you shall have him——He shall marry you this very night——I'll go for a license and a parson immediately. Zounds! Why do I stand arguing with you? An't I your father? Have not I a right to dispose of you? You shall have him.

Har. Sir!——

Rus. I won't hear a word. You shall have him.

[*Exit.*

Har. Sir!—Hear me!—but one word!—He will not hear me, and is gone to prepare for this odious marriage. I will die before I consent to it. You *shall* have him! O that fathers would enforce their commands by better arguments! And yet I pity him, while he afflicts me.—He upbraided me with Charles, his wildness and intemperance—Alas! but too justly ——I see that he is wedded to his excesses; and I ought to conquer an affection for him, which will only serve to make me unhappy.

Enter CHARLES *in a Frock, &c.*

Ha! What do I see!   [*Screaming.*

Char. Peace, my love!—My dear life, make no noise!—I have been hovering about the house this hour——I just now saw your father and Sir Harry go out, and have seized this precious opportunity to throw myself at your feet.   ?

Har. You have given yourself, sir, a great deal of needless trouble. I did not expect or hope for the favour of such a visit.

Char. O my dear Harriot, your words and looks cut me to the soul. You cann't imagine what I suffer, and have suffered since last night——And yet I have in some fond moments flattered myself, that the service I was so fortunate as to do you at Lady Freelove's, would plead a little in my favour.

Har. You may remember, sir, that you took a very early opportunity of cancelling that obligation.

Char. I do remember it with shame and despair. But may I perish, if my joy at having delivered you from a villain was not the cause! My transport more than half intoxicated me, and wine made an easy conquest over me.—I tremble to think lest I should have behaved in such a manner as you cannot pardon.

Har. Whether I pardon you or no, sir, is a matter of mighty little consequence.

Char. O my Harriot! Upbraid me, reproach me, do any thing but look and talk with that air of coldness and indifference. Must I lose you for one offence? when my soul dotes on you, when I love you to distraction!

Har. Did it appear like love, your conduct yesterday? To lose yourself in riot, when I was exposed to the greatest distresses!

Char. I feel, I feel my shame, and own it.

Har. You confess that you don't know in what manner you behaved. Ought not I to tremble at the very thoughts of a man, devoted to a vice which renders him no longer a judge or master of his own conduct?

Char. Abandon me, if ever I am guilty of it again. O Harriot! I am distracted with ten thousand fears and apprehensions of losing you for ever—— The chambermaid, whom I bribed to admit me to you, told me that when the two gentlemen went out, they talked of a license.——What am I to think? Is it possible that you can resign yourself to Sir Harry Beagle?——[Harriot *pauses.*]——Can you then consent to give your hand to another? No, let me once more deliver you——Let us seize this lucky moment! —My chariot stands at the corner of the next street —Let me gently force you, while their absence allows it, and convey you from the brutal violence of a constrained marriage.

Har. No!—I will wait the event, be it what it may.
—O Charles, I am too much inclined—They sha'n't
force me to marry Sir Harry——But your behaviour
——Not half an hour ago, my father reproached me
with the looseness of your character.   [*Weeping.*

Char. I see my folly, and am ashamed of it.   You
have reclaimed me, Harriot!—On my soul, you have.
——If all women were as attentive as yourself to the
morals of their lovers, a libertine would be an un-
common character.——But let me persuade you to
leave this place, while you may—Major Oakly will
receive us at his house with pleasure—I am shocked
at the thoughts of what your stay here may reserve
you to.

Har. No, I am determined to remain.——To leave
my father again, to go off openly with a man, of
whose libertine character he has himself so lately been
a witness, would justify his anger, and impeach my
reputation.

Char. Fool! fool! How unhappy have I made myself!——Consider, my Harriot, the peculiarity of
your situation; besides I have reason to fear other
designs against you.

Har. From other designs I can be no where so secure as with my father.

Char. Time flies——Let me persuade you!

Har. I am resolved to stay here.

Char. You distract me.   For Heaven's sake.

Har. I will not think of it.

Char. Consider, my angel!———

Har. I do consider, that your conduct has made it absolutely improper for me to trust myself to your care.

Char. My conduct!—Vexation! 'Sdeath!——But then, my dear Harriot, the danger you are in, the necessity———

Enter Chambermaid.

Chamb. O law, ma'am!——Such a terrible accident!——As sure as I am here, there's a press-gang has seized the two gemmin, and is carrying them away, thof so be one an 'em says as how he's a knight and baronight, and that t'other's a 'squire and a housekeeper.

Har. Seized by a press-gang! impossible.

Char. O, now the design comes out.——But I'll baulk his lordship.

Chamb. Lack-a-dasy, ma'am, what can we do? There is master, and John Ostler, and Bootcatcher, all gone a'ter 'em.———There is such an uproar as never was.   [*Exit.*

Har. If I thought this was your contrivance, sir, I would never speak to you again.

Char. I would sooner die than be guilty of it.— This is Lord Trinket's doing, I am sure. I knew he had some scheme in agitation, by a letter I intercepted this morning.

Har. [*Screams.*]

Char. Ha! Here he comes. Nay then, it's plain enough. Don't be frighted, my love! I'll protect you.——But now I must desire you to follow my directions.

Enter Lord TRINKET.

L. Trink. Now, madam.——Pox on't, he here again !———Nay, then, [*Drawing.*]come, sir ! You're unarmed, I see. Give up the lady : give her up, I say, or I am through you in a twinkling.

[*Going to make a pass at* Charles.

Char. Keep your distance, my lord ! I have arms. [*Producing a pistol.*] If you come a foot nearer, you have a brace of balls thro' your lordship's head.

L. Trink. How ? what's this ? pistols !

Char. At your lordship's service.——Sword and pistol my lord.——Those, you know, are our weapons.——If this misses, I have the fellow to't in my pocket.——Don't be frighted, madam. His lordship has removed your friends and relations, but he will take great care of you. Shall I leave you with him ?

Har. Cruel Charles ! You know I must go with you now.

Char. A little way from the door, if your lordship pleases.   [*Waving his hand.*

L. Trink. Sir !—'Sdeath ;—Madam !——

Char. A little more round, my lord.   [*Waving.*

L. Trink. But, sir !—Mr. Oakly !

Char. I have no leisure to talk with your lordship now.——A little more that way, if you please. [*Waving.*]—You know where I live.——If you have any commands for Miss Russet, you will hear of her too at my house.——Nay, keep back, my lord. [*Presenting.*] Your lordship's most obedient humble servant. [*Exit with* Harriot.

L. Trink. [*Looking after them, and pausing for a short time.*]——I cut a mighty ridiculous figure here, 'pon honour.——So I have been concerting this deep scheme, merely to serve him.——Oh, the devil take such intrigues, and all silly country girls, that can give up a man of quality and figure, for a fellow that nobody knows. [*Exit.*

ACT V. SCENE I.

Lady FREELOVE's *House. Enter Lord* TRINKET, *Lady* FREELOVE *with a Letter, and Captain* O'CUTTER.

Lord Trinket.

WAS ever any thing so unfortunate? Pox on't, captain, how could you make such a strange blunder?

O'Cut. I never tought of a blunder. I was to daliver two letters, and if I gave them one a piece, I tought it was all one, fait.

L. Free. And so, my lord, the ingenious captain gave the letter intended for me to young Oakly, and here he has brought me a challenge.

L. Trink. Ridiculous! Never was any thing so *mal-apropos.*——Did you read the direction, captain?

O'Cut. Who, me!——Devil burn me, not I. I never rade at all.

L. Trink. 'Sdeath! how provoking! When I had secur'd the servants, and got all the people out of the way—When every thing was *in train.*

L. Free. Nay, never despair, my lord! Things have happened unluckily, to be sure; and yet I think I could hit upon a method to set every thing to right again.

L. Trink. How? how? my dear Lady Freelove, how?

L. Free. Suppose then your lordship was to go and deliver these country gentlemen from their confinement; make them believe it was a plot of young Oakly's to carry off my niece; and so make a merit of your own services with the father.

L. Trink. Admirable! I'll about it immediately.

O'Cut. Has your lordship any occasion for my service in this expedition?

L. Trink. O no:——Only release me these people, and then keep out of the way, dear captain.

O'Cut. With all my heart, fait. But you are all wrong:—this will not signify a brass farding. If you would let me alone, I would give him a salt eel, I warrant you.——But upon my credit, there's noting to be done without a little tilting. *[Exit.*

L. Free. Ha, ha! poor captain!

L. Trink. But where shall I carry them, when I have deliver'd them?

L. Free. To Mr. Oakly's, by all means. You may be sure my niece is there.

L. Trink. To Mr. Oakly's!——Why, does your

ladyship consider? 'Tis going directly in the fire of
the enemy——throwing the *dementi* full in their teeth.

L. Free. So much the better. Face your enemies!
—nay, you shall outface them too. Why, where's the
difference between truths and untruths, if you do but
stick close to the point? Falsehood would scarce ever
be detected, if we had confidence enough to support it.

L. Trink. Nay, I don't want *bronze* upon occasion.
—But to go amongst a whole troop of people, sure,
to contradict every word I say, is so dangerous——

L. Free. To leave Russet alone amongst them,
would be ten times more dangerous. You may be
sure that Oakly's will be the first place he will go to
after his daughter, where; if you don't accompany
him, he will be open to all their suggestions. They'll
be all in one story, and nobody there to contradict
them: and then their dull truth would triumph,
which must not be. No, no,——positively, my lord,
you must battle it out.

L. Trink. Well, I'll go, 'pon honour——and if I
could depend on your ladyship as a *corps de reserve.*——

L. Free. I'll certainly meet you there. Tush! my
lord, there's nothing in it. It's hard, indeed, if two
persons of condition can't bear themselves out against
such trumpery folks as the family of the Oaklys.

L. Trink. Odious low people!——But I lose time
——I must after the captain——and so, till we meet
at Mr. Oakly's, I kiss your ladyship's hand.——You
won't fail me.

2

L. Free. You may depend on me.   [*Exit L.* Trink.

L. Free. So, here is fine work! This artful little hussy has been too much for us all: Well, what's to be done? Why, when a woman of fashion gets into a scrape, nothing but a fashionable assurance can get her out of it again. I'll e'en go boldly to Mr. Oakly's, as I have promised, and if it appears practicable, I will forward Lord Trinket's match; but if I find that matters have taken another turn, his lordship must excuse me. In that case I'll fairly drop him, seem a perfect stranger to all his intentions, and give my visit an air of congratulation to my niece and any other husband, which fortune, her wise father, or her ridiculous self has provided for her.   [*Exit.*

_____

SCENE II.

Changes to Mrs. OAKLY's *Dressing-Room.* *Enter Mrs.*
OAKLY.

Mrs. Oak.: This is worse and worse!——He never held me so much in contempt before.——To go out without speaking to me, or taking the least notice.—— I am obliged to the major for this.——How could he take him out? and how could Mr. Oakly go with him?——

Enter TOILET.

Mrs. Oak. Well, Toilet.

Toil. My master is not come back yet, ma'am.

K

Mrs. Oak. Where is he gone?

Toil. I don't know, I can assure your ladyship.

Mrs. Oak. Why don't you know?—You know nothing.—But I warrant you know well enough, if you would tell.—You shall never persuade me but you knew of Mr. Oakly's going out to-day.

Toil. I wish I may die, ma'am, upon my honour, and I protest to your ladyship, I knew nothing in the world of the matter, no more than the child unborn. There is Mr. Paris, my master's gentleman, knows—

Mrs. Oak. What does he know?

Toil. That I knew nothing at all of the matter.

Mrs. Oak. Where is Paris? What is he doing?

Toil. He is in my master's room, ma'am.

Mrs Oak. Bid him come here.

Toil. Yes, ma'am.   [*Exit.*

Mrs. Oak. He is certainly gone after this young flirt.——His confidence and the major's insolence provoke me beyond expression.

Re-enter Toilet *with* Paris.

Where's your master?

Par. *Il est sorti.*

Mrs. Oak. Where is he gone?

Par. Ah, madame, *je n'en scai rien,* I know noting of it.

Mrs. Oak. Nobody knows any thing. Why did not you tell me he was going out?

Par. I dress him—*Je ne m'en soucie pas du plus—*He go where he will—I have no bisness wis it.

                                                    I

Mrs. Oak. Yes, you should have told me——that was your business——and if you don't mind your business better, you shan't stay here, I can tell you, sir.

Par. Voila! quelque chose d'extraordinaire!

Mrs. Oak. Don't stand jabbering and shrugging your shoulders, but go, and enquire——go——and bring me word where he is gone.

Par. I don't know what I am do.——I'll ask John.——

Mrs. Oak. Bid John come to me.

Par. De tout mon cœur.——Jean! ici! Jean—Speak my ladi.   [*Exit.*

Mrs. Oak. Impudent fellow! His insolent gravity and indifference is insupportable ——Toilet!

Toil. Ma'am.

Mrs. Oak. Where's John? Why don't he come? Why do you stand with your hands before you? Why don't you fetch him?

Toil. Yes, ma'am,—I'll go this minute.——O, here, John! my lady wants you.

Enter JOHN.

Mrs. Oak. Where's your master?

John. Gone out, madam.

Mrs. Oak. Why did not you go with him?

John. Because he went out in the major's chariot, madam.

Mrs. Oak. Where did they go to?

John. To the major's, I suppose, madam.

Mrs. Oak. Suppose! Don't you know?

John. I believe so, but cann't tell for certain, indeed, madam.

Mrs. Oak. Believe, and suppose!—and don't know, and cann't tell!——You are all fools.——Go about your business. [John *going.*]—Come here. [*Returns.*] Go to the major's—no,—it does not signify—go along—[John *going.*]——Yes, hark'ee, [*Returns.*] go to the major's, and see if your master is there.

John. Give your compliments, madam?

Mrs. Oak. My compliments, blockhead! Get along. [John *going.*] Come hither. [*Returns.*] Cann't you go to the major's, and bring me word if Mr. Oakly. is there, without taking any further notice?

John. Yes, ma'am!

Mrs. Oak. Well, why don't you go, then? And make haste back.——And d'ye hear, John.

[John *going, returns.*]

John. Madam.

Mrs. Oak. Nothing at all—go along—[John *goes.*]—How uneasy Mr. Oakly makes me!——Hark'e, John! [John *returns.*]

John. Madam!

Mrs. Oak. Send the porter here.

John. Yes, madam. [*Exit.*

Toil. So, she's in a rare humour! I shall have a fine time on't.—[*Aside.*]——Will your ladyship choose to dress?

Mrs. Oak. Pr'ythee, creature, don't tease me with your fiddle-faddle stuff—I have a thousand things to think of.——Where is the porter? Why has not that booby sent him? What is the meaning——

Re-enter JOHN.

John. Madam, my master is this moment returned with·Major Oakly, and my young master, and the lady that was here yesterday.

Mrs. Oak. Very well. [*Exit* John.] Returned!—yes, truly, he is returned—and in a very extraordinary manner. This is setting me at open defiance. But I'll go down, and shew them I have too much spirit to endure such usage.—[*Going.*]—Or stay—I'll not go amongst his company—I'll go out.——Toilet!

Toil. Ma'am.

Mrs. Oak. Order the coach, I'll go out. [Toilet *going.*]——Toilet, stay,—I'll e'en go down to them ——No.——Toilet.

Toil. Ma'am.

Mrs. Oak. Order me a boil'd chicken——I'll not go down to dinner——I'll dine in my own room, and sup there——I'll not see his face these three days.

[*Exeunt.*

SCENE III.

Changes to another Room. Enter OAKLY, *Major* OAKLY, CHARLES, *and* HARRIOT.

Char. My dear Harriot, do not make yourself so uneasy.

Har. Alas! I have too much cause for my uneasiness. Who knows what that vile lord has done with my father?

K iij

Oak. 'Be comforted, madam; we shall soon hear of Mr. Russet, and all will be well I dare say.

Har. You are too good to me, sir:——But I can assure you, I am not a little concerned on your account as well as my own; and if I did not flatter myself with hopes of explaining every thing to Mrs. Oakly's satisfaction, I should never forgive myself for having disturbed the peace of such a worthy family.

Maj. Don't mind that, madam; they'll be very good friends again. This is nothing among married people.——'Sdeath, here she is!—No,—it's only Mrs. Toilet.

Enter TOILET.

Oak. Well, Toilet, what now? [*Toilet whispers.*] Not well?—Cann't come down to dinner?—Wants to see me above?——Hark'e, brother, what shall I do?

Maj. If you go, you're undone.

Har. Go, sir; go to Mrs. Oakly——Indeed you had better——

Maj. 'Sdeath, brother! don't budge a foot—This is all fractiousness and ill-humour——

Oak. No, I'll not go.—Tell her I have company and we shall be glad to see her here. [*Exit* Toilet.

Maj. That's right.

Oak. Suppose I go and watch how she proceeds?

Maj. What d'ye mean? You would not go to her? Are you mad?

Oak. By no means go to her—I only want to know how she takes it. I'll lie *perdue* in my study, and observe her motions.

Maj. I don't like this pitiful ambuscade work—this bush-fighting. Why cann't you stay here?——Ay, ay!—I know how it will be——She'll come bounce in upon you with a torrent of anger and passion, or, if necessary, a whole flood of tears, and carry all before her at once.

Oak. You shall find that you're mistaken, major. —Don't imagine that because I wish not to be void of humanity, that I am destitute of resolution. Now I am convinc'd I'm in the right, I'll support that right with ten times your steadiness.

Maj. You talk this well, brother.

Oak. I'll do it well, brother.

Maj. If you don't, you're undone.

Oak. Never fear, never fear. [*Exit.*

Maj. Well, Charles.

Char. I cann't bear to see my Harriot so uneasy. I'll go immediately in quest of Mr. Russet. Perhap, I may learn at the inn where his lordship's ruffians have carried him.

Rus. [*Without.*] Here? Yes, yes, I know she's here well enough. Come along, Sir Harry, come along.

Har. He's here?—My father! I know his voice. Where is Mr. Oakly? O, now, good sir, [*To the Major.*] do but pacify him, and you'll be a friend indeed.

Enter RUSSET, *Lord* TRINKET, *and* Sir HARRY BEAGLE.

L. Trink. There, sir—I told you it was so.

Rus. Ay, ay, it is too plain.——O you provoking

slut! Elopement after elopement! And at last to have your father carried off by violence! To endanger my life! Zounds! I am so angry, I dare not trust myself within reach of you.

Char. I can assure you, sir, that your daughter is entirely ————

Rus. You assure me? You are the fellow that has perverted her mind————That has set my own child against me————

Char. If you will but hear me, sir————

Rus. I won't hear a word you say. I'll have my daughter——I won't hear a word.

Maj. Nay, Mr. Russet, hear reason. If you will but have patience————

Rus. I'll have no patience—I'll have my daughter, and she shall marry Sir Harry to-night.

L. Trink. That is dealing rather too much *en cavalier* with me, Mr. Russet, 'pon honour. You take no notice of my pretensions, though my rank and family————

Rus. What care I for rank and family. I don't want to make my daughter a rantipole woman of quality. I'll give her to whom I please. Take her away, Sir Harry; she shall marry you to-night.

Har. For Heaven's sake, sir, hear me but a moment.

Rus. Hold your tongue, girl. Take her away, Sir Harry, take her away.

Char. It must not be.

Maj. Only three words, Mr. Russet. ————

Rus. Why don't the booby take her?

Sir H. Hold hard, hold hard! You are all on a wrong scent : Hold hard! I say, hold hard!—Hark ye, Squire Russet.

Rus. Well! what now?

Sir H. It was proposed, you know, to match me with Miss Harriot——But she cann't take kindly to me.——When one has made a bad bet, it is best to hedge off, you know—and so. I have e'en swopped her with Lord Trinket here for his brown horse Nabob, that he bought of Lord Whistle-Jacket for fifteen hundred guineas.

Rus. Swopped her? Swopped my daughter for a horse? Zouns, sir, what d'ye mean?

Sir H. Mean? Why I mean to be off, to be sure. —It won't do—I tell you it won't do——First of all I knocked up myself and my horses, when they took for London—and now I have been stewed aboard a tender——I have wasted three stone at least——If I could have rid my match, it would not have grieved me——And so, as I said before, I have swopped her for Nabob.

Rus. The devil take Nabob, and yourself, and Lord Trinket, and——

L. Trink. *Pardon! je vous demande pardon, Monsieur* Russet, 'pon honour.

Rus. Death and the devil! I shall go distracted. My daughter plotting against me—the——

Maj. Come, come, Mr. Russet, I am your man after all. Give me but a moment's hearing, and I'll engage to make peace between you and your daughter, and throw the blame where it ought to fall most deservedly.

Sir H. Ay, ay, that's right. Put the saddle on the right horse, my buck !

Rus. Well, Sir !—What d'ye say ?—Speak——I don't know what to do——

Maj. I'll speak the truth let who will be offended by it.——I have proof presumptive and positive for you, Mr. Russet. From his lordship's behaviour at Lady Freelove's, when my nephew rescued her, we may fairly conclude that he would stick at no measures to carry his point.—There's proof presumptive. —But, sir, we can give you proof positive too—proof under his lordship's own hand, that he, likewise, was the contriver of the gross affront that has just been offered you.

Rus. Hey ! how ?

L. Trink. Every syllable romance, 'pon honour.

Maj. Gospel, every word on't.

Char. This letter will convince you, sir !—In consequence of what happened at Lady Freelove's, his lordship thought fit to send me a challenge : but the messenger blundered, and gave me this letter instead of it. [*Giving the letter.*] I have the case which inclosed it in my pocket.

L. Trink. Forgery, from begining to end, 'pon honour.

Maj. Truth upon my honour.—But read, read, Mr. Russet, read and be convinced.

Rus. Let me see—let me see——[*Reading*]—Um—um—um—um—so, so!—um—um—um—damnation!—Wish me success—obedient slave—Trinket.——Fire and fury! How dare you do this?

L. Trink. When you are cool, Mr. Russet, I will explain this matter to you.

Rus. Cool? 'Sdeath and hell!—I'll never be cool again—I'll be revenged.—So my Harriot, my dear girl is innocent at last.—Say so, my Harriot; tell me you are innocent. *[Embracing her.*

Har. I am, indeed, sir; and happy beyond expression, at your being convinced of it.

Rus. I am glad on't—I am glad on't—I believe you, Harriot!—You was always a good girl.

Maj. So she is, an excellent girl!—Worth a regiment of such Lords and Baronets—Come, sir, finish every thing handsomely at once.——Come—Charles will have a handsome fortune.

Rus. Marry!—She durst not do it.

Maj. Consider, sir, they have long been fond of each other—old acquaintance—faithful lovers—turtles—and may be very happy.

Rus. Well, well—since things are so——I love my girl.—Hark'ye, young Oakly, if you don't make her a good husband, you'll break my heart, you rogue.

Char. Do not doubt it, sir! my Harriot has reformed me altogether.

Rus. Has she?—Why then—there—Heaven bless you both—there—now there's an end on't.

Sir H. So, my lord, you and I are both distanced —A hollow thing, damme.

L. Trink. N'*importe.*

Sir H. [*Aside.*] Now this stake is drawn, my Lord may be for hedging off mayhap. Ecod! I'll go to Jack Speed's, and secure Nabob, and be out of town in an hour.—Soho! Lady Freelove! Yoics! [*Exit.*

Enter Lady FREELOVE.

L. Free. My dear Miss Russet, you'll excuse——

Char. Mrs. Oakly, at your ladyship's service.

L. Free. Married?

Har. Not yet, madam; but my father has been so good as to give his consent.

L. Free. I protest I am prodigiously glad of it. My dear, I give you joy—and you, Mr. Oakly.—I wish you joy, Mr. Russet, and all the good company—for I think the most of them are parties concerned

Maj. How easy, impudent, and familiar! [*Aside.*

L. Free. Lord Trinket here too! I vow I did not see your lordship before.

L. Trink. Your ladyship's most obedient slave.

[*Bowing.*

L. Free. You seem grave, my lord!—Come, come, I know there has been some difference between you and Mr. Oakly—You must give me leave to be a mediator in this affair.

L. Trink. Here has been a small fracas to be sure, madam!—We are all blown, 'pon honour.

L. Free. Blown ! What do you mean, my lord ?

L. Trink. Nay, your ladyship knows that I never mind these things, and I know that they never discompose your ladyship—But things have happened a little *en travers*—The little billet I sent your ladyship has fallen into the hands of that gentleman—[*Pointing to* Char.]—and so—there has been a little *brouillerie* about it—that's all.

L. Free. You talk to me, my lord, in a very extraordinary stile—If you have been guilty of any misbehaviour, I am sorry for it; but your ill conduct can fasten no imputation on me.—Miss Russet will justify me sufficiently.

Maj. Had not your ladyship better appeal to my friend Charles here?—The Letter! Charles!——Out with it this instant!

Char. Yes, I have the credentials of her ladyship's integrity in my pocket.———Mr. Russet, the letter you read a little while ago was inclosed in this cover, which also I now think it my duty to put into your hands.

Rus. [*Reading.*] To the Right Honourable Lady Freelove———'Sdeath and hell!—and now I recollect, the letter itself was pieced with scraps of French, and madam, and your ladyship—Fire and fury ! madam, how came you to use me so? I am obliged to you then for the insult that has been offered me.

L. Free. What is all this? Your obligations to me, Mr. Russet, are of a nature that———

Rus. Fine obligations! I dare say I am partly

L

obliged to you too for the attempt on my daughter, by that thing of a lord yonder at your house. Zouns! madam, these are injuries never to be forgiven———— They are the grossest affronts to me and my family— All the world shall know them—Zouns!—I'll————

L. Free. Mercy on me! how boisterous are these country gentlemen! Why really, Mr. Russet, you rave like a man in Bedlam—I am afraid you'll beat me—and then you swear most abominably.——How can you be so vulgar?————I see the meaning of this low malice——But the reputations of women of quality are not so easily impeached—My rank places me above the scandal of little people, and I shall meet such petty insolence with the greatest ease and tranquillity. But you and your simple girl will be the sufferers.——— I had some thoughts of introducing her into the first company—But now, madam, I shall neither receive nor return your visits, and will entirely withdraw my protection from the ordinary part of the family. [*Exit*

Rus. Zouns, what impudence! that's worse than all the rest.

L. Trink. Fine presence of mind, faith!—The true French *nonchalance*——But, good folks, why such a deal of rout and *tapage* about nothing at all?——— Mademoiselle Harriot had rather be Mrs. Oakly than Lady Trinket——Why—I wish her joy, that's all.— Mr. Russet, I wish you joy of your son-in-law—Mr. Oakly, I wish you joy of the lady—and you, madam, [*To* Harriot.] of the gentleman——And, in short, I wish you all joy of one another, 'pon honour! [*Exit*

Rus. There's a fine fellow of a lord now! The devil's in your London folks of the first fashion, as you call them. They will rob you of your estate, debauch your daughter, or lie with your wife—and all as if they were doing you a favour—'pon honour!—

Maj. Hey! what now? [*Bell rings violently.*

Enter OAKLY.

Oak. D'ye hear, major, d'ye hear?

Maj. Zouns! what a clatter!——She'll pull down all the bells in the house.

Oak. My observations since I left you have confirmed my resolution. I see plainly, that her goodhumour, and her ill-humour, her smiles, her tears, and her fits, are all calculated to play upon me.

Maj. Did not I always tell you so? It's the way with them all——they will be rough and smooth, and hot and cold, and all in a breath. Any thing to get the better of us.

Oak. She is in all moods at present, I promise you.—I am at once angry and ashamed of her; and yet she is so ridiculous I cann't help laughing at her——There has she been in her chamber, fuming and fretting, and dispatching a messenger to me every two minutes—servant after servant—now she insists on my coming to her—now again she writes a note to intreat—then Toilet is sent to let me know that she is ill, absolutely dying—then, the very next minute, she'll never see my face again—she'll go out of the house directly. [*Bell rings.*] Again! now the storm rises!—

L ij

Maj. It will soon drive this way then—now, brother, prove yourself a man—You have gone too far to retreat.

Oak. Retreat!—Retreat!—No, no!—I'll preserve the advantage I have gained, I am determined.

Maj. Ay, ay!—keep your ground!—fear nothing —up with your noble heart! Good discipline makes good soldiers ; stick close to my advice, and you may stand buff to a tigress————

Oak. Here she is, by heavens!—now, brother!

Maj. And now, brother!—Now or never!

Enter Mrs. OAKLY.

Mrs. Oak. I think, Mr. Oakly, you might have had humanity enough to have come to see how I did. You have taken your leave, I suppose, of all tenderness and affection—but I'll be calm————I'll not throw myself into a passion—you want to drive me out of your house————I see what you aim at, and will be aforehand with you—let me keep my temper! I'll send for a chair, and leave the house this instant.

Oak. True, my love! I knew you would not think of dining in your own chamber alone, when I had company below. You shall sit at the head of the table, as you ought to be sure, as you say, and make my friends welcome.

Mrs. Oak. Excellent raillery! Look ye, Mr. Oakly, I see the meaning of all this affected coolness and indifference.

Oak. My dear, consider where you are————

I tell you I would cure all the disorders in your family? I beg pardon, sister, for taking the liberty to prescribe for you. My medicines have been somewhat rough, I believe, but they have had an admirable effect, and so don't be angry with your physician.

Mrs. Oak. I am indeed obliged to you, and I feel—

Oak. Nay, my dear, no more of this. All that's past must be utterly forgotten.

Mrs. Oak. I have not merited this kindness, but it shall hereafter be my study to deserve it. Away with all idle jealousies! And since my suspicions have been groundless, I am resolved for the future never to suspect at all.

EPILOGUE.

LAIDES! I've had a squabble with the Poet——
About his characters—and you shall know it.
Young man, said I, restrain your saucy satire!
My part's ridiculous—false—out of nature.
Fine draughts indeed of ladies! sure you hate 'em!
Why, sir!——My part is scandalum magnatum.

"Lord, ma'am, said he, to copy life my trade is,
And Poets ever have made free with ladies:
One Simon—the deuce take such names as these!
A hard Greek name——O—ay—Simonides—,
He shew'd——our freaks, this whim and that desire,
Rose first from earth, sea, air, nay, some from fire;
Or that we owe our persons, minds, and features
To birds, forsooth, and filthy four-legg'd creatures.

The dame, of manners various, temper fickle,
Now all for le assure, now the conventicle!

Who prays, then raves, now calm, now all commotion,
Rises another Venus from the ocean.
   Constant at every sale, the curious fair,
Who longs for Dresden, and old China ware;
Who dotes on pagods, and gives up vile man
For niddle-noddle figures from Japan;
Critic in jars and josses, shews her birth
Drawn, like the brittle ware itself, from earth.
  -The flaunting she, so stately, rich, and vain,
Who gains her conquests by her length of train;
While all her vanity is under sail,
Sweeps a proud peacock, with a gaudy tail.
   Husband and wife, with sweets! and dears! and loves!
What are they but a pair of cooing doves?
But seiz'd with spleen, fits, humours, and all that,
Your dove and turtle turn to dog and cat.
   The gossip, prude, old maid, coquette, and trapes,
Are parrots, foxes, magpies, wasps, and apes;
But she, with ev'ry charm of form and mind,
Oh! She's—sweet soul—the phœnix of her kind."
   This his apology!——'Tis rank abuse——
A fresh offront, instead of an excuse!
His own sex rather such description suits:
Why don't he draw their characters——The brutes!
Ay, let him paint those ugly monsters, men!
Mean time——mend we our lives, he'll mend his pen.